Mishnah's Theology of Tithing

Number 19

Mishnah's Theology of Tithing

by Martin S. Jaffee

MISHNAH'S THEOLOGY OF TITHING:
A Study of Tractate Maaserot

by

Martin S. Jaffee

Scholars Press

Distributed by
SCHOLARS PRESS
101 Salem Street
P.O. Box 2268
Chico, California 95927

Mishnah's Theology of Tithing

by
Martin S. Jaffee

Copyright © 1981
Brown University

Library of Congress Cataloging in Publication Data

Jaffee, Martin S
    Mishnah's theology of tithing.

    (Brown Judaic studies ; no. 19)
    "This study is a translation and exegesis of
Mishnah's tractate Maaserot (Tithes) and its
corresponding tractate of Tosefta."
    Bibliography: p.
    Includes index.
    1. Mishnah. Ma'aserot–Commentaries. 2. Tosefta.
Ma'aserot–Commentaries. 3. Tithes (Jewish law)
I. Mishnah. Ma'aserot. English 1981.
II. Tosefta. Ma'aserot. English. 1981. IV. Series.
BM506.M19J33   296.1'23   80-29333
ISBN 0-89130-459-2 (pbk.)

Printed in the United States of America
1 2 3 4 5
Edwards Brothers, Inc.
Ann Arbor, Michigan 48106

for Cher,
after five years

This book is published, in part, with the
support of The Max Richter Foundation, in
honor of Maurice Glicksman.

TABLE OF CONTENTS

This study is a translation and exegesis of Mishnah's Tractate
Maaserot (Tithes) and its corresponding tractate of Tosefta. The
goal of the study is to understand the laws of Maaserot (hereafter,
M.) as the tractate's creator(s) intended them to be understood.
I claim, then, to explain the meaning these laws conveyed to those
who, toward the end of the second century A.D., edited them into a
tractate on the subject of tithes. Consequently, the study makes
no effort to establish the meaning of the laws outside the context
provided by M. itself, e.g., prior to their formulation for use
in M., or afterward, in the subsequent history of Jewish legal
reflection. The reason for limiting the exegetical focus in this
way flows from the kind of information I seek from M. The tractate,
as part of Mishnah, is important evidence for the concerns which
engage Rabbinic Judaism at a point quite early in its history. By
offering an account of M.'s original meaning, I thereby contribute
to the larger task of describing and interpreting Mishnah, and,
ultimately, that form of Judaic religion which it so richly represents.

Both the translation of M. and its exegesis are carefully
designed to serve the specific task of understanding defined above.
They are intended, that is, to restrict the range of meaning to
that which can plausibly be ascribed to the editor(s) of the tractate. Thus the translation is as literal as readable English will
allow, and closely replicates the formal and syntactical traits of
the Hebrew. This method of translation prevents both translator
and reader from ignoring the critical, and often intentional,
ambiguities and difficulties of the text. At the same time, it
sensitizes the diligent reader to M.'s disciplined mode of expression and, therefore, enables the reader to permit the text itself
to define the limits of its own interpretation. My own judgment
regarding the text's meaning is offered in the exegesis, which
follows each discrete pericope of M. This exegesis emerges, first
of all, from careful analysis of those literary traits highlighted
by the translation. I attempt to show how the literary form in
which M.'s laws are cast yields sure access to the meaning they
are intended to convey. While the exegesis begins in literary
analysis, however, it moves rapidly to two further levels of analysis and explanation. The first is an account of each pericope's
clear sense, as this can be discerned by analysis of literary form

and conceptual content. The second is an identification of the
unarticulated assumptions of each pericope as well as a description
of the logical structure of ideas within which the law of each
pericope may be located. This analysis of the sense of each pericope, placed within the context of its legal assumptions and
logic, is what I identify as the original meaning of a given law.

Once the pericopae are fully explained and viewed in their
redacted sequence, it becomes possible to identify and explain the
larger problematic of the tractate as a whole. By "problematic"
I simply mean the underlying issue or preoccupation which generates reflection on the subject of tithes and shapes M.'s particular
exploration of that subject. Identification of this problematic
is the "pay off" for the historian of early Rabbinic Judaism, for
it leads the student into the motives and concerns which generate
the peculiar project of law found in Mishnah. These motives, I
argue, are distinctly theological. I offer detailed discussion of
M.'s problematic in the Introduction, which serves as well to
orient the reader within the tractate's factual data and range of
issues. The Introduction contains as well an extensive discussion
of the theoretical issues which determine the methods of translation and exegesis I employ. In addition, the reader will find a
guide to the technical apparatus used in the translation and an
explanation of the kinds of issues which I consistently raise in
my exegesis. This guide explains how to make best use of the
translation and exegesis, and should enable the reader to criticize
my own exegetical work from an independent perspective.

While M. is the primary focus of this study, I have seen fit
to translate and discuss all of Tosefta Maaserot (hereafter, T.)
as well. T. is an early and most important commentary to M., and
the only commentary which attempts to employ M.'s own formal and
conceptual framework for exegetical purposes. As such it is unlike
any commentary to M. I therefore present T.'s pericopae after the
pericopae of M. which they are intended to serve. While this mode
of presentation at times disrupts the redacted order of T., and
often disrupts the flow of ideas presented in M., the system best
highlights the exegetical utility of T. for the study of M. My
comments to T. are generally brief, intended simply to describe the
point T. wishes to make about M. Since my discussions of M.
routinely identify important contributions of T., the reader who
wishes to concentrate solely on Mishnah will not be at a disadvan-
tage if he or she chooses to ignore the translation and commentary
of T.

ACKNOWLEDGEMENTS

It gives me great pleasure to express my gratitude to those who have supported me in so many ways during the period in which I prepared this study. Above all, I wish to thank my parents, Abraham and Belle Jaffee, for all they have given me in my life, and for their faith in my ability to choose what was right for me. I hope that the appearance of this book will give them pleasure.

My teacher, Jacob Neusner, is responsible for whatever merits this book displays, for it was in his graduate seminars that the plan of the book took shape and its contents were first presented. Professor Neusner's criticism and insights have improved each page, such that I cannot imagine what kind of book I would have written without his guidance. To him I owe not only this book, but the education which made such a book possible, and the career which will issue from that education. If it is a truism that students are indebted to their teachers, it is true of me more than most.

The present volume was originally presented as a Brown University doctoral dissertation, and as such has benefited from passage under many eyes. I wish to thank, first of all, the official readers of my dissertation, Professors David M. Goodblatt (Haifa University) and William Scott Green (University of Rochester), both of whom made important suggestions and corrections which I have incorporated for publication. I must express as well my indebtedness to my colleagues in Professor Neusner's seminars over the past three years: Mr. Leonard Gordon, Professor Peter Haas (Vanderbilt University), Mr. Abraham Havivi, Professor Irving Mandelbaum (University of Texas), Mr. Alan Peck, Professor Richard S. Sarason (Hebrew Union College-Jewish Institute of Religion) and Ms. Margaret Wenig Rubenstein. Without their criticism, encouragement, and numerous kindnesses, the quality of this study would certainly have suffered.

I have received exceptionally generous financial support during, and immediately prior to, my residency at Brown University. The debt of longest standing is to the Max Richter Foundation, which supported my preliminary studies in Jerusalem from 1975-77 and provided timely assistance at crucial junctures thereafter, including provision of funds necessary for the publication of this volume. I wish to thank as well Brown University for naming me a University Fellow in 1977, and for extending to me a Religion Studies Fellowship in 1980. Finally, I am deeply grateful to the

Danforth Foundation, which appointed me Fellow in 1978, and since
then has shown genuine concern for my academic and personal well-
being.

This volume is dedicated to my wife, Cheryl Naomi Goldstein.
We met in Jerusalem, at the beginning of the journey which has
just now culminated in my first book. I am grateful to her for
choosing to commit herself to my journey, and for allowing me the
privilege of committing myself to hers. With the completion of
this book we conclude one journey and look forward with great
anticipation to embarking upon another.

June 1980   Martin S. Jaffee

Addendum: I wish to acknowledge with gratitude the generous help
of the Small Grants Committee of the University of Virginia
(Chairperson, Prof. Kenneth W. Thompson) towards defraying the
expenses of manuscript production.
      Additional thanks are due to Mr. Arthur Woodman for his
excellent work on the index, and to Ms. Joan Amatucci for a superb
job in typing an exceedingly difficult manuscript.

                        M.J.
                        Charlottesville, Va.
                        July 1981

ABBREVIATIONS AND BIBLIOGRAPHY

Ah.	= 'Ahilot
AJSR	= *Association for Jewish Studies Review*
Albeck	= Ḥanoch Albeck, *Shishah Sidrei Mishnah: Seder Zera^cim* (Jerusalem and Tel Aviv, 1957)
Albeck, "Hefqer"	= Sh. Albeck, "Hefqer," *EJ* 8:243
Allon, *History*	= Gedalyahu Allon, *A History of the Jews in Palestine During the Period of the Mishnah and Talmud* (Heb.) 2 vols. (Tel Aviv, 1961).
Arak.	= ^cArakhin
Aruch	= Alexander Kohut, ed., *Aruch Completum*, 8 vols. (Vienna, 1878-1892; second ed., 1926)
Applebaum, "Severan Empire"	= Shimon Applebaum, "The Province of Syria-Palestina as a Province of the Severan Empire," *Zion* XXIII (1958)
Avi-Yonah, *Jews*	= Michael Avi-Yonah, *The Jews of Palestine* (Oxford, 1976)
A.Z.	= ^cAbodah Zarah
b.	= *Babli*, Babylonian Talmud, cited by tractate and folio number of ed. Romm (Vilna, 1886); *ben*, "son of," as in *Simeon b. Gamaliel*
B	= Mishnah *Zera^cim*, MS. Berlin 93; see Sacks-Hutner, pp. 43, 77-78
BAR	= G. Ernest Wright and David Noel Freedman, eds., *The Biblical Archaeologist Reader* I (Ann Arbor, 1975, 1978)
B.B.	= Baba' Batra'
B.M.	= Baba' Meṣi^ca'
B.Q.	= Baba' Qamma'
Bek.	= Bekhorot
Ber.	= Berakhot
Bes.	= Beṣah

Bert.   = Obadiah b. Abraham of Bertinoro
                                 (fifteenth century), Mishnah Com-
                                 mentary in Romm ed. of Mishnah
                                 (Vilna, 1908)

Blackman   = Philip Blackman, *Mishnayot*, 2nd ed.,
                                 6 vols. (New York, 1964)

Britton-Brown   = H. A. Gleason, *The New Britton and*
                                 Brown Illustrated Flora of the
                                 North-Eastern United States and
                                 Adjacent Canada, 3 vols. (New York,
                                 1952)

Bunte   = G. Beer, C. Holtzmann, S. Krauss,
                                 K. Rengstorf, and L. Rost, eds.,
                                 Die Mischna: Text, Übersetzung und
                                 ausführliche Erklärung. Maaserot/
                                 Maaser Scheni (Vom Zehnten/Vom
                                 Zweiten Zehnten): Text, Übersetzung
                                 und Erklärung nebst einem text-
                                 kritischen Anhang, by Wolfgang
                                 Bunte (Berlin, 1962)

BZAW   = *Beihefte Zur Zeitschrift für die*
                                 Alttestamentliche Wissenschaft

C   = Mishnah, early printed edition of
                                 unknown origin, ca. 1516; cf. Sacks-
                                 Hutner, pp. 64, 82-83

Ca   = Mishnah, Ms. Cambridge 470, 1; see
                                 Sacks-Hutner, pp. 63, 67

Cohen   = Isadore Epstein, ed., *The Babylon-*
                                 ian Talmud: Seder Zera^{c}im II (Lon-
                                 don, 1948), "Maaseroth," tr. with
                                 notes by Phillip Cohen

Condit   = I. J. Condit, "Fig," *EB* 9:255

Dalman   = Gustav Dalman, *Arbeit und Sitte in*
                                 Palästina, 8 vols. (Gütersloh,
                                 1928-42)

Danby   = Herbert Danby, tr., *The Mishnah*
                                 (London, 1933)

Dem.   = Dema'i

Dt.   = Deuteronomy

E   = Tosefta, MS. Erfurt; see Lieberman,
                                 TZ, pp. 8-11

EB   = *Encyclopaedia Britannica*, 24 vols.
                                 (Chicago, 1968)

Ed.   = ^{C}Eduyyot

ed. princ.   = Tosefta, *editio princeps*, Venice,
                                  1521

Eissfeldt, *BZAW*   = Otto Eissfeldt, "Zum Zehnten bei
                                  den Babyloniern," *BZAW* 33 (Giessen,
                                  1918), pp. 163-174

Eissfeldt, *Erstlinge*   = Otto Eissfeldt, *Erstlinge und*
                                  Zehnten im Alten Testament
                                  (Leipzig, 1917)

Eissfeldt, *RGG*^{3} = Otto Eissfeldt, "Zehnten," *RGG*^{3}
                                  6:1877-1880

EJ   = *Encyclopaedia Judaica*, 16 vols.
                                  (Jerusalem, 1972), cited by volume
                                  and column (*EJ* 9:200)

Epstein   = Jacob N. H. Epstein, *Prologomenon*
                                  to the Text of the Mishnah (Heb.),
                                  2 vols., ed., E. Z. Melamed (Second
                                  ed., Jerusalem, Tel Aviv, 1964)

Erub.   = ^{C}Erubin

Ex.   = Exodus

Ez.   = Ezekiel

Feliks, *Haqla'ut*   = Yehudah Feliks, *Agriculture in*
                                  Palestine in the Period of the
                                  Mishna and Talmud (Heb.) (Jerusa-
                                  lem, Tel Aviv, 1963)

Feliks, *Plant World*   = Yehudah Feliks, *The Plant World of*
                                  the Bible (Heb.) (Tel Aviv, 1957)

Freedman   = Isadore Epstein, ed., *The Babylon-*
                                  ian Talmud: Seder Nashim (London,
                                  1936), "Nedarim," tr. with notes by
                                  H. Freedman

G   = Mishnah, MSS. from Cairo Genizah,
                                  listed and numbered in Sacks-
                                  Hutner, pp. 87-112

Gen.   = Genesis

Git.   = Gittin

Gereboff, *Tarfon*   = Joel Gereboff, *Rabbi Tarfon: The*
                                  Tradition, The Man, and Early
                                  Rabbinic Judaism (Missoula, 1979)

Goldenberg, *Meir*   = Robert Goldenberg, *The Sabbath Law*
                                  of Rabbi Meir (Missoula, 1979)

Goldschmidt   = Lazarus Goldschmidt, *Der Babylon-*
                                  ische Talmud, 12 vols. (Berlin, 1929)

Gordon, *M. Shebiit*   = Leonard Gordon, *A Study of Tractate*
                                Shebiit, Brown University doctoral
                                dissertation in progress, dir.
                                Jacob Neusner

GRA   = Elijah b. Solomon Zalman (1729-
                                1797), *Shanot Eliyahu*, Mishnah
                                Commentary in Romm ed. of Mishnah;
                                Tosefta emendations in Romm ed. of
                                Babylonian Talmud

Green, *Joshua*   = W. S. Green, *The Legal Traditions*
                                of Joshua ben Hananiah in Mishnah,
                                Tosefta, and Related Literature.
                                (Brown University dissertation,
                                1974)

Green, *Approaches*   = William S. Green, ed., *Approaches*
                                to Ancient Judaism I- (Missoula,
                                1979-   ), cited by volume and
                                page (*Approaches* I: 50)

Greenstone   = J. H. Greenstone, "Hefker," *JE*
                                6:316

Guthrie, "Tithe"   = H. H. Guthrie, Jr., "Tithe," *IDB*
                                4:654-655

Haas, *M. Maaser Sheni*   = Peter Haas, *A Study of Tractate*
                                Maaser Sheni. Brown University
                                doctoral dissertation in progress,
                                dir. Jacob Neusner

Hag.   = Ḥagigah
Hal.   = Ḥallah
Havivi-Eisenman   = Abraham Havivi and David Eisenman,
                                collaborating on *A Study of Trac-*
                                tate Hallah, in progress, dir.
                                Jacob Neusner

HD   = *Ḥasdei David.* David Samuel b. Jacob
                                Pardo (1718-1790), Tosefta Commen-
                                tary: *Sefer Ḥasdei David, Seder*
                                Zera^{c}im (Livorno, 1776; reprint
                                Jerusalem, 1970)

HY   = *Ḥazon Yeḥezqel.* Yeḥezqel Abramsky
                                (1886-1976), Tosefta Commentary;
                                Ḥazon Yeḥezqel, Seder Zera^{c}im
                                (Vilna, 1925; second ed.: Jerusalem,
                                1971)

Hor.   = Horayyot

Hul.	= Hullin
IDB	= *The Interpreter's Dictionary of the Bible*, 4 vols. (New York and Nashville, 1962), cited by volume and page (*IDB* 2:400)
JAAR	= *Journal of the American Academy of Religion*
Jastrow	= Marcus Jastrow, *A Dictionary of the Targumim, the Talmud Babli and Yerushalmi, and the Midrashic Literature*, 2 vols. (New York, 1895-1903; repr. New York, 1975), cited by entry and page (Jastrow, s.v., "*BGD*," p. 137)
JBL	= *Journal of Biblical Literature*
JE	= *The Jewish Encyclopedia*, 12 vols. (New York and London, 1901-1906; repr. New York, 1975), cited by volume and page (*JE* 2:400)
Jones	= Q. Jones, "Fenugreek," *EB* 9:176
Josephus, *Antiquities*	= Flavius Josephus, *Jewish Antiquities*, in *Works*, tr., H. St. J. Thackeray, R. Marcus, A. Wilkgren and L. H. Feldman, 9 vols. [Loeb Classical Library] (London and Cambridge, Mass., 1926-1965), vols. I-IX, cited by volume and paragraph (*Antiquities* IV:100)
JQR	= *The Jewish Quarterly Review*
JSJ	= *Journal for the Study of Judaism*
K	= Mishnah, MS. Kaufmann A 50; see Sacks-Hutner, pp. 63, 65-66
Kasovsky, *Mishnah*	= C. Y. Kasovsky, *Thesaurus Mishnae: Concordantiae verborum etc.*, 4 vols. (Tel Aviv, 1957, rev. 1967)
Kasovsky, *Tosefta*	= C. Y. Kasovsky, *Thesaurus Thosephthae: Concordantiae verborum etc.*, 6 vols. (Jerusalem, 1932-1961)
Kel.	= Kelim
Ket.	= Ketubot
Ker.	= Keritot
Kil.	= Kila'im

I. Klein   = Israel Klein, tr., *The Code of
                              Maimonides; Book Seven, The Book of
                              Agriculture* (New Haven, London,
                              1979)

S. Klein   = Samuel Klein, "Weinstock, Feigen-
                              baum und Sykamore in Palästina," in
                              Krauss, pp. 399-400

KM   = *Kesef Mishnah*. Joseph b. Ephraim
                              Karo (1488-1575). Commentary to
                              Maimonides' *Mishneh Torah*, in
                              standard editions of the latter

Kosovsky, *Mekhilta*   = B. Kosovsky, *Otzar Leshon Hattana'
                              im: Concordantiae verborum quae in
                              Mechilta D'Rabbi Ismael*, 4 vols.
                              (Jerusalem, 1966)

Kosovsky, *Sifra*   = B. Kosovsky, *Otzar Leshon Hatanna'
                              im: Concordantiae verborum quae
                              in Sifra aut Torat Kohanim*, 4 vols.
                              (Jerusalem, 1969)

Kosovsky, *Sifre*   = B. Kosovsky, *Otzar Leshon Hatanna'
                              im: Concordantiae verborum quae
                              in "Sifrei" Numeri et Deuteronomium*,
                              5 vols. (Jerusalem, 1974)

Krauss   = Samuel Krauss, ed., *Festschrift
                              Adolf Schwarz zum 70 Geburtstage*
                              (Berlin and Vienna, 1917)

Krauss, *TA*   = Samuel Krauss, *Talmudische Archäo-
                              logie*, 3 vols. (Leipzig, 1910-1912)

Krauss, "TBL"   = Samuel Krauss, "TBL: Eine neu
                              erschlossene hebräische Vokabel in
                              geschichtlichen Beleuchtung," in
                              Krauss, pp. 269-292

L   = Palestinian Talmud, MS. Leiden; see
                              Sacks-Hutner, pp. 63, 72

Levine, *Caesarea*   = Lee I. Levine, *Caesarea Under Roman
                              Rule* (Leiden, 1975)

Lv.   = Leviticus

Liddell-Scott   = H. G. Liddell and R. Scott, *A
                              Greek-English Lexicon*, revised and
                              augmented by H. S. Jones and R.
                              McKenzie (Oxford, 1925-1940)

Lieberman, *Hellenism*   = Saul Lieberman, *Hellenism in Jewish
                              Palestine* (New York, 1950)

Lieberman, "Palestine"   = Saul Lieberman, "Palestine in the
                                  Third and Fourth Centuries," *JQR*
                                  XXXVII-XXXVIII (1946-47)

Lieberman, *TK*   = Saul Lieberman, *Tosefta Ki-fshuta:*
                                  A Comprehensive Commentary on the
                                  Tosefta, I. *Order Zera^{c}im,* 2 vols.
                                  (New York, 1955), cited by volume,
                                  page and line (*TK* II:600.1-4)

Lieberman, *TM*   = Saul Lieberman, ed., *The Tosefta*
                                  According to Codex Vienna with
                                  Variants from Codex Erfurt, Geni-
                                  zah MSS. and Editio Princeps, II.
                                  The Order of Mo^{c}ed (New York, 1962)

Lieberman, *TZ*   = Saul Lieberman, ed., *The Tosefta*
                                  According to Codex Vienna with
                                  Variants from Codex Erfurt, Geni-
                                  zah MSS. and Editio Princeps, I.
                                  The Order of Zera^{c}im (New York,
                                  1955)

Löw   = Immanuel Löw, *Aramaeische Pflanzenna-*
                                  men (Leipzig, 1881)

Löw,   = Immanuel Löw, *Die Flora der Juden,*
                                  4 vols. (Vienna and Leipzig, 1924-
                                  1934)

M   = Babylonian Talmud, Codex Munich
                                  95; see Sacks-Hutner, pp. 63, 69-
                                  70

M.   = Mishnah (e.g., M. Maaserot, M.
                                  Kelim, etc.)

Ma.   = Ma^{c}aserot

MacDonald   = W. L. MacDonald, "Tyros," *Princeton*
                                  Encyclopaedia of Classical Sites
                                  (Princeton, 1976), p. 944

Maim., *Comm.*   = Maimonides (1135-1204), Mishnah
                                  Commentary; edition used: *Mishnah*
                                  ^{c}im perush rabbenu Moshe ben Maimon,
                                  Hebrew translation of the Arabic,
                                  introduction and notes, by Joseph
                                  D. Kappaḥ, I. *Zera^{c}im-Mo^{c}ed*
                                  (Jerusalem, 1964)

Maim., *Tithes*   = *Hilkhot Ma^{c}aser,* codification of
                                  tithing laws in Maimonides' *Mishneh*
                                  Torah, standard ed., cited by

	chapter and paragraph (*Tithes* 3:5). This edition is the source of references to Maim., *Heave-Offering, Second Tithe and Fourth Year Fruit, Seventh Year and Jubilee* and *Uncleanness of Foodstuffs*
Mal.	= Malakhi
Mak.	= Makkot
Makh.	= Makhshirin
MB	= *Minḥat Bikkurim*. Samuel Avigdor b. Abraham Karlin (nineteenth century), Tosefta Commentary in Romm ed. of Babylonian Talmud
Me.	= Me^{C}ilah
Meg.	= Megillah
Melamed, *DeVries*	= E. Z. Melamed, *Benjamin DeVries Memorial Volume* (Heb.) (Jerusalem, 1968)
Men.	= Menaḥot
MH	= *Mar'eh Hapannim*. Moses Margolioth (eighteenth century), supercommentary to the author's commentary to the Jerusalem Talmud (*Penei Moshe*; see *PM*), the Zhitomir edition (1860-1867)
Mid.	= Middot
M.Q.	= Mo^{C}ed Qaṭṭan
MR	= *Mishnah Rishonah*. Ephraim Isaac of Premysla (nineteenth century), Mishnah Commentary in Romm edition of Mishnah
M.S.	= Ma^{C}aser Sheni
MS.	= manuscript
MS	= *Melekhet Shlomo*. Solomon b. Joshua Adeni (ca. 1600), Mishnah Commentary in Romm edition of Mishnah
N	= Mishnah, *ed. princ.*, Naples 1492; see Sacks-Hutner, pp. 64, 81-82
Naz.	= Nazir
Ned.	= Nedarim
Neusner, *Appointed Times*	= Jacob Neusner, *A History of the Mishnaic Law of Appointed Times*, 5 vols. (Leiden, 1981), cited by volume (*Appointed Times* I)

Neusner, *Cults*   = Jacob Neusner, ed., *Christianity,*
                                      Judaism and Other Greco-Roman
                                      Cults: Studies for Morton Smith at
                                      Sixty, 4 vols. (Leiden, 1975),
                                      cited by volume and page (*Cults*
                                      II:25)

Neusner, *Damages*   = Jacob Neusner, *A History of the*
                                      Mishnaic Law of Damages, 5 vols.
                                      (Leiden, 1982), cited by volume
                                      (*Damages* I)

Neusner, *Eliezer*   = Jacob Neusner, *Eliezer ben Hyrcanus:*
                                      The Tradition and the Man, 2 vols.
                                      (Leiden, 1973), cited by volume
                                      and page (*Eliezer* I:25)

Neusner, "Form and Meaning"   = Jacob Neusner, "Form and Meaning:
                                      Mishnah's System and Mishnah's
                                      Language," *JAAR* 45 (1977), pp. 27-
                                      45

Neusner, *Holy Things*   = Jacob Neusner, *A History of the*
                                      Mishnaic Law of Holy Things, 6
                                      vols. (Leiden, 1978-1979), cited by
                                      volume (*Holy Things* I)

Neusner, *Judaism*   = Jacob Neusner, *Judaism: The Evidence*
                                      of the Mishnah (Chicago, 1981)

Neusner, *Pharisees*   = Jacob Neusner, *The Rabbinic Tradi-*
                                      tions About the Pharisees Before
                                      70, 3 vols. (Leiden, 1971) cited by
                                      volume and page (*Pharisees* I:25)

Neusner, *Purities*   = Jacob Neusner, *A History of the*
                                      Mishnaic Law of Purities, 22 vols.
                                      (Leiden, 1974-1977), cited by
                                      volume and page (*Purities* I:25)

Neusner, "Redaction"   = Jacob Neusner, "Redaction, Formula-
                                      tion, and Form: The Case of Mish-
                                      nah," *Jewish Quarterly Review* 70
                                      (1980), pp. 1-22

Nid.   = Niddah
Nu.   = Numbers
O^1 = MS. Oxford 366, Babylonian Talmud,
                                      Orders *Zera^{c}im* and *Mo^{c}ed*; see Sacks-
                                      Hutner, pp. 63, 67-69
O^2 = MS. Oxford 393, Mishnah *Zera^{c}im*
                                      with Maimonides' Commentary; see
                                      Sacks-Hutner, pp. 63, 76-77

Oppenheim, "Temple"   = A. Leo Oppenheim, "The Significance
                               of the Temple in the Ancient Near
                               East, II. The Mesopotamian Temple,"
                               BAR I:158-168

Oppenheimer, *^cAm Ha-aretz*   = Aharon Oppenheimer, *The ^cAm Ha-
                               Aretz: A Study in the Social History
                               of the Jewish People in the Hellen-
                               istic-Roman Period* (Leiden, 1977)

Oppenheimer, "First Tithe"   = Aharon Oppenheimer, "The Separation
                               of First Tithe During the Second
                               Temple Period: Fact vs. Theory"
                               (Heb.), in Melamed, *DeVries*, pp.
                               70-83

Orl.   = ^cOrlah

P   = Mishnah, MS. Parma DeRossi 138; see
                               Sacks-Hutner, pp. 64, 79

Par.   = Parah

Peck, *M. Terumot*   = Alan Peck, *A Study of Tractate
                               Terumot*, Brown University disserta-
                               tion in progress, dir. Jacob
                               Neusner

Pes.   = *Pesaḥim*

Porton, "Dispute"   = Gary G. Porton, "The Artificial
                               Dispute: Ishmael and Aqiba," in
                               Neusner, *Cults* IV:18:29

Porton, *Ishmael*   = Gary G. Porton, *The Tradition of
                               Rabbi Ishmael*, I. *The Non-Exegeti-
                               cal Materials* (Leiden, 1976)

Press   = Isaiah Press, *A Topographical-
                               Historical Encyclopedia of Pales-
                               tine*, 4 vols. (Jerusalem, 1955)

PM   = *Penei Moshe*. Moses Margolioth
                               (eighteenth century), Commentary
                               to the Jerusalem Talmud, Zhitomir
                               edition (see *MH*)

Primus, *Aqiva*   = Charles Primus, *Aqiva's Contribution
                               to the Law of Zera^cim* (Leiden, 1977)

Qid.   = Qiddushin

Qin.   = Qinnim

R   = Jerusalem Talmud, MS. Rome 133;
                               Sacks-Hutner, pp. 63, 73

R.   = Rabbi

Rabad	= Abraham b. David of Posquieres (ca. 1120-1198), glosses to Maimonides' *Mishneh Torah*, in standard editions of the latter
RDBZ	= David ibn Zimra (1479-1589), super-commentary to Maimonides' *Mishneh Torah*, in standard editions of the latter
Rashi	= Solomon b. Isaac of Troyes (1040-1105), commentary to Babylonian Talmud, Romm edition
RGG^3	= *Die Religion in Geschichte und Gegenwart*, 3rd edition, 6 vols. (Tübingen, 1957-1962), cited by volume and page (RGG^3 6:200)
R.H.	= Rosh Hashanah
Ribmaṣ	= Isaac b. Melkhiṣedeq of Siponto (ca. 1090-1160), Mishnah Commentary in Romm edition of the Babylonian Talmud
Rosh	= Asher b. Yeḥiel (1250-1327), Mish-nah Commentary in Romm edition of Babylonian Talmud
S	= MS. British Museum 403, Palestinian Talmud, *Zera^{c}im*, with commentary of Sirillo; see Sacks-Hutner, pp. 63, 73-75
Sa	= Mishnah Zera^{c}im, MS. Sassoon 531; see Sacks-Hutner, pp. 63, 68
Sacks-Hutner	= *The Mishnah with Variant Readings, Order Zera^{c}im*, 2 vols., ed. Nissan Sacks (Jerusalem, 1972-1975)
Sammter	= A. Sammter, tr., *Mischnajot: die sechs Ordnungen der Mischna, hebräischen Text mit Punktation, deutschen Übersetzung und Erklärung*, I. *Sera^{c}im*, 6 vols., 3rd edition (Basel, 1968)
San.	= Sanhedrin
Sarason, *M. Demai*	= Richard S. Sarason, *A History of the Mishnaic Law of Agriculture: A Study of Tractate Demai, Part One* (Leiden, 1979)

Sarason, "Mishnah and   = Richard S. Sarason, "Mishnah and
   Scripture"   Scripture: Observations on the Law
                                       of Tithing in *Seder Zera^{c}im*," in
                                       W. S. Green, ed., *Approaches* II
                                       (Chico, 1980)

Schürer-Vermes-Millar   = Emil Schürer, *The History of the
                                       Jewish People in the Age of Jesus
                                       Christ*, rev. and ed. by G. Vermes
                                       and F. Millar, Vol. I (Edinburgh,
                                       1973)

Sens   = Samson b. Abraham of Sens (twelfth-
                                       thirteenth centuries), Mishnah
                                       Commentary in Romm edition of
                                       Babylonian Talmud

Shab.   = Shabbat
Shabu.   = Shabu^{c}ot
Sheb.   = Shebi^{c}it
Sheq.   = Sheqalim
Sifra   = *Sifra debe Rab, hu' Sefer Torat
                                       Kohanim*, ed., I. H. Weiss (Vienna,
                                       1892; repr. New York, 1946)

Sifre Nu.   = *Siphre de'be Rab, Fasciculus primus:
                                       Siphre ad Numeros adjecto Siphre
                                       Zutta*, ed. H. S. Horovitz (Leipzig,
                                       1917; repr. Jerusalem, 1966)

Sifre Dt.   = *Siphre ad Deuteronomium*, ed., L.
                                       Finkelstein, with H. S. Horovitz
                                       (Berlin, 1939)

Sirillo   = Solomon b. Joseph Sirillo (d. 1558),
                                       Commentary to Palestinian Talmud,
                                     Zera^{c}im (Jerusalem, 1963)

Sot.   = Soṭah
Sperber   = Daniel Sperber, *Roman Palestine
                                       200-400: Money and Prices* (Ramat
                                       Gan, 1974)

Sperber, "Pyrgos"   = Daniel Sperber, "On the *Pyrgos* as a
                                       Farm Building," *AJSR* 1 (1976),
                                       pp. 359-361

Strack   = Hermann L. Strack, *Introduction to
                                       the Talmud and Midrash* (New York,
                                       1974)

Suk.   = Sukkah

Sussman, "Inscription"	= Jacob Sussman, "A Halakhic Inscription from the Bet Shean Valley" (Heb.), *Tarbiz* 43 (1973-74)
T.	= Tosefta
Ta.	= Ta^{c}anit
Tam.	= Tamid
Tarbiz	= *Tarbiz: A Quarterly for Jewish Studies*
TAS	= *Tosefot Anshei Shem*, anonymous collection of novellae on the Mishnah (nineteenth century) in Romm edition of Mishnah
Tem.	= Temurah
Ter.	= Terumot
Theophrastus, *Enquiry*	= Theophrastus, *Enquiry into Plants*, tr. Sir Arthur Hart, 2 vols. [Loeb Classical Library], cited by book, chapter and paragraph (e.g., *Enquiry* I. ii.9-10)
Toh.	= Tohorot
TYT	= *Tosefot Yom Tob*. Yom Tob Lippmann Heller (1579-1654), Mishnah Commentary in Romm edition of Mishnah
TYY	= *Tif'eret Yisra'el Yakin*. Israel b. Gedaliah Lipshcütz (1782-1860), Mishnah Commentary in Romm edition of Mishnah
Uqs.	= ^{c}Uqṣin
V	= Tosefta, MS. Vienna Heb. 20; see Lieberman, *TZ*, pp. 11-12
Weinfeld, "Tithes"	= Moshe Weinfeld, "Tithes," *EJ* 15: 1156-1162
White, *Roman Farming*	= K. D. White, *Roman Farming* (Ithaca, N.Y., 1970)
Wright, "Temple"	= G. Ernest Wright, "The Significance of the Temple in the Ancient Near East, III. The Temple in Palestine-Syria," *BAR*, I:167-174
y.	= Yerushalmi, Jerusalem Talmud, *ed. princ.*, Venice (1520-1523), cited by tractate, pericope, folio and column (y. Ma. 1:1[48d])

Y.T.   = Yom Tob

Yad.   = Yada^{c}im

Yeb.   = Yebamot

Z   = Mishnah, MS. Paris 362, with com-
                                   mentary of Sens; see Sacks-Hutner,
                                   pp. 64, 79-80

Zab.   = Zabim

Zeb.   = Zebaḥim

Zahavy   = Tzvee Zahavy, *The Traditions of
                                   Eleazar ben Azariah* (Missoula, 1977)

Zuckermandel   = *Tosephta, based on the Erfurt and
                                   Vienna Codices*, M.S. Zuckermandel
                                   (Trier, 1881-1882; rev. with sup-
                                   plement by Saul Lieberman, Jerusalem,
                                   1936-1939; reprint, Jerusalem, 1970)

Addendum: In the year which has elapsed since the completion of
the manuscript, two Brown University dissertations cited in this
study have been published or sent to press. Following are the
bibliographical citations of those dissertations as used in this
volume in addition to the published titles:

Haas, *M. Maaser Sheni*   = P. Haas, *A History of the Mishnaic
                                   Law of Agriculture: Maaser Sheni*
                                   (Chico, 1980)

Peck, *M. Terumot*   = A. Peck, *The Priestly Gift in
                                   Mishnah* (Chico, in press for 1981)

TRANSLITERATIONS

א	=	'	ל	=	l
ב‬,בּ	=	b	מ‬,ם	=	m
ג‬,גּ	=	g	נ‬,ן	=	n
ד‬,דּ	=	d	ס	=	ś
ה	=	h	ע	=	ᶜ
ו	=	w	פ‬,פּ‬,ף	=	p
ז	=	z	צ‬,ץ	=	ṣ
ח	=	ḥ	ק	=	q
ט	=	ṭ	ר	=	r
י	=	y	שׁ	=	š
כ‬,כּ‬,ך	=	k	שׂ	=	s

ת‬,תּ = t

    Transliterations represent the consonantal structure of the
Hebrew word, with no attempt made to vocalize. We do not distinguish between the spirantized and non-spirantized forms of *b*, *g*,
d, *k*, *p*, and *t*. Verbal roots are indicated by capitalization,
e.g., *BGD*. When, on occasion a word is vocalized, the following
notation is used:

a = *qamaṣ*, *pataḥ*   i = *ḥiriq*
ei = *ṣere-yod*   o = *ḥolem*, *ḥolem ḥaśer*,
e = *ṣere*, *śegol*, vocal *šewa'*   *qamaṣ qaṭan*
           u = *šuruq*, *qubbuṣ*

Quiescent *šewa'* is not represented. Proper names and commonly
used words are reproduced in their most frequent English usage,
e.g., Eleazar, Mishnah, etc.

INTRODUCTION

A. *The Issues of Tractate Maaserot*

Tractate Maaserot (Tithes) defines the class of produce which
is subject to Scripture's diverse agricultural taxes,[1] and determines when payment of these taxes is due. It thus amplifies, in
rather predictable ways, those aspects of Scripture which are
likely to interest Israelites concerned with the proper tithing
of their food. That is, the tractate tells its audience what to
tithe, and stipulates when they must remove the offerings from
food they wish to eat. Where Scripture is clear on these matters,
Mishnah is content to repeat and highlight the obvious. Thus in
regard to the kinds of produce which must be tithed, Maaserot
simply affirms Scripture's view that these gifts, the priestly
dues and tithes,[2] are to be offered from all produce grown in the
fields of the Land of Israel (cf. Dt. 14:22).

Maaserot receives little scriptural guidance, however, regarding its second, and major, focus of interest, the removal of the
offerings from produce which is ready for the use of its owner.
Scripture's interest in this question is colored by its overriding
concern for the needs of those who are to receive the various
offerings. Scripture simply stipulates, therefore, that the tithes
must be paid each year. It goes not, however, elaborate how this
is done. By contrast, Tractate Maaserot is primarily interested
in the concerns of the common Israelites who want to eat their
food. The tractate's questions, accordingly, reflect those concerns. That is: When, in the course of a crop's growth, may it
be used to satisfy the obligation to tithe? When, further, in the
course of the harvest of the crop, must the tithes actually be
paid?

Mishnah's answer to this two-fold question is generated by
Scripture's assumption that the agricultural offerings of the Land
of Israel are a sacred tax which Israelites owe to God for the
property they take from his Land (Lv. 27:30).[3] Accordingly, the
tractate points out that produce *may* be tithed as soon as it
ripens, for at this point the crop becomes valuable as property.
Payment of the tithes is not due, however, until the farmer or
householder actually claims his harvested produce as personal
property. This occurs, in Maaserot's view, whenever a person
brings untithed produce from his field into his home, or when he
prepares untithed produce for sale in the market. Produce

1

appropriated in this fashion is forbidden for consumption until it
is tithed. Having claimed the produce for his own personal use,
the farmer must remove those portions which belong to God before
he may use it himself.

The framers of the tractate, however, are troubled by their
own notion that produce need be tithed only after it has been
claimed as property. What disturbs them is that now there normally
will be a lengthy period of time--beginning with the ripening of
the crop and extending until well after the harvest--during which
the produce will remain untithed. It is precisely during this
indeterminate period prior to tithing, however, that some of the
produce is likely to be eaten by those who harvest it or who are
otherwise involved in its processing or transport. This is what
concerns Tractate Maaserot, for untithed produce presents a tax-
onomical problem. On the one hand, such produce is not sacred
food, restricted for the use of priests, for the dues have not yet
been designated within the produce and set aside from it for their
meals. On the other hand, the produce cannot be used as profane
or common food, for it is capable of yielding offerings which stand
under the claim of God. Untithed produce, it follows, is subject
to a special set of rules which take account of its ambiguous
character. The problematic of Maaserot, as it articulates these
rules, is to regulate the use of produce which is neither sacred
nor profane, neither wholly God's nor wholly man's.[4]

Maaserot's basic principle for regulating the use of untithed
produce is simple. Since untithed produce is taxonomically ambiguous, neither sacred nor profane, it may not be eaten as priests
eat their sacred offerings or as common folk eat their daily food.
That is, untithed produce may not be eaten in meals.[5] This does
not mean, however, that untithed produce is entirely forbidden for
use as food. To the contrary, it is permitted for random eating
as a snack or in any other informal manner. The point is that the
anomalous character of untithed food prevents it from serving the
normal purpose of food which is sanctified to priests or of tithed
food which is available for the use of commoners. As long, however, as a person eats his untithed food in a manner which respects
its anomalous character, he may do so without removing any offerings. Should he, to the contrary, wish to use the produce in a
meal, he must tithe forthwith. He must make the food fit for
normal use by designating the sacred offerings in the produce and
removing them from the remainder. Thereafter, the produce is
thoroughly profane, and is fit for use as its owner desires.

The bulk of the tractate is concerned to apply this principle
to the use of untithed produce from the moment it ripens in the
field, through the harvest season, and ultimately to the point at
which it is brought into the home or sold in the market. At issue
throughout is to determine whether untithed produce eaten during
this period of transition is intended to serve as a meal or as a
snack. If the former, the householder is forbidden from eating
the produce at all until he tithes. If, however, the owner of the
produce simply wishes to snack on the untithed fruit, he may do so
without obligation. How, then, do we distinguish a meal from a
snack? One possible criterion, scarcely explored by Maaserot,
might be the quantity eaten and the context of the act of eating.
A meal, that is, requires a substantial amount of food and is
eaten at a table. A snack, to the contrary, consists of a small
amount of food eaten, so to speak, on the run. Maaserot prefers,
instead, a more subtle criterion, namely, the intentions of the
person who actually eats the food. The tractate rules that what
a person intends to eat as a snack, however great the quantity,
is indeed a snack, and is permitted without the removal of tithes.
Correspondingly, what a person intends to eat as a meal, however
minimal in quantity, is deemed a meal, and is forbidden for such
use until tithes are removed. The liability of a particular batch
of produce to the removal of tithes, then, is determined solely
by what its owner intends to do with it. To be sure, Maaserot
recognizes that intentions must usually be inferred by what people
actually do. To a great extent, therefore, its discussion of
intention is actually an essay in the interpretation of human
actions. Thus the tractate will rule, for example, that a farmer
who cooks untithed produce on a field stove clearly intends to
make a meal of it, for food used in meals is normally cooked. Had
he simply left the produce in the field to ripen, however, no such
intention could be inferred. Any uncooked food eaten in the field
by such a person would be deemed a snack unless the owner's subsequent actions indicated a change of intention. It would, of
course, be exempt as well from the removal of tithes.

This summary of the tractate's basic conceptions yields a
curious result. The criteria which determine that produce must be
tithed appear to be independent of each other. Produce is liable
to the removal of tithes either at the time it is intended for
use as a meal or at the time it is claimed as private property,
whichever happens to come first. It is appropriate, then, to ask
what these two criteria have in common. The answer, of course,

is that in both instances a human being has appropriated for his
personal benefit produce against which God has a claim. God's
claim is violated, in other words, whenever an Israelite farmer or
householder prepares to use untithed produce as if he had full
rights regarding its disposition. Whether he prepares it for a
meal out in the field, or brings raw food into his home for the
use of his family, he has claimed rights of ownership which in
fact are still God's. Accordingly, the Israelite must give to God
his due before exercising his own property rights.

We see then that the taxonomic ambiguity which shapes the
problematic of Maaserot--the anomalous character of untithed pro-
duce--masks a theological problem as well. That is to determine,
and then to adjudicate, the respective claims of man and God to
the produce of the Land of Israel. At stake, in other words, is
the relationship of Israel to the lord of its ancestral land.
The theological agendum emerges most clearly if, from our present
standpoint, we return to the key points which interest Mishnah
as produce passes from the field of the Israelite farmer to his
table. We recall that produce first becomes subject to the law
of tithes when it ripens in the field. God's claim to the tithes
of the produce, that is, is made only when the produce itself
becomes of value to the farmer. Only after produce has ripened
may we expect the farmer to use it in his own meals, or sell it to
others for use in theirs. Thus God's claim to it is first provoked, and must therefore be protected, from that point onward.
As we have seen, the produce is permitted as food only if the
farmer acknowledges God's prior claim, e.g., by refraining from
eating it as he would his own produce. Should the farmer overreach
his privilege, however, either by preparing to make a meal of the
produce in his field or by claiming to be its sole owner, he loses
his privilege to eat altogether, until he tithes. Once God's
claim against the produce is satisfied by the removal of the
tithes, the produce is released for use in all daily meals. It
is now common food.

What is striking in all this is that the entire mechanism of
restrictions and privileges, from the field to home or market, is
set in motion solely by the intentions of the common farmer.
Priests cannot claim their dues whenever they choose, and God himself plays no active role in establishing when the produce must
be tithed. Indeed, the framers of Maaserot assume a profound
passivity on the part of God. For them, it is human actions and
intentions which move God to affect the world. God's claims
against the Land's produce, that is to say, are only reflexes of

those very claims on the part of Israelite farmers. God's interest
in his share of the harvest, as I said, is first provoked by the
desire of the farmer for the ripened fruit of his labor. His claim
to that fruit, furthermore, becomes binding only when the farmer
makes ready to claim his own rights to its use, whether in the
field or at home or market.

The fundamental theological datum of Masserot, then, is that
God acts and wills in response to human intentions, God's invisible
action can be discerned by carefully studying the actions of human
beings. This datum must now be assessed in the context of the
time and place in which Tractate Masserot is constructed. With
the Mishnah as a whole, Maaserot comes into being in second-century
Palestine, at a time in which Israel's hopes for God's victory over
his enemies have been abandoned, and in a place in which his
Temple, the visible symbol of his presence, no longer stands.[6]
In such a time and place, both Maaserot's loyalty to Scripture's
ancient tithing law, and its distinctive innovations upon that
law, are equally suggestive. Fundamentally, Maaserot affirms an
essential continuity of God's lordship over the Land of Israel.
It presents Scripture's command to tithe all the fruit of the
field as an obligation which extends even to the present. God's
ancient tax on the Land must still be offered in its proper season,
as it was when the Temple still stood and its priestly officiants
brought God's blessing from heaven into the Land. At a time in
which God's inability to protect his Land or its inhabitants has
long been clear, this is a bold claim indeed. Maaserot asserts
that historical catastrophe has left the sacred economy of Israel
undisturbed. While the Temple is gone, the Land remains holy and
its fruit is still under the claim of God. Those remaining in
the Land, it follows, remain bound by the ancient system of obligations which their ancestors accepted in covenant with God.

The very law which affirms the continuity of God's lordship
over Israel, however, reveals how much has truly changed, both in
the Land and in the imagination of some of its inhabitants. Unlike the theologians of Scripture's priestly laws, Maaserot's
authorities can no longer turn to the visible evidence of God's
presence, the Temple, in order to legitimate the collection of
agricultural taxes. Rather, the framers of Maaserot must locate
the play of God's power, and the foundation of his claims upon
the Land, in an invisible realm immune from the hazards of history.
This, as we have seen, is the realm of human appetite and intention, as they are aroused in the mundane course of daily affairs,
and as they are directed toward the produce of God's Land. In

Maaserot's view, the law by which God's lordship is affirmed is
itself set in motion by those who continue to affirm that he is
Lord. As I have pointed out, the God of Israel acts and wills in
Maaserot only in reaction to the action and intention of his
Israelite partner on the Land. Nowhere do the framers of Maaserot
expect--or allow for--unilateral or uncontrollable actions proceeding from the initiative of God. As in the time of the Temple,
then, God remains Lord of the Land of Israel, and owner of its
fruits. But when his Temple no longer stands and his Land has been
defiled, his status as Lord depends upon the action of his remaining people. That is the whole point of linking God's claim upon
the tithes to the social rhythms of the agricultural enterprise.
Those who impose upon themselves the task of reconstructing the
human and social fabric of Israelite life make effective the holiness of the Land and make real the claims of its God. This reci-
procity between Israel and its God, the near parity between two
partners in the task of re-creation, is what distinguishes the
vision of Maaserot's thinkers from that of the priestly theoreti-
cians of Scripture, from whom Mishnah inherits and transforms the
law of tithes.

B. *The Structure of the Tractate*

Maaserot's concern to link invisible, supernatural events to
the common intentions of Israelite farmers during the course of
the agricultural cycle is clearly reflected in the structure of
the tractate.[7] All of its laws may be subsumed under three topical headings, which discuss, in turn, the status of produce under
the law during (1) the natural cycle of agriculture, (2) in the
course of the activities which bring produce from field to table,
and (3) ambiguous cases in which the status of the produce is in
doubt because the intentions of its owner are uncertain. Unit I
(M. 1:1-4) is concerned with the conditions under which produce
becomes subject to the law of tithes, and its consumption is
limited to random snacks. Unit II (M. 1:5-4:5A), by far the
largest and most complex of the tractate's units, investigates
four activities which complete the farmer's appropriation of harvested produce for his own use, and so impose upon him the obligation to tithe. Unit III (M. 4:5B-5:8) is dependent upon both of
the foregoing units. It investigates the farmer's obligation to
tithe his produce in cases in which the natural conditions of
ripeness (unit I) are unmet, or the normal processes of appropriation (unit II) are imperfectly accomplished. Thus the unit
explores the application of the law in cases in which clear

criteria of liability do not emerge from the facts provided in the
major portion of the tractate. Maaserot's study of these issues
is best clarified by a survey of the tractate's main units and
their subtopics.

I. *Conditions under which produce becomes subject to the law*
   (M. 1:1-4)

A. *General conditions* (M. 1:1)

    M. 1:1A All produce which is edible, privately-owned, and
            which grows from the earth must be tithed.

    M. 1:1B Produce is subject to the law as soon as it becomes
            edible.

B. *Specific conditions* (M. 1:2-4)

    M. 1:2 At what point in their growth do various kinds of
          produce become subject to the law?
          (+ list of ten: Figs--when they ripen, etc.)

    M. 1:3 (ten further items: Carobs--when they become spotted,
          etc.)

    M. 1:4 Cucumbers, gourds, melons are tithed at any point in
          their growth (+ dispute, Simeon)

    Unit I sets the context for the entire tractate. All produce
which becomes liable to the removal of tithes is presumed to have
first met both the general and specific criteria enumerated at A
and B. A points out that only agricultural produce useful as food
need be tithed, while B's list offers an exhaustive set of examples
in which criteria relevant to specific kinds of produce are defined.

II. *Procedures by which harvested produce is rendered liable to
    the removal of tithes* (M. 1:5-4:5A)

A. *Processing and storage of untithed produce* (M. 1:5-8)

    M. 1:5 At what point in its processing is produce rendered
          liable to the removal of tithes?
          (+ list of four: cucumbers and gourds--when he removes
          the fuzz, etc.)
          Under what conditions? When he intends to market the
          produce. But if he intends to bring it home, he
          snacks on the produce without tithing until he arrives
          at his home, at which point he must tithe.

    M. 1:6 (four further items continue M. 1:5: dried fruit--
          when he piles it up, etc.)

    M. 1:7 Wine--when he skims it; oil--when it flows into the
          vat

M. 1:8 Fig cakes--when he glazes them; dried figs--when he
        presses them (+ dispute, Yose)

B. *Acquisition of another's untitled produce in four modes*
   (M. 2:1-3:4)

   1. *Gifts* (M. 2:1-4)

   M. 2:1 One who says, "Take figs for yourselves"--the reci-
           pient makes a snack of them without tithing until he
           arrives home, at which point he tithes (+ comple-
           mentary case demonstrating the principle).

   M. 2:2 If men were in a shop and a passer-by said, "Take
           figs," they make a snack without tithing, but the
           shopkeeper must tithe before eating, for the shop
           is like his home (+ gloss, Judah).

   M. 2:3 A transporter of untithed produce makes a snack,
           but must tithe anything he eats after reaching his
           destination (+ gloss, Judah).

   M. 2:4 Unprocessed produce from which heave-offering is
           removed--Eliezer prohibits a snack/Sages permit.

   2. *Purchases* (M. 2:5-6)

   M. 2:5 One who purchases five figs for an *issar* may not
           eat them without tithing: Meir. Judah: he may
           eat them one by one without tithing, but must tithe
           if he gathers the purchase together as a batch.

   M. 2:6 One who purchases ten figs, a grape-cluster, a
           pomegranate, a melon eats one by one without tithing
           (+ complementary case in which the principle is
           questioned).

   3. *Barter* (M. 2:7-3:3)

   M. 2:7 One who hires a harvester--the harvester eats during
           his labor without tithing, because the Torah gives
           him this privilege (+ statement of the principle).

   M. 2:8 Those who trade figs with each other--both parties
           must tithe what they receive (+ gloss, Judah).

   M. 3:1 One who brings unprocessed produce into his court-
           yard--his dependents eat without tithing, but his
           workers must tithe if they depend upon him for their
           board.

   M. 3:2 One who brings workers to the field--if they depend
           upon him for their board, they eat one by one from
           the tree.

   M. 3:3 One who hires gardeners--they eat one by one from
           the tree.

4. *Lost produce found by another* (M. 3:4)

    M. 3:4 If one found figs in the road--they are permitted
            for untithed use unless they were processed prior to
            being lost.

C. *Bringing produce from the field into the courtyard or home*
    (M. 3:5-10)

    M. 3:5 What kind of courtyard renders liable produce brought
            within it?

            (+ five opinions: Ishmael, Aqiba, Nehemiah, Yose, Judah)

    M. 3:6 Roofs, gate-houses, etc., which stand within the court-
            yard--they do/do not share the status of the courtyard
            itself.

    M. 3:7 Storage-huts, watch-towers, etc., outside the courtyard
            do not render liable produce brought within them. Yose;
            any building which is not a year-round home has no power
            to render liable the produce of its owner.

    M. 3:8 A fig-tree standing in a courtyard--the householder
            eats one by one from the tree without tithing (+ gloss,
            Simeon).

    M. 3:9 A vine growing in a courtyard--he eats an entire cluster
            of grapes without tithing: Tarfon. Aqiba: he eats
            one grape at a time without tithing.

    M. 3:10 A fig-tree standing in a courtyard, with its bough
            extending into the garden--he may eat fruit from that
            bough as he pleases, but only one by one from the part
            of the tree within the courtyard.

D. *Preparation of untithed produce for use in a meal* (M. 4:1-5A)

    M. 4:1 One who pickles, boils or salts untithed produce in
            the field is required to tithe before eating.

    M. 4:2 Children who hid untithed figs, intending to eat them
            on the Sabbath, but forgot to tithe them--after the
            Sabbath the figs remain liable to the removal of
            tithes (+ dispute, Houses).

    M. 4:3 Untithed olives which are being softened for pressing--
            he eats one by one from the bin without tithing, but
            if he salts a small batch he must tithe (+ gloss,
            Eliezer).

    M. 4:4 Untithed wine which is drunk at the vat--Meir permits
            him to drink without tithing, Eleazar b. Sadoq forbids.
            Sages forbid only if he mixes the wine with hot water
            before drinking it.

    M. 4:5A Untithed barley--he may husk and eat one kernel at a

time without tithing (+ matching case demonstrating
identical principle).

This large unit follows logically from unit I. Produce which
has ripened and become subject to the law (unit I) has now been
harvested, and awaits its final disposition. We recall that,
while it is forbidden for use in meals at this point, the untithed produce is nevertheless permitted for nibbling in random
fashion. A-C take up discussion of three common means by which
the farmer or householder appropriate such produce for their own
use, and incur thereby the obligation to tithe it. The sequence
of topics at A-C is explained chronologically. A's interest is in
the farmer's rights to use the produce between the time he processes it for storage and the moment it is actually stored in his
home or prepared for sale. B discusses the liability of such
produce which never reaches the farmer's home, but rather is
acquired by another as a gift or in some other formal or informal
transaction. The problem is to determine when the recipient is
deemed the new owner, and therefore responsible for tithing whatever he eats. At C the farmer himself finally reaches his home
with the untithed produce. Now it is necessary to determine which
areas surrounding his home are deemed part of the home itself.
Produce brought into such areas must be tithed before it is eaten.
The issue of D, the final subunit of unit II, cuts through all
chronological considerations, and is equally appropriate at the
beginning of the end of the unit. If the householder follows none
of the procedures of A-C, but immediately sets the produce aside
for use as a normal meal, it is liable at that point to the removal
of tithes, regardless of all other considerations.

The sequence of pericopae within each sub-unit yields few
difficulties. A begins with a simple question (M. 1:5), and
supplies a cogent answer in an exhaustive, heavily-glossed, list
(M. 1:5-8). The most ambitious sub-unit, B, raises the most
literary problems. The sequence of topics--gifts (B1), purchases
(B2), barter (B3), lost produce (B4)--appears to have no particular meaning. The logic emerges only from the content of the
specific cases. B1 begins with informal transactions in the
marketplace, and is followed at B2 with discussion of commercial
transactions in the marketplace. B3 then asks about commercial
transactions performed outside the marketplace, e.g., in the
field. B4, finally, concludes with informal transactions outside
the marketplace, i.e., lost produce found in the road. The
redactor's sequence, then, is: transactions in the market--

informal and commercial/transactions outside the market--commercial
and informal. Of the pericopae distributed within these four
topical units, only M. 2:3-4 seem out of place. They are located
within the category of gifts because the problem of each pericope,
like that of M. 2:1-2, is to determine the point at which the
householder's privilege to snack on his produce ceases, and his
obligation to tithe is imposed. The remainder of the unit offers
no difficulties. C is in two parts, M. 3:5-7 and M. 3:8-10. The
former is interested solely in structures which may or may not be
deemed homes, while the latter investigates the interplay of laws
appropriate to produce harvested in the field with those governing
produce which is brought into the home or courtyard. D's discussion begins with a general rule of thumb (M. 4:1), and proceeds
to explore ambiguous cases and possible exceptions (M. 4:2-5A).

III. *Unmet conditions and incomplete procedures: ambiguities in
      application of the law* (M. 4:5B-5:8)

  A. *Unmet conditions: produce which is edible, but is normally
       not deemed food* (M. 4:5B-4:6)

    M. 4:5B If coriander is sown for seed, the leaves are exempt
               from the law. If it is sown for the leaves, both
               seeds and leaves are subject to the law.

    M. 4:6   Pods of fenugreek, etc., are subject to the law:
               Gamaliel. Caper is tithed for its pods, berries and
               flowers: Eliezer. Aqiba: only the berries are
               tithed, for they are the normally-eaten part.

  B. *Incomplete procedures: produce taken from the field prior
       to the harvest of the crop* (M. 5:1-2)

    M. 5:1   One who uproots shoots for transplanting need not
               tithe. If he purchased produce before the harvest,
               or sent it to a friend before the harvest, he need
               not tithe (+ gloss, Eleazar b. Azariah).

    M. 5:2   One who uproots turnips and radishes as a seed crop
               must tithe, for this is their harvest (+ complemen-
               tary case).

  C. *Unmet conditions: produce which is sold or purchased while
       inedible* (M. 5:3-5)

    M. 5:3   A man shall not sell his produce, once it ripens, to
               one who is untrustworthy to remove tithes. He may
               take the ripe fruit for his own use, however, and
               sell the unripened remainder to whomever he wishes.

    M. 5:4   A man shall not sell his straw, olive-peat or grape-
               lees to one who is untrustworthy. He may, however,

remove what is edible and sell the rest to whomever
he wishes.

M. 5:5   One who purchases a field of greens in Syria--if he
         bought it before the crop ripened, he need not tithe
         once the crop ripens.

         (+ glosses, Judah, Simeon b. Gamaliel)

         Rabbi: he tithes the percentage of produce which
         ripens under his ownership.

D. *Incomplete procedures: produce which is insufficiently processed, or produce the processing of which is in doubt*
   (M. 5:6-7)

M. 5:6   One who soaks grape-lees for their liquid--if he
         extracted the same amount of water which he added,
         the water need not be tithed as wine. Judah: he
         must tithe.

M. 5:7   Ant-holes beside a stack of grain--grain within the
         holes is liable to the removal of tithes, for it
         is presumed to have been processed with the adjacent
         stack.

E. *Unmet conditions: produce which is not grown in the Land of
   Israel, or which is not food* (M. 5:8)

M. 5:8   Garlic of Baalbek is exempt. Inedible seeds are
         exempt.

M.'s concluding unit takes up the facts of the first two, and
explores ambiguities in their application. The theory of I and
II is that natural conditions of ripeness must exist before human
procedures of appropriation can render produce liable to the
removal of tithes. Two problems now arise. On the one hand, it
is necessary to determine the farmer's obligation in cases in
which the natural condition of edibility is deemed of no concern
to the farmer (A), or indeed is not met at the time that the
farmer appropriates the crop (C, E). On the other hand, there are
cases in which the produce involved is perfectly edible and
desirable to the farmer, but his appropriation of it has not
followed normal procedure. That is, he has taken produce from
the field before the time of the harvest (B) or processed it insufficiently for use as a table commodity (D). In each set of
circumstances we must decide how the farmer's obligation to tithe
is modified by the fact that one or another set of necessary conditions is lacking.

The above outline demonstrates the cogency with which the
creators of Tractate Maaserot undertake their inquiry. They

clearly wish to limit the consumption of produce at two critical
junctures in its passage from the field to the table. They direct
attention to these junctures by organizing their tractate's laws
into thematic units relevant to each. The earliest juncture, the
ripening of the produce, provides an occasion for laying the conceptual groundwork of all that follows. A supernatural claim to
the tithes is made upon produce grown by Israelites at the precise
moment at which they wish to use it. The second juncture, the
farmer's appropriation of the produce, offers an opportunity to
explore issues involving the nature of ownership and the effects
of human intentions in effecting ownership. These reflections on
the tension between the farmer's right to his produce and his
duty to satisfy supernatural claims upon it before he eats it
comprise the bulk of the tractate. With all its principles fully
articulated, Maaserot concludes with a series of exercises in
their application to cases in which it is unclear whether both
human and supernatural claims have been made upon a specific
batch of produce.

C. *Theory of Text and Exegesis*
     With the argument and structure of Tractate Maaserot before
us, it remains to explain the interpretive work which, in the
first place, permits identification of argument and discovery of
structure. We turn, then, to the goals and methods of my commentary to Maaserot. The goal is to uncover the original meaning
which the creator(s) of the tractate intended to convey to their
immediate (and, to us, unknown) audience. Isolation of the original meaning of Maaserot yields important insight into the concerns which find expression in this early product of Rabbinic
Judaism, and thus throws important light upon the nature of
Rabbinic Judaism in its formative period. This fundamentally
historical goal shapes the particular theory of meaning with which
the text of the document is approached. This theory, the method-
ological foundation of the commentary, is that the way in which
Mishnah's creator(s) formulate their ideas for literary purposes
is the key to the meaning those ideas were expected to convey.
That is, the form of mishnaic discourse is inseparable from its
original meaning and governs the method by which that meaning is
discovered.[8] The commentary, then, is an attempt to elicit from
Mishnah's distinctive literary traits the meaning of the ideas
expressed within those conventions.
     A fundamental assumption of my commentary is that the text
of Maaserot reflects only the ideas of those who cast it into its

present form. While the tractate (with Mishnah as a whole)
regularly cites authorities presumed to have flourished over a
period of some centuries prior to the formation of Mishnah, the
document as a whole appears to have been produced by a circle of
late-second-century contemporaries. The reason is that the document follows a self-conscious aesthetic and intellectual program
uniquely its own. The text conforms to consistent canons of
literary taste and style, and is constructed so as to obscure,
rather than point out, any diachronic literary development. There
can be no "source-criticism" of Mishnah because its sources have
been systematically homogenized by those who, in the brief period
of a generation or two, produced the text before us.[9] The sum of
these observations is that the text of Maaserot is formulated in
order to be used in the tractate as we have it. It is not a
pastiche of early literary materials gathered together under a
single rubric, but a masterful effort of stylistic taste and judgment. It is for this very reason that the literary conventions
of the document are central to its exegesis. Maaserot, to paraphrase William S. Green,[10] tells us what it wants us to know only
in the way it wants us to know it. Study of the tractate's
literary conventions, then, is crucial in the interpretation of
what it has to say.

Accordingly, my exegesis of Tractate Maaserot is shaped by
the most obvious characteristics of the text. First among these,
as I have already pointed out, is that the text is highly forma-
lized. Nearly all of its ideas are framed within a small number
of stereotyped linguistic patterns, which exhibit easily-recognized
syntactical characteristics.[11] The fundamental requirement of
exegesis, then, is to discern the meaning which the form of a
statement imposes upon its content. As I shall explain below,
the imposition of standard forms of expression upon diverse kinds
of ideas, and the repetition of specific linguistic patterns
throughout a series of apparently unrelated rules, indicates an
editorial judgment about the unity of principle to be discerned
in the apparent diversity of facts. The task of the exegete is to
discern that unity and explain the facts through which it is
articulated.

Secondly, while the editor(s) of the text take pains to
impose standard patterns upon their discourse, there are clear
indications that materials of unknown provenance have been reworked
for inclusion in a specific unit of the tractate (cf. M. 1:2-4).[12]
The editorial standardization of the text, in other words, is not
always perfect, and at times suggests that ready-to-hand literary

materials have been altered for use in the text. Where the edi-
tor(s) have sought to impose their own stylistic conventions upon
earlier materials, it is possible as well that they have also
imposed their own ideas upon those materials. Here analysis of
Mishnah's formal traits permits us to isolate the editorial work
from the prior material, and to trace how the editorial imposition
of form shapes as well the meaning conveyed by the material. While
it remains impossible to know the nature of such prior materials
or their origins, such criticism permits us to appreciate the
role of the editor(s) in shaping an intellectual agendum of their
own.

A final observation issues from both of the above. The
editorial principle of Mishnah is that inquiry into a particular
theme or problem generally proceeds within a single dominant
pattern of formulation. That is, a shift in the tractate's topic
is normally signalled by a shift in literary style. We recall
from the foregoing outline of the tractate, for example, that the
first unit of Maaserot, which defines the kinds of produce which
are subject to tithing, is composed almost entirely of lists. As
the interests of the editor(s) move to the topic of liability to
tithing, however, conditional sentences and disputes become the
preferred mode of discourse. Attention to the literary traits of
the text, therefore, enables the interpreter to control the work
against the very canons of conceptual coherence employed by the
editor(s). This prevents us from conflating ideas or principles
which the framers of the document viewed as unrelated.

With the above considerations in mind, let us turn to the
major exegetical foci of the commentary. These are, in turn,
(1) the pericope and its formal traits, (2) the aggregation of
pericopae into formal-thematic units, and (3) the tractate itself
as a coherent essay. As we shall see, each of these foci shapes
the others, for analysis of the tractate builds from a study of
its smallest parts, to a discussion of the units to which they
belong. Ultimately, it concludes with the foregoing introduction,
a description of the tractate as a whole.

(1) *The pericope and its formal traits.* The pericope is the
smallest literary unit of the tractate.[13] Normally it consists
of a number of rules or cases which examine a specific principle
of law within one or more of Mishnah's typical stylistic conventions. The elements of the pericope, sentences and rulings, may
be interpreted in the first instance only within the immediate
context of the pericope in which they are located. It is from
this perspective that a critique of the pericope's formal traits

is crucial. The distinctive formulation of the pericope's rules
is commonly the formulator's way of directing attention to the
issue or principle deemed central to the discussion. There are
two common literary techniques for directing the reader's attention. These are, in turn, the use of a fixed form[14] or the
repetition of a distinctive formulary pattern.[15]

We begin with the common forms of Tractate Maaserot. These
are, primarily, the list and the dispute. The list consists of a
superscription followed by a series of substantives or brief
clauses, which respond to the superscription. Thus a list of
twenty items in M. 1:2-3 begins in the following way:

> When is produce subject to the law of tithes?
> Figs--when they begin to ripen.
> Grapes and wild grapes--when...
> Sumac and mulberry--when...

The superscription links the diverse items appended to it into a
single category subject to a common principle. The task of exegesis, accordingly, is to deduce from the listed items that
principle which accounts for their collection beneath the superscription. In the above example, the problem is to determine,
first, why various sorts of produce become subject to the law when
they do, and, second, what the various criteria have in common
with each other. Recognition of how the list functions to convey
principles is central in the criticism of those lists which appear
to include items unsuited to the superscription. When the rules
of list-formation appear to be violated (cf. M. 1:4A-B), there are
two interpretive possibilities. On the one hand, the formulator
of the pericope may be directing attention to the critical problem
of the law. The exegete, accordingly, must carefully study the
relationship of the anomalous item to both the superscription and
the other items in the list. On the other hand, the pericope
itself may have been disturbed at some point in the post-mishnaic
transmission of the text. If so, MS. evidence may turn up a
better version of the form, which will itself have to be evaluated.[16] However, the issue is resolved, the exegetical decision
emerges from careful attention to the normal use of the form.

The second major form consistently employed in Maaserot is
the dispute. Like the list, it is introduced by a superscription.
Unlike the list, however, only two items are appended to the
superscription. While the formulation of these items varies,
they are normally attributed to specific individuals, exhibit
metrical balance, and present direct or indirect modes of discourse linked by the conjunction *w-* ("and" or "but"). Thus (M. 2:4):

> A basket of figs from which one separated heave-offering--
> R. Simeon permits making a random snack of it.
> But Sages forbid making a random snack of it.

The dispute is a remarkably compact means of conveying a great
deal of information. The superscription, with its particular
substantive concerns, provides the context within which the conflicting opinions are to be understood. The exegetical task is to
discern the principle at issue between the disputants, that is,
the position which explains both the connection of each opinion
to the superscription as well as the relationship of the opinions
to each other. Identification of the divisive issue, in turn,
uncovers the ground of shared opinion which, in the first place,
brings the disputants into (editorial) conversation with each
other. A dispute, therefore, yields three sorts of information.
The first, presented in the superscription, is the moot issue itself, pointing toward an ambiguity in a principle which at first
appears uncontroversial. Secondly, the actual disputing opinions
suggest the principles of resolution which the editor(s) deem
relevant to the particular problem. Third, identification of these
principles points toward the shared assumptions out of which the
dispute itself has emerged. These, most probably, are the assumptions of the dispute's framer.

Forms, as I have said, are only one common way in which the
editor(s) signal what is of interest to them. A far more common
method in Tractate Maaserot is the repetition and variation of
stereotyped formulary patterns in the expression of cases and
rules. Where the same syntactical construction informs a series
of rules (e.g., "If he found X, it is Y," repeated three times at
M. 3:4), we learn first of all that, according to the editor of
the pericope, the principle of interpretation is identical for all
rules. Thus, even though the substance of each might appear amen-
able to varying principles of interpretation, attention to syntax
permits us to locate the meaning imposed by the editor. Such
criticism is particularly useful when, as in M. 1:5-8, the imposition of a standard formulary pattern on a series of rulings has
clearly imposed a standard meaning on originally diverse observations.

When, as often happens, rules displaying careful formal
balance contain matching, but contradictory apodoses, the exegetical problem is to determine the issue which yields the contrast
in the rulings. Suppose, as in M. 4:1, that a pericope contains
a catalogue of rules in the following pattern (One who X is A/B):

A. One who pickles produce in the field is required to tithe.

      B. One who buries produce in the ground is exempt from
         tithing.
      C. One who seasons produce in the field is exempt from
         tithing.

A asserts that produce treated in a certain way must be tithed,
while B and C are clear that produce treated in different fashion
is exempt from tithing. Exegesis of the pericope emerges from the
contrast between A and B-C. In what way is pickling different
from burying or seasoning, and how are burying and seasoning like
each other but different from pickling? The answer to the question will yield the principle at issue in the entire catalogue.

    (2) *The formal-thematic unit*. Once a pericope is thoroughly
explained on the basis of its internal traits, a further problem
of exegesis remains. That is to discern the meaning imposed upon
the pericope by the context in which it is placed. For the most
part, individual pericopae do not stand in isolation, but are
constituent parts of larger, more ambitious constructions. Normally, the formal traits of these larger constructions are consistent. That is, the pericopae of which they consist share
similar patterns of formulation. Further, the unit explores a
single theme or problem, to which each pericope makes its distinctive contribution. The problem is to define the limits of the
formal-thematic unit, identify the issue which accounts for its
creation, and explain the role of the pericopae within the overall
construction.[17]

    Two exegetical concerns are served in this work. First, the
identification of a group of pericopae as a unit prevents the
arbitrary ascription of one unit's principles to pericopae found
in a separate unit on some quite independent theme. The formal-
thematic unit, like the pericope itself, has its own integrity.
It must therefore be interpreted within its own editorial conventions. Secondly, as I have suggested, identification of the
formal-thematic units helps to trace the levels of meaning which
the editor(s) impose upon the pericopae within a given unit. When
a pericope appears to make one point in isolation from its context
and a second point within that context, we discern at work the
essentially exegetical method of Mishnah's editor(s). In Mishnah
the creation of novel literary contexts for an idea is a means of
testing that idea and expanding it beyond its former range of
meaning.

    (3) *The tractate as an essay*. Identification and interpreta-
tion of the tractate's formal-thematic units leaves unexplained
the relationships among the units and the larger program which

they serve. The purpose of the editor(s), self-evidently, is to
produce a tractate on the topic of tithes. By understanding the
relationships which bind the diverse units into a single literary
project, we discover how the creators of the document themselves
understood the topic of interest to them. We learn, in other
words, more than the sum of all the tractate's laws. Rather, we
decipher the larger statement which the collection of laws is
intended to make. I view Tractate Maaserot, therefore, as an
essay, a construction of ideas which pursue a particular problematic. This problematic is the unstated question to which the
tractate, the essay, provides an answer. As I have already
demonstrated in part I of this introduction, the question of the
tractate is discernible only on the basis of the form and structure of the answer. Once, therefore, the laws of the tractate are
fully understood, and the relationship among different units of
law is clear, the final task is to explain the law as a coherent
product of its parts.

The foregoing remarks on the exegetical theory and method of
my commentary should appear peculiar in one important respect.
The discussion proceeds as if Tractate Maaserot had been recently
dug up from an ancient library and had never been subject to exegesis. In fact Tractate Maaserot, with the rest of Mishnah, has
been the subject of nearly two millenia of continuous and acute
exegetical labor. Why, then, is a new exegesis of Maaserot,
complete with hermeneutical introduction, a necessary enterprise?
The reason is that the goal of the present exegesis, to achieve
historical understanding of Maaserot from within its own conventions of expression, differs from the goals of all earlier studies
of the tractate. Let us, then, turn to the dominant exegetical
methods which have been applied to the tractate, the goals of such
methods, and the contribution of such work to the present study.

The oldest, and from the present perspective, the most important exegetical tradition is that of rabbinic exegesis, a tradition which begins with Tosefta and evolves in unbroken lines
through two Talmuds, the medieval academies of Babylonia, Europe
and North Africa, and into the present day in the United States
and the State of Israel.[18] The methods of rabbinic exegesis are
shaped by the Torah-theology of rabbinic Judaism. This asserts
that the Oral Torah, consisting of Mishnah and the literature
generated by Mishnah, is a revealed complement to the Written
Torah, Scripture. Together, these two Torahs are one wholly
coherent, internally consistent, eternally binding Torah, a law of
life. This theological perspective has important consequences for

the methods and goals of rabbinic exegesis of Mishnah, for at issue
now is the interpretation of revelation. A law of Mishnah must
not only make coherent sense in its own setting but it must also
be harmonious in principle with all other revealed law on that
same subject.   That is so whether such law is found elsewhere in
Mishnah or anywhere else in the ever-growing literature of Oral
Torah, e.g., the Babylonian Talmud (sixth century), Maimonides'
Code (twelfth century), or the *Shulhan* ^{C}*Arukh* (sixteenth century).
The goal of such exegesis, accordingly, is to juxtapose and harmonize Mishnah's laws with the entire corpus of revealed law, as
well as that body of exegesis of revealed law which is deemed
normative.   Thus its dominant method is the atomization of a
tractate's text into discrete laws, the fundamental units of
revelation, and the harmonization of these laws with principles
adduced by legal philosophers who lived and worked as much as 1500
years after the formation of Mishnah, yet who are deemed to parti-
cipate in the unfolding of revelation.

Clearly, rabbinic exegetes, at any particular stage in their
own evolving tradition, interpret a text far different in character
from the text I find before me. Their text is the single, revealed
law, which finds its natural context within the entire body of
Oral Torah, early and late, relevant to the subject of that law.
My text, to the contrary, is the unit of meaning constituted by
the formal limits of a pericope, which is itself to be understood
solely within the context of the single tractate. Thus, where
rabbinic exegetes find in Tractate Maaserot a collection of diverse
laws under the rubric of tithes, I find an "essay," systematically
exploring a carefully defined problematic. A mode of exegesis
which, through honoring the single law, ignores the immediate intellectual structure which shapes that law, ignores precisely what
I wish to recover--the historical meaning of Maaserot. This, of
course, is no loss at all to those who wish to articulate the
eternally cogent system of revelation; it is a great loss, however,
to the historian of Judaism, for whom the earliest meaning of the
law is crucial for the interpretation of all that comes later.

To the extent, therefore, that the methods and goals of my
commentary differ from those of prior exegesis, my use of the
results of such exegesis is selective. The Talmuds of Babylonia
and Palestine, and those later exegetes who base their work upon
the programs of the Talmuds (e.g., MS, Sirillo, TYT), offer indis-
pensable guidance in identifying the subtle issues of logic which
emerge from any careful reading of the text from any perspective.
Insofar as I share the rabbinic concern to discern the structure

and relationships of ideas, the rabbis are thoughtful and helpful
partners in conversation. I am particularly indebted to the work
of Maimonides' *Commentary*, the first and only rabbinic commentary
(after Tosefta) which takes Mishnah seriously within its own
documentary limits. The considerations of Maimonides' and the
reflections of his later critics (e.g., KM, MR) frequently exhaust
the entire range of meanings, plausible and implausible, which a
particular pericope can support. From these, on the basis of my
own independent formal analysis, I am generally bound to choose.
The reader will note my frequent dependence upon Maimonides or MR
for a clarification of an otherwise murky logical conundrum. Indeed, there is little in my interpretation of individual pericopae
which is entirely unprecedented within the rabbinic exegetical
tradition. Where I claim to improve upon such exegesis is in my
ability to control the work on the basis of formal analysis. I
thus gain a grasp of the document as a whole, and a sense for the
interplay of ideas *within* the tractate. This is often lost in the
atomistic exegesis of the tractate's rules.

In recent times, within the past century, the exegesis of
Mishnah has interested individuals outside of the institutional
framework of Rabbinic Judaism.[19] Mishnah contains data of great
interest to linguists, historians of antiquity, and students of
ancient Judaism and early Christianity. For numerous reasons, it
has fallen to philologists to make Mishnah's data available to a
broader scholarly community. Most often the work consists of
translations of Mishnah with brief explanatory comments and philological observations (e.g., Goldschmidt, Sammter, Danby, Cohen,
Bunte, Blackman). University scholarship in Hebrew foregoes the
translation, but maintains the general goal of appending to the
text (of a selected MS. with appropriate text-critical apparatus)
brief clarifications and expansions, as well as historical and
philological observations (e.g., Albeck). This work has proved
useful in my own exegesis insofar as translations and philology
add new perspectives to individual words and phrases. Such
efforts, nevertheless, are disappointing, for they share the
shortcoming of atomistic rabbinic exegesis, but not its exegetical
brilliance. I have found no academic commentary to Tractate
Maaserot which advances the rabbinic discussion in any way, apart
from clarifying the meaning of words and, particularly in Maaserot,
the precise kinds of fruit or buildings referred to in the course
of legal inquiry. In this regard, I intend my work to replace
philological commentaries of this sort, a goal unthinkable in
regard to rabbinic exegesis. I address the original and appropriate

audience of the philological commentary, the student of the human-
ities in general and the historian of religion and culture in Late
Antiquity in particular. For those who approach Mishnah as a
datum of culture and a construction of human meaning, I offer an
exercise in the explication and interpretation of that meaning.

D. *Guide to the Use of the Commentary*
     The theoretical perspective outlined above has a profound
affect upon the form of the commentary itself. The commentary
consists of a translation of each pericope of the tractate, followed by an exegetical essay devoted to that pericope. Thus a
dialogue between pericope and exegesis is established and main-
tained. The translation provides the information upon which the
exegesis is based and by which the exegesis may be evaluated.
The exegesis, in turn, articulates the sense of the pericope and
shows how that sense emerges from the words, clauses and formal
traits of the pericope.
     The technique of the translation is determined by the formu-
laic character of Mishnah. In order to highlight that character,
and make it available for exegetical purposes, the translation
closely replicates the characteristic syntax of the text. The
goal is not elegance of English style, but loyalty to the aesthe-
tics and rhetoric of the Hebrew. Where necessary, I have interpolated explanatory language or essential stylistic phrases into
the text. These appear in brackets. Where the translation is
unavoidably paraphrastic, or reflects a problematic *Vorlage*, I
have transliterated the Hebrew within parentheses immediately following the relevant English passage. Important MSS. variants
appear as well within parentheses, and are coded by Latin letters.
This code is explained in the bibliography.
     Essential to understanding the text is the ability to identify
the basic compositional units employed in the construction of the
pericope, as well as extraneous materials which may have been
interpolated or glossed into the unit. In order to facilitate
recognition of a pericope's building blocks I have divided each
into individual stichs and have appended to the left margin of
each stich a Latin letter (i.e., A, B, C, etc.). The exegetical
remarks following each pericope regularly refer to each stich by
the designated letter, e.g., "A introduces the topic of the pericope, and is elaborated at B-C."
     Beneath each translated pericope the reader will find a list-
ing of parallel passages in Mishnah, Tosefta, the halakhic mid-
rashim and the Talmuds. I offer these for convenience only and

make no claim to provide an exhaustive list. The parallels are interesting primarily for the information they provide concerning the interpretation of the pericope in later rabbinic documents.

My own exegesis of the pericope immediately follows the translation. The exegetical essay regularly addresses three issues. Most often, the essay begins with a description of the formal traits and structure of the pericope. This description provides the literary framework within which the work of exegesis must proceed. The central task of the essay is to explain the clear sense of the pericope, and to identify its main point. This includes an account of the legal issues it addresses and the assumptions which make such issues important to the framers of the tractate. The problem is to explain the intellectual agendum served by any particular law. Where possible, the exegesis attempts as well to describe the larger perspective upon the world which the law takes for granted. Not all pericopae yield this sort of information, nor need it be stressed in each case. Nevertheless, at crucial turns in the argument I offer my own judgment of what is ultimately at stake in the law.

For reasons of convenience the chapter divisions of the commentary follow those which have been imposed upon the tractate by its copyists and printers. Thus the commentary is divided into the traditional five chapters, even though the tractate itself consists of three basic divisions among which are distributed some six clear-cut formal/thematic units. The introductions to each chapter locate the reader in the unfolding argument of the tractate. The first task of each introduction is to present an overview of the chapter's central issues and the formal-thematic units within which these issues are articulated. There follows a more wide-ranging set of reflections upon the issues which exegesis reveals to lie at the heart of the law. In sum, then, the chapter introduction prepares the reader to follow the tractate's major turns of argument as well as the assumptions upon which that argument is based.

Following the exegetical comments to each pericope of the tractate, I translate and explain the relevant pericopae of Tosefta Maaserot. This document, redacted between the third and fifth centuries, is the only commentary to Mishnah which pays attention to the formal characteristics of the latter and which systematically employs them in the interpretation of its law. The insights of Tosefta Maaserot, therefore, are often especially illuminating for my own work, and deserve full attention and comment.

The translation of Tosefta Maaserot follows the same method
employed in Mishnah. The only difference is that where Tosefta
cites Mishnah I reproduce that citation in italics and indicate
the specific passage in brackets at the end of the stich. This
highlights the exegetical method of Tosefta most clearly. My
comments to Tosefta, which follow each pericope, are limited to a
description of the latter's relationship to Mishnah and to the
point Tosefta wishes to make about Mishnah's law. Normally,
Tosefta adds supplementary or explanatory materials. Where this
is the case, I explain the point of the supplement or amplification.
At times, Tosefta will contradict or criticize Mishnah's view.
Here as well I try to explain the grounds on which Tosefta differs.
In general, these grounds emerge from Mishnah itself. Tosefta thus
affords rich insight into the interpretive possibilities of Mishnah's rulings. Finally, Tosefta presents relatively few pericopae
which stand entirely apart from the literary or substantive characteristics of Mishnah. Here I provide extensive comments which
attempt to explain not only the law, but the reason that the pericope has been included in a commentary to Mishnah Maaserot. An
invaluable aid in such cases, as well as in all matters of Tosefta
exegesis, is Saul Lieberman's *Tosefta Ki-fshuta*. Lieberman's
encyclopaedic talmudic learning and his mastery of the documents
of hellenistic civilization often shed important light on obscure
passages of Tosefta.

In the preparation of the commentary to Mishnah I have made
use of the entire range of texts and translations available to me.
The translation is based upon the text of Tractate Maaserot provided in Albeck, with constant reference to the variant readings
catalogued in Sacks-Hutner. My translation has benefitted from
the earlier translations of Goldschmidt, Sammter and Bunte (in
German) as well as the more well-known English translations of
Danby, Cohen and Blackman. The translation of Tosefta Maaserot,
the first into English, is based upon MS. Vienna, as reproduced
in Lieberman, *The Tosefta*.

CHAPTER ONE

MAASEROT CHAPTER ONE

Chapter One commences M.'s discussion of the law of tithes at the logical foundation of the subject. Of primary interest is the establishment of basic facts regarding 1) what sorts of produce must be tithed (M. 1:1B), 2) when such produce becomes suitable for the removal of tithes (M. 1:1D-H, 1:2-3+4), and 3) how the owner of the produce incurs the obligation to tithe it (M. 1:5-8). As a whole, the chapter offers a self-contained unit of law which regulates the consumption of produce at all points in its growth, processing and preparation for the table. The purpose of these regulations is to prevent produce from being eaten in daily meals until all agricultural offerings have been removed.

The chapter begins with a pair of rulings, M. 1:1B and 1:1D-H, which the redactor identifies as "general rulings." These establish the theory of tithes within which the subsequent details of the chapter are to be understood. M. 1:1B limits the removal of tithes to agricultural produce alone. Its limitation of the range of the law to food cultivated by man reflects the scriptural postulate that the produce of the Land of Israel is a gift of God, for which Israel expresses its gratitude by the presentation to God of sanctified offerings (Lv. 27:30, Dt. 26:14-15).[1] Tithes represent God's claim against each season's harvest, a claim which, according to M. 1:1B, can be satisfied only by the offering of produce grown by man on the land. The second "general rule," M. 1:1D-H, adds that tithes need be removed from produce only after it becomes edible. If it is edible early in its growth, as are greens (T. 1:1b), it is subject to the law of tithes at this early stage (M. 1:1D-F); if, on the other hand, produce is not edible until a relatively late stage of its growth, it is not subject to the law until it is edible (M. 1:1G-H). The point is that God's claim is made upon the produce at the precise moment that it becomes of value to man and, consequently, is likely to be eaten by him. It is necessary, at that point, to adjudicate the respective rights of God and man to the produce. This is precisely what the law of tithes, as presented in Chapter One, proposes to do.

The chapter balances the farmer's right to consume the fruit of his labor against the right of God to a portion of the land's

25

yield. This balance is defined and elaborated within the limits
of two formulaically identical catalogues, M. 1:2-3 and M. 1:5-8,[2]
each of which answers an important question. M. 1:2A asks at what
point produce growing in the field becomes subject to the law, a
question for which M. 1:1D-H has already provided a general
answer. The subsequent catalogue, M. 1:2B-3P, now offers a detailed exemplification of the familiar principle. The catalogue
provides information regarding the point at which twenty kinds of
produce are deemed edible and, therefore, subject to the law. The
point is that prior to ripening, the catalogued items may be eaten
without the removal of tithes. After ripening, however, they may
not be eaten unless they are tithed. Since God claims the produce
in its ripeness, man must satisfy that claim before he consumes
the produce.

M. 1:4, joined to the foregoing by the disjunctive *waw*
("but"), is clearly foreign to the catalogue. It presents a list
of produce followed by the single apodosis, "are subject to the
law whether they are large or small." The apodosis breaks the
formulary pattern established at M. 1:2-3, recalling instead
M. 1:1D-F's ruling that produce edible early in its growth is
"subject to the law whether it is small or large." M. 1:4, therefore, supplements the latter, rather than M. 1:2-3. If we dis-
miss the *waw* as a copyist's addition, however, the difficulty is
removed. The redactor of the chapter has laid out his materials
in the following pattern:

        M. 1:1D-F: produce edible small or large   (a)
        M. 1:1G-H: produce edible after it ripens   (b)
        M. 1:2-3:   examples of 1:1G-H   (b)
        M. 1:4:   examples of 1:1D-F, large or small   (a)

The whole, therefore, is a single well-constructed redactional
unit, introduced by M. 1:1A-B+C. Its theme, the point at which
produce growing in the field becomes subject to the law of tithes,
is exhaustively examined, both in terms of guiding principles and
particular details.

M. 1:5A, introducing the chapter's second catalogue, asks an
entirely fresh question. M. 1:5A wants to know how long produce
may remain untithed beyond the point at which it ripens. The
question assumes that while produce *may* be tithed at its ripening,
it need not be tithed until some later point.[3] As we shall see,
M. 1:5-8 claims that the farmer's own acts determine when he is
obliged to tithe produce which has become suitable for tithing.
A series of extensively glossed rulings points out that ripened

produce need not be tithed until it is harvested and processed
for storage. The processing, which removes natural impurities
from the produce, indicates the owner's intention to store the
produce for use as food. The owner has claimed the produce as
his own and intends to use it in his daily meals. Precisely at
this point he is prohibited from using the produce until he tithes
it (T. 1:1a). Having established his claim to the produce, he
must now offer to God what is His.

A significant qualification of this general position is made
at M. 1:5L-M, an interpolation into the catalogue. The ruling
states that processing the produce obliges the owner to tithe it
only if he intends to sell it afterward. The owner's intention
to sell indicates that he considers himself in control of the
crop's disposition--that he is, in fact, sole owner. Thus he may
neither eat the produce himself nor sell it to another (M. Dem. 2:2)
unless, by tithing, he acknowledges God's proprietorship. If, to
the contrary, the owner intends to bring the processed goods home
for domestic use, he need not tithe until he gets home, and may
even snack on the produce until that point. Since he will not
establish his claim to the produce until arriving home, he may,
without tithing, make limited use of it, in the interim between
field and home. The notion that a farmer makes a random snack of
produce he has not appropriated is the assumption which underlies
the bulk of Chapters Two through Four. M. 1:5L-M, while it is
introduced rather abruptly into M. 1:5, is nevertheless one of
M.'s most crucial rulings.

It is not difficult to attribute the construction of Chapter
One to a specific generation of Mishnah's authorities. Ushan
glosses at M. 1:2 (Judah) and M. 1:4 (Simeon) engage the central
principles of their unit, and therefore attest the construction
of M. 1:1-4 to Usha. Judah and Yose, both Ushans, gloss M. 1:7-8
as well, but their materials, as we shall see, are extraneous to
the catalogue in which they appear. In themselves, therefore,
they yield no information regarding M. 1:5-8's provenance. On
thematic and formal grounds, however, the unit must be deemed
Ushan, for it develops the issue of M. 1:1-4 in a significant way,
employing the same formulary pattern as the earlier catalogue of
M. 1:2-3. The chapter as a whole, then, is created at Usha and
reflects the conception of the law current among that generation
of authorities.

The entire first chapter of Tosefta is devoted to Chapter
One of M. T.'s editor closely follows the thematic sequence of
M., with the single exception of T. 1:1a. That pericope, one of

four autonomous pericopae designated in MSS. and printed editions
as T. 1:1, introduces T. with a general definition of the point
at which produce must be tithed. The ruling is congruent with,
and indeed is an abstract formulation of, M. 1:5ff. The placement
of T. 1:1a is sound judgment on the part of T.'s redactor, for
the bulk of M., Chapters Two through Four, is concerned with the
proper disposition of produce which has become liable to the removal of tithes by some act of appropriation. Rules relevant to
produce growing in the field, while central in Chapter One, play
a relatively minor role thereafter. T., therefore, presents its
understanding of major principles at the outset. Only thereafter
does it proceed to supply a series of rulings complementary to,
and in the sequence of, M.'s major units. Without exception,
these add little to the law as found in M., generally remaining
content to refine M.'s principles or improve its formulation (e.g.,
T. 1:1b vs. M. 1:1D-H).

                              1:1

A.   A general principle they stated concerning tithes:
B.   anything (*kl š-*) that is
     (1) food (*'kl*),
     (2) cultivated (*nšmr*),[4]
     (3) and which grows from the earth
     is subject to [the law of] tithes (*ḥyyb bm^c srwt*).[5]
C.   And yet another general principle they stated:
D.   anything (*kl š-*) which at its first [stage of development][6]
     is food and which at its ultimate [stage of development]
     is food (e.g., greens: T. 1:1b)--
E.   even though [the farmer] maintains [its growth] in order to
     increase the food [it will yield]--
F.   is subject [to the law of tithes whether it is] small or large
     (i.e., at all points in its development).
G.   But (*w-*) anything (*kl š-*) which at its first [stage of develop-
     ment] is not food, yet which at its ultimate [stage of develop-
     ment] is food (e.g., the fruit of trees: T. 1:1b)
H.   is not subject [to the laws of tithes] until it becomes
     edible.

                         M. 1:1 (A: cf. b. Shab. 68a,
                         y. Shab. 7:1[8d]; B=b. Nid. 50a,
                         cf. M. Pe'ah 1:4)

     The tractate begins with two rulings, B and D-H. The former
concerns the range of produce to which the law of tithes applies,

while the latter treats the moment in the growth of such produce
at which the law actually takes effect. The rulings are formally
and substantively autonomous, but the order of presentation and
the superscriptions (A, C) transform them into a complementary
pair, inviting us to read D-H in light of B.

The three criteria enumerated at B point out that all plants
cultivated by man as food are subject to the law of tithes.[7] When
such agricultural produce is harvested, the householder must
designate a fixed percentage of it as heave-offering and tithes.[8]
These offerings are deemed sanctified and are therefore set aside
from the rest of the harvest for the use of priests and others to
whom such offerings are due (M. Ter. 3:5-8). Only after the removal of these offerings is the remaining produce deemed "unconsecrated," and permitted for general consumption.

The subject of this process of sanctification and deconsecration is food (B1) that exhibits two distinguishing characteristics.
As agricultural produce, it is the focus of the Israelite farmer's
labor on his own land (B2), and as plant-life, it grows from land
given to Israel by God (B3).[9] According to B, then, the law of
tithes applies only to food which man labors to produce from land
leased from God. Sanctification, in other words, pertains only to
produce which issues from land over which both God and man have
legitimate claims. Man's claim is justified by his need and his
labor, God's by his ultimate ownership of the land and all its
fruits.[10] Claims on both sides are satisfied by the separation
of a portion of the produce for God. With God's portion removed,
the remainder is deemed fit for human consumption. In Mishnah's
technical language, it is now *ḥulin metuqanin*, food which has
been made suitable for common use by the removal of offerings.

The second unit of M., D-H, assumes the criterion of edibility stated at B1, but raises an independent issue. It points out
that agricultural produce need be tithed only after it has
actually become edible. While C identifies D-H as a single rule,
the unit actually contains two well-balanced rulings, D+F and G-H.
An interpolation at E upsets this balance, but provides important
exegetical guidance.

We begin with D+F. The rule takes for granted that only
produce grown for food is subject to the law. Its claim is that
the law goes into effect only at the point in the growth of the
produce at which it is deemed to be food. It follows, then, that
produce which can be eaten as soon as the edible portion develops
(MR), such as leafy vegetables, is subject to the law when these
portions appear. It remains subject to the law throughout its

future growth, or as long as these portions remain edible (y.
Ma. 1:1[48d], s.v., *'mr rby ywnh*). G-H adds the logical complement of D+F. If the produce remains inedible until a relatively
advanced point in the development of the portion usually eaten,
as is the case with most fruit, the produce is exempt from the
law until the portion in question becomes edible. If for some
reason the produce is eaten before it is normally deemed to be
food, it need not be tithed at all.

E, inserted between D and F, adds a new consideration which
will become central to later developments in the tractate. It
points out that once produce is edible it is subject to the law
even if the farmer does not deem it worthy of harvest until the
yield is greater. At issue is the criterion for determining
when a crop is deemed to be food. Such a criterion can be based
upon either the actual condition of the produce, i.e., its edibility, or the actions of the farmer, i.e., his harvest of the
crop for food. E rules that the edibility of the produce is the
normative criterion, for its edible condition permits us to assume
that the farmer deems the produce useful as food. The alternative
criterion is that we deem the crop to be food only when it is
harvested as such. This would permit the farmer to use the produce prior to the harvest without removing tithes. By rejecting
this alternative, E stresses the fact that food is food whether
man intends to harvest it as such or not. It is subject to the
law when it is edible, regardless of human intentions. As we
shall see, the problem of establishing when the objective condition of produce imposes upon it the strictures of the law, and
when, on the other hand, the subjective intentions of the owner
are determinative, proves to be a recurrent concern of the tractate (cf. M. 4:5-6).

D. (1) *Anything which at its first [stage of development] is*
        food and which at its ultimate [stage of development]
        is food [= M. 1:1D],
E. such as green vegetables (*yrq*),[11]
F. *is subject [to the law of tithes]* at its first [stage of
        development] and at its ultimate [stage of development]
        [cf. M. 1:1F].
G. (2) Anything which at its first [stage of development] is
        food but which at its ultimate [stage of development]
        is not food,
H. such as one who prolongs [the growth] of green vegetables for
        [their] seed (*hmqyym yrq lzr^c*) [cf. M. 1:1E],

I.   is subject [to the law of tithes] at its first [stage of
     development] but is exempt [from the law upon reaching] its
     ultimate [stage of development].

J.   (3) *Anything which at its first [stage of development] is not*
     food but which at its ultimate [stage of development] is
     food [= M. 1:1G],

K.   such as the fruits of the tree,

L.   is exempt [from the law of tithes] at its first [stage of
     development] but is subject to [the law of tithes] upon
     reaching its ultimate [stage of development].

                         T. 1:1b (p. 227, l. 2-5)
                         (G-I: cf. y. Ma. 1:1[48d])

     T. 1:1, of which only T. 1:1b is before us, is composed of
four entirely autonomous pericopae. We shall discuss each in
connection with its appropriate pericope of M. T. 1:1b's triplet
is clearly a commentary to M. 1:1D-G, citing, glossing and reform-
ulating the latter at D-F and J-L. G-I, generated by M. 1:1D-F,
exploits the potential of M.'s logic in order to stake out yet a
third ruling exemplifying the principle that produce is subject
to the law only if it is edible.

     D-F and J-L clarify M. 1:1D-G. First we are told the kinds
of produce which M. has in mind (E, K). Then M.'s unbalanced
apodoses (M. 1:1F, G) are placed in perfect balance both with each
other (F, L) and with their respective protases (D, J). Only G-I
offers something new. If a man, in order to harvest seeds for
future sowing, prolongs the growth of edible produce past its
point of edibility, it is subject to the law only as long as it
remains edible. As in M., the objective state of the produce,
rather than the intentions of the farmer, determine its status
under the law. Since the man has no intention of using the produce for food, we might expect the produce to be exempt from the
law at the outset. T., following M., rules otherwise. Despite
the farmer's intentions, the crop remains subject to the law as
long as it is edible, and must be tithed if it is used as food
during that time. It follows that any produce eaten at the time
of the seed-harvest, however, is exempt from the law (HY). The
seeds are exempt, for they are not to be eaten,[12] and the produce
is exempt, for it is not suitable as food.[13]

(G. *You shall tithe all the yield of your seed, which comes*
        forth from the field year by year [Dt. 14:22].)[14]

H.   Is it possible (*ykwl*) that something which grows from the
     earth, such as woad (*śtyś*)[15] or madder (*qwṣh*),[16] is subject

[to the law of tithes]? Scripture says: *You shall tithe*
(Dt. 14:22) and *You shall eat* (Dt. 14:23).

I.   Is it possible that even honey and milk [are subject to the
     law of tithes]? Scripture says: *which comes forth from
     the field year by year.*

J.   Conclude from this (*'wmr m^{c}th*) [that Scripture prescribes
     tithing only for] something which comes from the domain of
     the field (*hywṣ' mršwt ṣdh*: GRA emends: *hywṣ' mn hṣdh wn'kl*,
     "which comes from the field and is eaten").

                              Sifre Dt. 105b (ed. Finkelstein,
                              p. 164) (cf. y. Ma. 1:1[48d])

     Like M. 1:1B, Sifre restricts the law of tithes to produce
which is edible, cultivated, and which grows from the earth.
Sifre's point is to demonstrate that the restrictive nature of
the ruling is congruent with the explicit meaning of Scripture.
Sifre inaugurates the tradition of exegesis, followed by me, which
perceives M. 1:1B as a restrictive rule designed to exclude from
the law produce which is neither anchored in God's land (I) nor
produced by agricultural labor (J).

                              1:2-3

A.   From what time is fruit (*prwt*)[17] subject to [the law of]
     tithes?

B.   (1) Figs--when they have begun to ripen (*msbḥlw*);[18]

C.   (2) grapes and (3) wild grapes (*'bšym*)[19]--when their seeds
     have become visible inside them (*mšhb'yšw*);[20]

D.   (4) sumac[21] and (5) mulberry[22]--when they have become red;

E.   and (6) all red [berries]--when they have become red;

F.   (7) pomegranates[23]--when they have become soft;

G.   (8) dates--when they have begun to swell;

H.   (9) peaches[24]--when they have developed red veins;[25]

I.   (10) walnuts[26] (S adds: "and almonds")[27]--when they have
     developed a chamber.

J.   R. Judah says "Walnuts and almonds--when they develop a husk."

                              M. 1:2 (B = b. Nid. 48a; cf. M.
                              Sheb. 4:7; C: cf. M. Sheb. 4:8;
                              G: cf. T. Dem. 1:1, y. Dem. 1:1
                              [21c])

K.   (11) Carobs--when they have become speckled;

L.   (12) and all black [produce, e.g., myrtle berries: y.]--
     when it has become speckled;

M. (13) pears, and (14) crustumenian pears,[28] and (15) medlar,[29]
    and (16) crab-apples[30]--when they have become smooth;
N. (17) and all white produce [31]--when it has become smooth;
O. (18) fenugreek[32]--when the seeds are able to sprout;
P. (19) grain and (20) olives--when they reach a third of their
    mature growth (mšyknyšw šlyš).

> M. 1:3 (O-P = b. R. H. 12b; P: cf.
> M. Sheb. 4:9, y. Sheb. 2:7[34a],
> M. Hal. 1:3, y. Hal. 1:3[57d],
> b. Git. 47a)

The superscription A introduces a catalogue of twenty kinds
of produce and the point at which each is deemed ripe (B-P). The
pericope, in its present redactional context, is a detailed explication of the rule at M. 1:1G-H, that produce which is inedible
at its first stage of growth becomes subject to the law as soon
as it is edible. As A announces, we are now given criteria for
determining when various kinds of produce have indeed become edible
and, therefore, may no longer be eaten freely unless they are
tithed (MR).

From a literary-critical perspective, the pericope is a
unitary construction. Any sources upon which the pericope's
redactor may have drawn have been totally reshaped for use in the
present context. Fourteen separate stichs (B-I, K-P), incorpor-
ating twenty substantives, are cast into the identical formulary
pattern (substantive + mš- + imperfect plural) and placed into
context by A. Indication that the principle of redaction is the
number of substantives, rather than the number of stichs, comes
at J, where Judah's lemma breaks the catalogue into two units of
ten items each. Further, items such as E, L, and N, which add
little new information, seem to be included solely for the purpose
of reaching the desired number of items in the catalogue.[33] I
cannot explain, however, why twenty items in particular are
desired.

While the redactor has crafted his sources into a unified
literary whole, certain inconsistencies in the pericope suggest
that the sources do not entirely agree as to what the various
signs of ripeness indicate. As we have already pointed out, A,
in juxtaposition with M. 1:1G, leads us to expect that the signs
of B-P indicate the point at which produce is edible, and therefore subject to the law of tithes. This is most plausible for
the items of B-H and K-N, for all point to a relatively advanced
stage in the ripening of the respective kinds of produce,[34] an
appropriate point at which they may be deemed edible. This is not

however the case at I-J. At issue in the dispute is the point
at which the fruit itself is deemed to have been formed (cf.
Ribmaṣ vs. Maim., *Comm.*). I claims that the walnut has been
formed when the nutmeat is distinguishable from the shell. Judah
(J), on the other hand, holds that the separated nutmeat is not a
piece of fruit in its own right until it forms a husk, i.e., its
own individual skin, around the meat. It is only within the context established by A that the issue is understood to relate to
the point at which the produce is edible. If I-J is originally
formulated in response to a problem concerning the law of tithes,
its claim is that produce becomes subject to the law when the
fruit forms, some time earlier than the point at which the produce
may be eaten.

We meet similar problems at O and P. Fenugreek seeds, used
primarily for medicinal purposes, can meet these purposes as soon
as the seeds form.[35] O, however, states that they are not subject
to the law until they have become fertile. Edibility, therefore,
is hardly at issue. Rather, the seeds become subject to the law
when they can reproduce, i.e., when they become recognizable
representatives of their species. Interpretation of P depends
upon the meaning of the *terminus technicus*, "reaching a third"
(*KNŚ/BW' šlyš*).[36] M. Sheb. 4:9 indicates that, in reference to
olives, the term defines the point in their growth at which one
se'ah of young olives will yield a third of the oil they would
yield if fully-grown (i.e., one *log* instead of three *logs*: y.
Sheb. 4:7[35c]). At issue, then, is the yield, not edibility.
The point is the same for grain, which becomes subject to the law
only when it can yield a worthwhile, if smaller than average,
harvest. According to P, then, at least one sort of produce
becomes subject to the law when it becomes an economically feasible harvest.

It is clear, then, that while M.'s redactor certainly wants
us to understand all the signs he has listed to indicate edibility, his sources reveal the existence of rather different opinions.
I-J and O suggest that produce becomes subject to the law when
the edible portion becomes an independent entity, while P indicates
that produce must become economically useful before it becomes
subject to the law.[37]

M.   R. Ishmael b. R. Yose said in his father's name, "Even if the
      seeds had become visible in only one grape of the bunch, the
      entire bunch indeed is subject [to the law of tithes]" (*ḥyyb*;
      y. and y. Dem. 1:1 read: *hybwr lm^c srwt*, "connected for the
      purpose of tithing")[38] [cf. M. 1:2C].

N. Hazelnuts[39] and peaches (*hpršqyn*; Lieberman, following y. and
    commentaries, suggests *h'pštqyn*, "pistachio nuts"),[40] and
    cedar nuts[41]--when they have developed a husk;

O. *walnuts* and almonds--*when they have developed a chamber*
    [= M. 1:2I].

P. *R. Judah says, "When they have developed a husk"* [M. 1:2J].

Q. Of which husk did they speak? Of the netherhusk which is
    upon the nutmeat (*'wkl*; lit., "food").

                          T. 1:1c (p. 227, ls. 5-8) (N: cf.
                          y. Dem. 1:1[21c], y. Ma. 1:1[48d];
                          N-Q: cf. y. Ma. 1:2[48d])

    T. consists of two autonomous units, M and N-P+Q, both of
which supplement M. 1:2. M assumes the ruling of M. 1:2C, that
grapes are subject to the law when their seeds become visible.
The natural question which arises is whether, in the case of
grapes, which are normally harvested in bunches, the ripening of
a single grape indicates that the entire bunch stands under the
law. At bottom, the question is whether the "fruit" is considered
to be the bunch of grapes, or rather, the individual grape (cf.
M. 3:9, Tarfon vs. Aqiba). Yose, as Ishmael reports, argues that
the grape is deemed part of a larger fruit, the bunch, following
Tarfon's earlier view. Therefore as soon as one grape, i.e.,
one *part* of the fruit, is ripe, the entire bunch is subject to
the law.[42]

    N-P, autonomous of the foregoing, places M. 1:2I-J in a new
context, created by N. At issue is whether walnuts and almonds
are deemed one with other nuts (N), and subject to the law when
they develop a husk (Judah, P), or whether, to the contrary, they
stand within a special category, becoming subject to the law only
when they develop a chamber (O). Q, glossing P, indicates that
all nuts are judged by the development of their husk, for it
defines the precise husk in question.

A. Savory,[43] sweet marjoram,[44] and thyme[45]--when they develop
    berries[46] (*mšyybynw*; ed. *princ.* and HD read *mšynyşw*, "when
    they blossom");

B. and all (*wkl*; E reads *wkn*, "and also") red sprouts (*h'wbyn*[47]
    'dwmyn; HD emends to *h'zwbyn h'dwmyn*, "red marjoram")--
    when they develop berries (*ed. princ.*; *mšynyşw*).

                          T. 1:4 (p. 228, ls. 12-13)
                          (Cf. y. Sheb. 7:6[37c])[48]

The pericope supplements the catalogue of M. 1:2-3. The
formulary pattern is familiar from M. 1:2D-E, M. 1:3K-L and M-N.
Following HD's emendation of B, the rule states that four types
of herb become subject to the law of tithes when they develop
seed-bearing berries. Since the herbs are edible prior to the
development of the berries, it is clear that T. reflects a conception of the law similar to that of M. 1:2/O--that ability to
reproduce, rather than edibility, determines the point at which
produce becomes subject to the law.

A.   [If] it was the second [year of the Sabbatical cycle] and the
     third year began (*wnknŝh ŝlyŝ*), lo, [the crops] belong to the
     third year.
B.   [If] it was the eve of the seventh year [of the Sabbatical
     cycle] and the seventh year began, lo, they belong to the
     seventh year.[49]
C.   Rabban Simeon b. Gamaliel says, "The House of Shammai and the
     House of Hillel did not differ that [fruit reaching] maturity
     (*hgmwr*) [before the New Year] belongs to the past [year]
     (*lŝ^{c}br*) [even if it is harvested in the New Year (HY)], and
     that [fruit] which has not blossomed [before the New Year]
     belongs to the coming [year] (*l^{c}tyd lbw'*).
D.   "Concerning what did they differ? Concerning sprouts (*'wbyn*;
     Lieberman emends to *'ybwn*, "the development of berries")
     [before the New Year].
E.   "For the House of Shammai say, 'to the past [year]',
F.   "and the House of Hillel say, 'To the coming [year]'."

                              T. 1:5a (p. 228, ls. 13-18)
                              (A-B: cf. y. Sheb. 7:6[37c];
                              C-F = T. Sheb. 2:6)

     The pericope is composed of two independent units. A-B is a
rule consisting of a balanced pair of declarative sentences, while
C-F revises a Houses-dispute not before us. C-F also appears at
T. Sheb. 2:6, where it glosses M. Sheb. 2:8. There too no
Houses-dispute is at hand.[50] In its present context, the juxtaposition of C-F and A-B is intended to indicate that the latter
is an imperfect transmission of a tradition which is properly to
be attributed to the Houses. I cannot explain, however, the
motive behind such a claim. That motive is certainly not the
clarification of M., for T.'s interest in M. is at best tangential.
     While M.-T. has thus far concerned itself with defining the
point at which fruit becomes subject to tithes, A-B turns its
interest to a problem which arises concerning the actual separation

of tithes. It maintains that the decision concerning which tithes
to separate is determined by the particular tithing schedule applicable to the year in which it is picked.[51] That is, if crops
are planted in the second year of the Sabbatical cycle but are
not picked until the third year, the owner must separate poorman's
tithe (along with heave-offering and first tithe), since poorman's
tithe is removed only in the third and sixth years of the cycle.
Had the produce been picked in the first, second, fourth or fifth
year, the owner would be required to separate second tithe instead
of poorman's tithe. Should the crops be planted in the sixth
year, however, the advent of the seventh year before their harvest
exempts them from the tithes entirely, since produce of the
seventh year is technically ownerless (Lev. 25:6-7; M. Sheb. 7:3,
9:4-9) and thus not subject to the removal of tithes (M. Sheb.
4:7-10).

The addition of C-F, which is formulated in response to a
pericope other than A-B, is intended by the redactor to revise
the conception of A-B outlined above.[52] C is meant to show that
A-B is a statement of law based upon the Hillelite position in
the following hypothetical dispute:

A. If it was the second year and the third began:
   the House of Shammai say, "To the past year,"
   and the House of Hillel say, "To the coming year" (= A).
B. If it was the eve of the seventh year and the seventh began:
   the House of Shammai say, "to the past year,"
   and the House of Hillel say, "to the coming year" (= B).

Having established that A-B is a Houses tradition, C continues to
revise the entire agendum of the dispute. As Simeon b. Gamaliel
phrases the matter, the Houses agreed that if crops ripen before
the new year, they are tithed according to the year of ripening
and not according to that in which they are picked; if they have
not yet blossomed before the advent of the new year, they are to
be tithed in the new year, for that is when they will eventually
mature. This agreement that a stage in the growth of the crop
at the new year determines its tithing year assumes a conception
of the law which entirely excludes the original issue of A-B
from consideration. Details concerning the acts of sowing and
harvesting are simply irrelevant once we assert that the system
hinges upon the growth of the crop.

Now that C has defined the parameters of the issue, D-F
records the "correct" version of the dispute--whether the appearance of berries[53] after blossoming, but before maturity, determines

the tithing year. The Hillelite opinion, which assigns the appearance of berries "to the coming year," can now be read back into a
thoroughly revised understanding of A-B. That is, if berries
develop in the second year and the third year begins, the crop is
tithed according to the third year. The reason apparently is that
the appearance of berries is not a sufficient sign of maturity.
To summarize, the redactional juxtaposition of A-B and C-F has
accomplished two goals. First, it has established that the anonymous rule of A-B accords with the Hillelite view of the law.
Second, it has completely revised the agendum of the dispute in
order to locate the objective criteria for establishing the tithing
year in the events of the natural economy rather than in the actions
of the owner.

A question remains concerning the interpretation of D-F.
For what type of crop is the appearance of berries a debatable
issue? T. 1:4 has already told us that savory, sweet marjoram,
red marjoram and thyme become subject to the laws of tithes when
they bear the berries which contain their seed. In the absence
of evidence that the appearance of such berries is a significant
stage in the growth of other crops, we must assume that the issue
of D-F also concerns the berries of herbs. If so, in the present
context, D-F seeks to revise T. 1:4 as well as A-B. The berries
not only indicate the beginning of liability to tithes, but also
determine the tithing year of the herbs.[54]

K. Since it is said: *And before the lord your God, in the place
    he will choose, to make his name dwell there, you shall eat
    the tithe of your grain (dgnk), of your wine (tyršk) and of
    your oil (yṣhrk)*...(Dt. 14:23), is it possible that one
    obligates nothing but (*'yn lḥyyb 'l'*) grain, wine and oil
    [to the laws of tithes]?

L. On what basis (*mnyn*) [do I know] to include (*lrbwt*) other
    types of fruit (*š^{c}r pyrwt*)? Scripture says: *(all) the yield
    (tbw't) of your seed (zr^{c}k)* (Dt. 14:22).

M. This must be stated (*y'mr zh*),[55] for (*š-*

N. If so (*'ylw kn*; R, O, B and GRA read *š'lmly kn*, "for if it
    were not so") I should say: Just as grain (*tbw'h*) is dis-
    tinctive in that one places it in storage (GRA omits:) and
    it is normally eaten as it is (Finkelstein emends: "and it
    is *not* normally eaten as it is"), so too I need include only
    similar items.

O. What, then, do I include? Rice and millet and panicum
    (*prgym*)[56] and sesame.

P. On what basis do I include other types of pulse ($š^c r$ $qtnywt$)[57]?
    Scripture says: *you shall tithe (all the yield of your seed)*.

Q. (B omits this entire passage:) Shall I include pulse which
    is normally eaten as it is, yet not include lupine (*twrmwś*)[58]
    and mustard seed which are not normally eaten as they are?
    Scripture says: *you shall tithe (all...that comes forth
    from the field)* (Dt. 14:22).

R. Is it possible [that they are subject to the law] even though
    they have not taken root? Scripture says *and you shall eat*.

S. On what basis [do I know] to include green vegetables (*yrqwt*)
    among produce subject to the laws of tithes? Scripture says:
    all the tithe of the land (Lev. 27:30).

T. *Of the seed of the land* (Lev. 27:30)--to include (O adds "the
    seeds of") garlic, pepperwort[59] and field rocket.[60]

U. Should I include (Neṣib and GRA add, "the seeds of") turnip,
    radish and garden seeds (so Jastrow, p. 414, for $zr^c ny$ $gynh$)
    which are not eaten? Scripture says: *of (m-) the seed of
    the land*, but not all (*kl*) the seed of the land.

V. Of the fruit of the trees (*mpry* $h^c ṣ$) (Lev. 27:30)--to include
    the fruits of trees (*pyrwt h'yln*).

W. Should I include sycamore pods[61] (*ḥrwby sqmh*; O, B, R, Neṣib
    and GRA read: *ḥrwby šyṭh*, "acacia pods),[62] carobs [from the
    area of] Ṣalmonah and carobs [from the area of] Gedurah which
    are not eaten? Scripture says: *of (m-) the fruit of the
    trees*, but not all (*kl*) the fruit of the trees.

>   Sifre Dt. 105c (ed. Finkelstein,
>   pp. 164-65, ls. 10-13, 1-9).
>   (K-W: cf. y. Ma. 1:1[48d]; O:
>   cf. M. Sheb. 2:7; R: cf. M. Sheb.
>   2:7; S-W = Sifra Beḥuqotai 12:9)

I discern three distinct units in the pericope, each of which
interprets the scope of Scripture's tithing regulations. None of
the units exhibits dependence upon M. K-L shows that while only
the tithes of grain, wine and oil must be brought to Jerusalem,
Scripture is clear that all fruits are tithed. N-R is separate
from the foregoing, yet is linked to it by the clumsy joining
language at M.[63] As the unit stands before us, N's "if so"
refers back to the word "yield" of L. Thus, following the emendation of the MSS, the sense of the passage is: "If Scripture had
not modified the word 'yield' by the word 'seed,' I could have
reasoned...." The unit extends the tithing laws to pulse by
establishing an analogy between pulse and grain based upon the
need to prepare both before eating (N-O). P-Q completes the

extension to *all* types of pulse by reference to Scripture. R
glosses N-Q with a new issue. Presumably since it is impossible
to eat pulse before the plant itself has taken root, it is not
subject to the law until that time. S-W is an exegesis of Lev.
27:30, and in fact appears in Sifra Behuqotai 12:9. In Sifra,
T-W precedes S. While K-R have been interested in expanding the
application of Scripture's rules, S-W seeks scriptural warrant for
limiting the kinds of fruit to which the law applies.

                                1:4

A. And among green vegetables (*wbyrq*)--
B. cucumbers,[64] and gourds,[65] and chatemelons,[66] and muskmelons[67]
    (Sirillo adds: "are subject [to the law of tithes whether
    they are] large or small" [= D]).
C. (O^2, B and G^1 read: "and") Apples and citrons[68]
D. are subject [to the law of tithes whether they are] large or
    small.
E. R. Simeon exempts citrons which are immature (*bqṭnn*).
F. That which is subject [to the law] among bitter almonds [i.e.,
    the small ones] is exempt among sweet [almonds] (*hḥyyb bšqdym*
    hmrym pṭwr bmtwqym).
G. That which is subject [to the law] among sweet almonds [i.e.,
    the large ones] is exempt among bitter [almonds].[69]
                              M. 1:4 (E = b. Suk. 36a, y. Suk.
                              2:7 [53a]; F-G = M. Hul. 1:6;
                              cf. b. Hul. 25b)

     M. supplements and concludes M. 1:2-3's catalogue. The
pericope consists of two autonomous units, A-D+E and F-G, each of
which must be discussed separately.

     Imperfect literary transmission obscures the fact that A-D+E
is itself a composite of two separate units, A-B and C-D+E. The
superscription at A introduces a list, B, but the required apodosis has dropped from the text. Thus we do not know what point
the ruling of A-B originally made. Since the material immediately
follows M. 1:2-3, however, it seems intended to extend M. 1:2-3's
catalogue of produce and relevant signs of edibility. Most commentators solve the literary problem by interpolating D at B (so
Sirillo), or by reading C-D as a continuation of A-B (Maim.,
Comm.). The resulting rule is that the items of B and C are subject to the law whether they are large or small. The problem
with this unitary reading, however, is that A, which promises a
list of green vegetables, now includes among these apples and

citrons, which do not fall within M.'s category of *yrq*. Clearly,
then, we cannot conflate the two rulings. The point of A-B must
remain obscure.[70]

C-D, glossed at E, presents no problems. Apples and citrons
are subject to the law when the fruit is "small," i.e., at the
beginning of its formation (MR), and remains so throughout its
later growth. The ruling is congruent with M. 1:2I-J which, as
we have seen, claims that produce is subject to the law when the
portion normally eaten is fully formed. It disagrees, however,
with the dominant thesis of M. 1:1D-H and M. 1:2-3, that produce
becomes subject to the law only when it is edible. Simeon (E),
on the other hand, represents the opinion of M. 1:1G-H. He
exempts small citrons from the law, presumably because they are
not edible until a later point in their growth. I cannot explain
why he does not exempt small apples as well (but cf. T. 1:1d,
below).

A pair of perfectly balanced declarative sentences, F-G, is
entirely autonomous of the foregoing. The ruling assumes we know
that bitter almonds are edible only when small, while sweet
almonds are edible only when large (so T. Hul. 1:24). The point
is that when the small bitter almonds are subject to the law, the
sweet counterparts, which are still inedible, remain exempt. By
the time the almonds become large, the sweet ones are subject to
the law while the bitter ones are now exempt. F-G is a rather
elegant conclusion to M.'s first major thematic unit, for the
ruling permits us to apply the criterion of edibility to a concrete problem in the growth of produce.[71]

R. Nahorai b. Shinayya said in the name of R. Simeon, "Small
    apples are exempt [from the law of tithes].
S. "Honey apples[72] (*tpwḥy nmylh*; E reads: *tpwḥy my nmlh*, "apples
    from Namlah") are subject [to the law of tithes] whether they
    are large or small."

                    T. 1:1d (p. 227, ls. 9-10)
                    (cf. y. Ma. 1:4[49a])

T. completes Simeon's opinion of M. 1:4E, Nahorai b.
Shinayya pointing out that Simeon differs from M. about apples
as well as citrons. S qualifies R, and must be read as a continuation of Simeon's tradition. While regular apples are not
subject to the law of tithes when small, honey apples are tithable
at all stages of development, and are therefore subsumed under the
rule of M. 1:4C-D.

A.   R. Simeon exempts muskmelons which are immature
B.   when (*mš-*; HY and Lieberman emend to *^{c}d š-*, "until") they
     become smooth (*yqrḥw*).

                              T. 1:3 (p. 228, 1. 12)

     A's formulary pattern is identical to that of M. 1:4E: *rby*
X pwṭr Y bqṭnn. B is a gloss qualifying A. The unit supplements
Simeon's opinion at M. 1:4E. At A Simeon exempts small muskmelons from the law, the third instance in which he differs from
M. 1:4A-B (cf. M. 1:4E and T. 1:1d[A]). B narrows the difference
between Simeon and M. 1:4B. He does not flatly exempt all small
melons. Rather he exempts only those which have not yet become
smooth.[73] Apparently, this is the point at which he deems the
melons to be edible.

A.   (Lieberman, following *ed. princ.*, inserts the following:)
     [R. Ishmael b. R. Yose said in his father's name,[74] "Bitter
     almonds are subject[75] to the law whether large or small;]
B.   "sweet almonds--when (*mš-*; y. Ma. 1:4 reads: *^{c}d š-*, "until")
     their outer shell (*qlyptn hḥyṣwnh*) separates [from the meat,
     forming a chamber:PM]."

                              T. 1:2 (p. 227, ls. 10-11)   (cf.
                              y. Ma. 1:4[49a] and b. Hul. 25b)

     T. presents two rules defining the point at which the almonds
mentioned at M. 1:4F-G become subject to the law. A, which states
that bitter almonds are subject to tithes at all stages of their
growth, makes no contribution to M. 1:4F-G; rather it ignores M.'s
clear assumption that bitter almonds are not tithable at all times,
and simply asserts that they are tithable both large and small.
For its part, B simply asserts that the separation of the shell
determines the point at which sweet almonds become subject to the
law. Thus it, too, falls outside the range of M. 1:4F-G's vision.[76]
     T.'s disinterest in M.'s problem suggests that the pericope
is not formulated in response to M. at all, but is rather an
autonomously formulated unit with its own set of concerns. Indeed, a *baraita* cited in y. Ma. 1:4[77] raises the possibility that
T. might indeed refer to T. Hu. 1:24 which reads:

A.   Bitter almonds--small [ones] are subject [to the law],
     large [ones] are exempt.
B.   And sweet almonds--large [ones] are subject [to the law],
     small [ones] are exempt.
C.   *Thus (nms't 'wmr): [That which is] subject [to the law] (ḥyyb*
     b-) among bitter almonds is exempt among sweet [almonds].

[*That which is*] *subject* [*to the law*] *among sweet* [*almonds*] *is exempt among bitter* [*almonds*][78] [= M. Hul. 1:6 and M. 1:4F-G].

Reading T. 1:2 as a gloss of T. Hul. 1:24, we find that T. 1:2A disputes the explicit rule of T. Hul. 1:24A, accepting the latter's terminology but departing from its concrete rule. The relation-ship of T. 1:2B to T. Hul. 1:24B remains less clear-cut. The former simply proposes a criterion different from the rule of T. Hul. 1:24B without explicitly acknowledging it. It exhibits no closer relationship to T. Hul. 1:24 than it does to M. Thus we can reach no conclusive opinion about the original reference of T. 1:2 and must remain satisfied with the observation that the pericope is autonomous of M.

1:5-8

A. At what point after the harvest must tithes be removed from produce (*'yzhw grnn lm^{c}srwt*)?[79]

B. (1) Cucumbers and gourds--after they remove the fuzz [from them] (*mšypqśw*).[80]

C. But if (*w'm*)[81] he does not remove the fuzz, [tithes are re-moved] after he stacks them up (*mšy^{c}myd ^{c}rymh*).[82]

D. (2) Chatemelons--after he scalds [them in order to remove the fuzz] (*mšyšlq*).[83]

E. But if he does not scald [them] [tithes need not be removed] until he makes a store [of melons] (*^{c}d šy^{c}sh mwqsh*).[84]

F. (3) Green vegetables which are [normally] tied in bunches--after he ties [them].

G. If he does not tie them, [tithes need not be removed] until he fills the vessel [into which he places the picked greens].

H. But if he does not fill the vessel [tithes need not be re-moved] until he collects all he needs.

I. (4) [The contents of] a basket [need not be tithed] until he covers [the basket].

J. But if he does not cover [it], [tithes need not be removed] until he fills the vessel.

K. But if he does not fill the vessel [tithes need not be removed] until he collects all he needs [in that basket].

L. Under what circumstances [do these criteria apply]? If he is bringing the produce to market.

M. But (*'bl*) if he is bringing it home [it is not liable to the removal of tithes, and] he eats some of it as a random snack

($'wkl\ mhm\ {}^{c}r'y$) until he reaches home.

M. 1:5 (A-B = b. B.M. 88b;
A-C = b. Bes. 13b; F = b. Hul. 7a;
F-G = b. R.H. 12a)

N.   (5) Dried split-pomegranates (prd),[85] raisins and carobs--
after he stacks them up.

O.   (6) Onions--after he strips off [the peels].

P.   But if he does not strip off the peels, [the onions must be
tithed] once he stacks them up.

Q.   (7) Grain--after he evens [the pile on the threshing-floor]
(so TAS for $m\check{s}ymrh$).

R.   But if he does not even [the pile on the threshing-floor]
[the grain need not be tithed] until he stacks it up [in
the bin].

S.   (8) Pulse--after he sifts it.

T.   But if he does not sift it, [it need not be tithed] until he
evens [the pile].

U.   Even though he has evened [the pile], he takes ($nwtl$) [edible
kernels] from those which are not properly threshed ($qt^{c}ym$),[86]
from the sides [of the smoothed pile], and from whatever is
[left] in the straw,

V.   and eats [without tithing].

M. 1:6 (N = y. Ter. 1:9[41a];
O-P: cf. b. Bes. 13b;
Q = Sifre Nu. Huqqat 123)

W.   (9) Wine--after he skims [the scum from the fermenting
juice in the receiving tank] ($m\check{s}yqph$).[87]

X.   Even though he has skimmed, he collects ($qwlt$) [liquid] from
the upper vat [where the grapes are trod] and from the duct
[which connects the latter to the receiving tank],

Y.   and drinks [without tithing].

Z.   (10) Oil--after it has flowed (yrd) into the trough [from
the press].

AA. Even though it has flowed, he takes [oil] from the pressing
bale (^{c}ql),[88] from (wmn)[89] the press-beam (mml),[90] and from
between the boards [of the pressing vat],

BB. and puts [the oil] into a plate ($hmth$)[91] or dish ($tmhwy$).

CC. However ($'bl$), he shall not place [the oil] into a pan or pot

DD. when [their contents] are boiling [unless he tithes].

EE. R. Judah says, "Into anything may one put [oil], except what
has vinegar or brine [in it.]"

M. 1:7 (W = Sifre Huqqat 121, y.
Ma. 2:6[50a]; X-Y = b. A.Z. 56a,
cf. b. B.M. 92b; BB-EE: cf. M.
Shab. 3:5, b. Shab. 42b)

FF. (11) A [fig] cake--after he glazes its surface.

GG. They glaze with [the juice of] figs or grapes which are liable
to the removal of tithes (*šlṭbl*) [and need not tithe the juice].

HH. R. Judah forbids [the use of untithed juice as a glaze].

II. One who glazes with [the juice of] grapes--

JJ. [that which he glazes] has not been made susceptible to uncleanness (*l' hwkšr*).

KK. R. Judah says, "It has been made susceptible to uncleanness."

LL. (12) Dried figs--after he presses [them into a storage jar],[92]
and molded figs (so Sens for *mgwrh*)--after he presses them
with a roller.

MM. [If] he was pressing [them] into a jar or rolling [them] in
a mold,

NN. [and] the jar broke or the mold cracked,

OO. he shall not make of them a random snack.

PP. R. Yose permits [him to make a random snack].

                                M. 1:8 (II-KK = b. Shab. 145b;
                                LL-MM = y. Bes. 4:1[62c])

This catalogue of twelve heavily glossed rulings is the
second and final unit of Chapter One. It commences, at A, the
problem which occupies the bulk of Chapters Two through Four: to
determine the point at which produce must be tithed. On the basis
of M. 1:1-4 we have assumed that produce is to be tithed no
earlier than the point at which it ripens and no later than its
harvest. Now we learn (M. 1:5L-M) that produce may remain untithed until a relatively late stage in its passage from field to
table--as long as the owner has not established his own claim to
the produce (cf. M. 1:1B and discussion, pp. 29-30). At issue,
then, is to determine when such a claim has been made. In view
of the prolixity with which M. 1:5-8 introduces this issue, our
analysis of the unit proceeds in two steps. First, we discuss
the unit's distinct rulings and identify their glosses, pointing
out the literary traits and basic propositions distinctive to each.
This exercise permits us to isolate the various conceptual elements of the unit and examine how they have been combined into a
coherent statement of law. Following this preliminary exegesis,
we engage in more detailed analysis of the unit's several literary
and substantive difficulties.

A. *Literary and Substantive Analysis*

Each ruling of the catalogue follows the identical formulary
pattern (substantive + *mš-/ᶜd š-* + imperfect: cf. M. 1:2-3),
framed in response to the question at A. Each, likewise, makes

the same point: the farmer is obliged to tithe his produce as
soon as he removes inedible impurities from it (B) or otherwise
makes it available for general consumption (e.g., by preparing it
for convenient sale: F). At the completion of such processing
the produce is deemed *ṭebel*[93] (T. 1:1a), and is forbidden for the
farmer's consumption until heave-offering and tithes are removed.
The point is that the produce, while edible at its harvest, is not
genuinely desirable as food until it is processed. Once processed,
however, the produce is deemed desirable, and therefore must be
tithed.

This understanding of matters serves as the point of depar-
ture for a series of formulaically disciplined glosses. Each
significantly qualifies its ruling by revising the context within
which the act of processing is to be understood. The first series,
C, E, G-H, J-K, P, R, and T,[94] is based upon the formulary pattern
and verb choice of the rulings themselves: *w'm 'ynw* + operative
verb, *mš-/ᶜd š-*.... The glosses point out that if no processing
is contemplated, produce must be tithed as soon as it is stored
up. By storing the produce away, the owner establishes his claim
to it. According to this series of glosses, then, processing is
the earliest possible indication of the owner's intention to
appropriate the produce for his own use. If, however, he does
not process the produce, his storage of the crop indicates his
intention to establish his claim to it, for we assume that the
owner contemplates no processing after he stores the goods.

The first series of glosses is interrupted by the interpolation of L-M, the only item in the entire unit without a formal
mate.[95] L-M further qualifies the rulings of B, D, F, and I in
light of the newly introduced issue of appropriation. It points
out that processing imposes the obligation to tithe only if the
owner intends to market the produce in question. Since he intends
to profit from it, we assume he will offer the produce for sale
as soon as feasible (y. Ma. 1:1[49a], s.v., *mh byn mwlk lbytw*).
His appropriation of the produce, therefore, is deemed complete
as soon as it is processed, for now it is suitable for sale. If,
to the contrary, the owner intends the produce for personal use,
he may make a random snack of it until he brings it home, at which
point he must cease eating until he tithes. His clear intention
to make use of the produce at home renders inconsequential any
snacks he may make while transporting the produce. Since the
farmer as yet has made no claim upon the entirety of the produce,
his random snacking indicates no pretension to sole ownership.
Matters, of course, change as soon as the man brings the produce

home, for produce inside a man's home must be tithed regardless
of how it is intended to be eaten.[96]

The notion that the owner may make a snack of produce which
is as yet unclaimed is the key assumption of the second series of
glosses, U-V, X-Y, and AA-BB. These employ an entirely new
formulary pattern (*'p ^{c}l py* + verb, *nwṭl/qwlṭ*... + participle),
and depend upon their respective rulings for their operative verbs
alone (*MRḤ, QPH, YRD*). Each points out that the owner may make a
random snack of any unprocessed remnants of a batch of processed
produce, e.g., kernels found in straw after the grain has been
winnowed and piled. The point is that the act of processing renders liable only that part of the batch which has actually been
affected by the owner's labor. Even if failure to process all of
the produce is a result of inattention, as in the case of the
kernels, the unprocessed produce remains permitted as a random
snack, for its condition does not conform to the desires of the
owner. His claim, in other words, affects only that which he is
deemed to desire--the processed portion. Whatever is unprocessed
remains unclaimed and may be eaten without tithing.

The final series of glosses, four disputes (CC-EE, GG-HH,
II-KK, MM-PP), is the most difficult. The first three, all of
which involve Judah, are substantively unrelated to the unit's
central issues. CC-EE, as we shall demonstrate in a more detailed
discussion below, is neither a true dispute, nor is it related in
any way to GG-HH and II-KK. The unit is a revised version of
M. Shab. 3:5, originally concerned with the prohibition against
cooking on the Sabbath. There Judah's lemma glosses an already-
completed unit, which appears here at BB+CC-DD. GG-HH and II-KK,
while formally unrelated, are both interested in the role of
human intention in establishing whether a substance is 1) deemed
to be food (GG-HH), and 2) capable of rendering food unclean (II-
KK). Only the final dispute, MM-PP, clearly responds to the ruling to which it is appended (LL). At issue is whether produce,
the processing of which has been interrupted, is considered processed or unprocessed, i.e., forbidden as a random snack or
permitted. Yose (PP) rules in accord with U-V ff. A man's
intention to process his produce affects only that part of the
batch which he is able to process. Once the mold is broken, all
the dried figs are deemed unprocessed, and are permitted as a
random snack (cf. T. 1:11).

Let us now stand back and view the unit's content as a
whole. We see that M. 1:5-8 systematically examines three basic
propositions: 1) the owner must tithe his produce when it is

desirable as food (twelve rulings); 2) the owner must tithe his
produce when he appropriates it for profit or personal use
(glosses C-T); 3) as long as produce is unclaimed the owner may
make a random snack of it without incurring the obligation to
tithe (L-M, U-V, X-Y, AA-BB, MM-PP). The striking fact about
these propositions is that they have no intrinsic connection with
each other. Propositions 1) and 2) are obviously independent in
conception, for each proposes an entirely coherent, self-sufficient
criterion for determining when a man must tithe his produce. They
have nevertheless been made to complement each other by the introduction of 2), as a series of glosses, into the exegesis of 1),
the catalogue's rulings. Proposition 3) also stands on its own.
In the present construction its basic task is to answer the
central question left open by the juxtaposition of M. 1:5-8 with
M. 1:1-4. That is, What are the owner's rights of consumption
between the time his produce becomes subject to the law and the
moment he is obliged to tithe it? We learn that during this period
the produce enters an indeterminate status in which it is no
longer permitted for free consumption (as it was prior to ripening),
but is not yet prohibited for consumption as a regular meal (as
it shall be when the owner establishes his claim to it). During
this time the produce, which is technically unclaimed, may be
eaten as a random snack only.

B. *Special Literary and Substantive Problems*

With the basic literary traits and substantive issues of
M. 1:5-8 in our grasp, we may now turn to more detailed literary
and conceptual problems. We begin with the organization of the
rulings themselves. These are organized into three topical units
of four rulings each: fresh produce (M. 1:5); non-perishable
produce (M. 1:6); and manufactured produce (M. 1:7-8). There are
indications, however, that the neatly arranged twelve-count is
artificial. M. 1:5I, for instance, is hardly in phase with the
other items of the catalogue, for it identifies a mode of processing rather than a type of produce. Indeed, the ruling could
be read as a further gloss of M. 1:5F+G-H. This route is impossible, however, for J-K proceeds to gloss I as if it were a
legitimate item of fresh produce, an intrinsic item of the catalogue. Clearly, the redactor of these materials intends them to
be understood as a ruling + gloss, the fourth such sequence to
his first topical unit (cf. MS and Sens).

A second difficulty in the catalogue occurs at LL. Here we
have two rulings, each consisting of its own protasis and apodosis.

The gloss, however (MM-PP), treats these rulings as a single unit, for it incorporates the operative verb of each ruling ($DW\check{S}$, ^cGL) into the protasis of its own dispute ($hyh\ d\check{o}\ b\text{-}\ldots wm^cgl\ b\text{-}\ldots$). It appears, then, that the redactor wishes LL to be read as a single ruling. As at I+J-K, the redactor's use of glosses has helped us to identify his conception of what is to be considered a distinct element of his basic catalogue.

In view of the importance of these glosses, let us look at them more closely. The first series, except for the interpolated item at L-M, presents no problems.[97] L-M, for its part, might better have been placed at the very end of the construction, for it applies, in principle, to all cases. Its present location is explained by two considerations, one formal and one substantive. Formally L-M concludes the first series of four rulings + glosses with a general observation relevant to the whole. Substantively, L-M introduces the problem of a random snack, the issue implicit in the second series of glosses and explicit at MM-PP. L-M's present location, therefore, is the most convenient in light of the formal and conceptual tasks which the redactor has set for himself.

The second series of glosses is far more problematic. U-V, which follows S-T, is clearly out of place. Its concern for kernels buried in straw is relevant only to grain (Q: cf. MS). I can only explain the clumsy arrangement by pointing out that the redactor clearly wants his glosses in consecutive series. He cannot, therefore, append U-V to Q, for the fourth ruling of the sub-unit (S) is then glossed by T, which belongs to the first series of glosses. This does not explain, however, his failure to reverse the order of Q-R and S-T, a solution which yields a more sensible flow of ideas.

A more serious problem arises at AA-BB+CC-EE, the transition from the second series of glosses to the third. Note that BB breaks the formulary pattern established at V and Y. These conclude their respective rulings with a single verb, while BB adds an entire clause. There is no substantive reason for this, for Z+AA-BB makes the same point as S+U-V and W+X-Y: a random snack is permitted of unprocessed remnants of processed produce. The problem, rather, is literary. BB, in fact, is originally independent of AA. It has been appended to the latter, along with CC-EE, to effect a transition to the third series of glosses. The unit as a whole has been moved here, in slightly revised form, from its original context in M. Shab. 3:5. There we read:

D.   The pan or pot which one has taken off the stove while it is
     boiling--

E.   one may not put spices in it (cf. CC-DD).

F.   But he may put [spices] into [hot food which is] in a plate
     or dish (BB).

G.   R. Judah says, "Into anything may one put [spices], except
     what has vinegar or brine in it" (= EE).[98]

Neusner points out that, in M. Shab., the unit is concerned with
the prohibition against cooking food on the Sabbath. At issue
is whether heating by indirect heat is considered cooking, and
therefore forbidden on the Sabbath. D-F assumes that food boiling
from the original source of heat cooks whatever is poured into it.
Thus putting spices into such food on the Sabbath is forbidden.
If the spices are poured into hot food in a cold plate, however,
the heat is no longer deemed sufficient to cook the spices. This
unit, reworked for use in M., now refers to the unprocessed oil
of Z+AA. A man may use unprocessed oil placed in a dish without
tithing it, for such use is deemed a snack (Maim., *Comm.*). Oil
placed in a pot of boiling food, however, is considered to be
part of a regular meal, for it has been cooked. As M. 4:1 will
tell us, use of any untithed produce in a regular meal, whether
or not such produce is processed, is strictly forbidden. The
oil, therefore, must be tithed before it may be placed in boiling
food. Judah now disputes DD. He argues that the oil may be put
into any receptacle, even one containing boiling food, unless
the vessel contains vinegar or brine. Apparently, such substances
flavor the oil and make it desirable for use in a meal. Maim.,
Comm., Bert., *et al.* explain that Judah holds that the brine aids
the boiling of the food. Such food removed from the fire will be
"hotter" for the brine than were the brine absent. While such
an explanation may be appropriate to M. Shab. 3:5, I do not see
how it helps us here.

    Judah's lemma, despite its obscurity in the present location,
has been preserved for formal reasons alone. As we have pointed
out above, BB-EE inaugurates a series of four disputes, of which
the first three involve Judah. We turn now to Judah's disputes
at GG-HH and II-KK, both of which are entirely independent of FF,
to which they are appended. The sole link between ruling and
glosses is the issue of the juice of grapes used as a glaze.
The glosses, however, are both informed by the same principle
regarding the role of human intention in determining whether fruit
juice is deemed a food.

At GG-HH we learn that it is permitted to glaze fig cakes with the juice of untithed grapes. Since the owner of the grapes is interested in eating the fruit itself, any juice which happens to exude from it will not be used for drinking, but will go to waste (MR). Since there is no intention to use the juice as food, it is not liable to the removal of tithes, even though the grapes themselves are liable. When such juice is used to glaze fig cakes, there is thus no concern that untithed produce is being used as food. The juice was never considered food by the owner and its function as a glaze is not deemed to be a use as food. Judah objects (HH). He understands the juice, which comes from the grapes, to share the status of the grapes. The juice, therefore, may not be used as a glaze unless the grapes themselves are tithed. According to Judah, then, since the grapes are deemed food, all products derived from them, accidentally or intentionally, are subject to the law of tithes as food.

Related issues are worked out at II-KK, this time concerning the problem of susceptibility to food-uncleanness. The ruling at II-JJ holds that grape juice applied to fig cakes does not render the cakes susceptible to uncleanness. Since M. Makh. 6:4 and M. Ter. 11:3 are clear that the juice of grapes, like water, renders food susceptible to uncleanness (cf. Lv. 11:38), the exception here must be based upon the assumption which stands behind GG. That is, the grape juice has not been intentionally squeezed and preserved, but has rather exuded on its own (M. Toh. 9:1-3). Underlying the ruling, then, is the principle of M. Makh. 1:1. As interpreted by Maimonides,[99] the principle is that liquid has the power to render foodstuffs susceptible to uncleanness only if it has intentionally been detached from its source (e.g., a pond) and then intentionally applied to the food. Since the naturally exuding grape juice has not been extracted to serve some purpose, it cannot become capable of rendering food susceptible to uncleanness even when it is later put to some use, such as glazing fig cakes (cf. Bert., MR). Judah (KK) disagrees on the basis of principles he has articulated at M. Makh. 3:5-7. That is, the final disposition of the liquid by the owner determines the character of his intention at the time it was detached from its source.[100] Since the juice has ultimately been put to use, therefore, it is deemed to have been desirable from the moment it exuded, and thus renders the fig cakes susceptible to uncleanness.

A. [The stage in processing for] storage [addressed by the law of] tithes (*grnn lm^c srwt*)--

B.   [which] imposes upon [the owner] (*lḥyyb ᶜlw*) [the obligation
     to tithe all produce which is as yet] untithed (*mšm ṭbl*)--
C.   [occurs] when its processing or its storage is complete.

                              T. 1:1a (p. 227, ls. 1-2)
                              (cf. b. B.M. 88b)

     The pericope begins Chapter One of T. with an explanation of
the term *grnn lmᶜsrwt* (M. 1:5A),[101] proposing an abstract definition (B-C) which covers the various acts of processing and storage
listed at M. 1:5B - M. 1:6T. By beginning its tractate with a
clarification of M. 1:5, T. departs significantly from the order
of issues found in M. T.'s redactor argues that the primary
business of the tractate is the proper disposition of produce
which has become liable to tithes. He places the issue, therefore, at the very head of his tractate.

G.   [If] he was removing the fuzz (*hyh mpqš*) from the very first
     [cucumber or gourd],
H.   or was scalding the first [watermelon]--
I.   as soon as (*kywn š-*) he finished all he needs,
J.   lo, it is [rendered] liable [to tithes].

                              T. 1:5b (p. 228, l. 18)
                              (Cf. y. Ma. 1:5[49a])

     T. raises a question concerning M. 1:5B+D, which has told us
that cucumbers, etc., are considered fully processed when their
fuzz is removed. The problem is whether liability to tithes
falls upon each individual piece of fruit as it is processed or
whether all remain exempt until the entire batch is processed.
I-J takes the latter position.[102] It follows, then, that T.'s
rule would permit the first melon to be eaten without removal of
tithes as long as the last one of the batch remained unprocessed.
The principle is that of M. 1:6U-V and M. 1:8MM-PP: produce is
liable when the owner's intention to process is fulfilled. In
the present case, since the owner's intention is to process a
large batch, he becomes liable for individual pieces of fruit only
when the whole conforms to his wishes.

A.   One separates heave-offering (*twrmyn*) [from] cucumbers and
     gourds even though [he has not][103] removed the fuzz [from
     them];
B.   [from] chatemelons and muskmelons even though he has not
     scalded [them].
C.   Muskmelons which are to be removed from the vat [in which
     they are being scalded]--

D. he is not required [to tithe them] until he removes them from
    the vat.

E. Green vegetables which he tied [in bunches] in the field

F. and which are to be made into a small bundle (*ṣynwq*) for
    scalding (*lšlwq*; GRA and Lieberman, following E, emend: *lšwq*,
    "for market")--

G. as soon as he has tied them [in the field: MB], lo, this one
    is [rendered] liable [to tithes].

H. One who gathers vegetables in the field--

I. as soon as he has gathered all he needs, lo, this [i.e., the
    contents of the gathering basket] is [rendered] liable [to
    tithes].

T. 1:6a (p. 228, ls. 19-22)
(E-G: cf. y. Ma. 1:5[49a])

T. is a series of discrete glosses to M. 1:5. A-B gives a
rule relevant to M. 1:5B-E. Although separation of heave-offering
(which must be removed prior to other offerings: M. Ter. 3:6-7)
is required from produce which is completely processed, T. says
that one is permitted to remove the heave-offering, and presumably
the rest of the tithes, before the completion of processing.[104]
The point is obvious, for despite its lack of desirability (i.e.,
it is unprocessed), the produce is edible and therefore subject to
the law in principle. As M. 1:5-8 has labored to point out in
detail, processing is the act which *imposes* the obligation to
tithe; it is not, however, a *precondition* for the removal of
tithes. C-D also glosses M. 1:5B-E. The rule is simply that the
produce is rendered liable when processing is complete and not
before. The principle is that adduced at T. 1:5b (= M. 1:6U-V,
M. 1:8MM-PP). E-G glosses M. 1:5F. Once the picker has tied the
vegetables into bundles, they are irrevocably rendered liable to
the removal of tithes, even if he later undoes his labor in order
to make smaller bunches (Lieberman, TK, II:672, 21). This, of
course, contradicts Yose's position at M. 1:8 PP. H-I requires
no comment.

J. If he was going to braid garlic or tie onions, he is not
    required [to tithe them] until he braids [the garlic] or ties
    [the onions].

K. [Unwinnowed] ears [of grain] which find their way (*pwlṭwt*)
    from the threshing floor into the pile of grain, and inferior
    kernels (*mḥpwrwt*)[105] in the pile, and pods (so Jastrow,
    p. 1408, for *qṣṣyn*) of pulse--

L. when the [pile] is smoothed [on] the threshing floor, he may
    not eat [anything in the pile] until he removes tithes.
M. *Pulse is [rendered liable] when he sifts [it]* [= M. 1:6S].
N. [y. Ma. 1:6 adds *'bl*, "But"] he takes (*nwṭl*) [pulse] from
    beneath the sieve and eats [without tithing].

T. 1:6b (p. 228, l. 22-p. 229,
ls. 1-3) (E = y. Ma. 1:6[49b])

J continues the interests of T. 1:6a (C-H) and T. 1:5b,
stipulating that an intended act of processing must actually be
complete before liability is incurred. Although J mentions onions,
as does M. 1:6/O, it shows no interest in M.'s problem, and is
therefore probably an autonomous formulation placed here primarily
to continue T.'s interests while maintaining a superficial relation to M. K-L demonstrates agreement with the principle of M
M. 1-6U-V by outlining an exactly inverse case. In M. the edible
odds and ends have been excluded from the smoothed pile and are
therefore permitted. In T. the normally undesired items, despite
all precautions, have remained in the pile and have been processed
along with the rest of the pile.[106] For this reason they are
forbidden, while M.'s edible items, because they are unprocessed,
are permitted. M quotes M. 1:6S, and N glosses. Now the principle of K-L and M. 1:6U-V is refined further. On the one hand,
the pulse has all been processed; yet, the smaller beans have
fallen through the sieve into the dirt. Thus they are both
desirable (M.), and processed (T.), yet are still in need of
further processing since they have fallen back into the dirt.
The owner may therefore eat the pulse even though its processing
is completed, since the product itself is not in the cleaned condition which is the goal of its processing.[107]

Maimonides (*Tithes* 3:13) combines M. 1:6S-T and T. 1:6bN
into a single rule: "Pulse [is rendered liable] when he sifts
[it]. And he [may] take pulse from beneath the sieve and eat.
If he does not sift, [the pulse is not liable] until he evens the
pile."

A. One who consecrates a vat [of wine solely for Temple use]
    before drawing [the waste from it] (*ŠLH* or (w-) skimming
    [the waste off the top],
B. [GRA deletes:] and after he has drawn it or (w-) skimmed it
    the Temple treasurer (*gzbr*) came,
C. and he [i.e., the original owner] redeemed it--
D. [the wine] is liable [to tithes] (*ḥyyb*).
E. [If] he consecrated it before drawing or skimming,

F.   and the Temple treasurer came and drew or skimmed [on his
     own],

G.   and afterwards [the original owner] redeemed it--

H.   since at the moment [in which] the liability [to tithes]
     should have been incurred], [the wine was] exempt (*hw'yl*
     wbš᷉ᶜt ḥwbtw pṭwr),

I.   [it remains] exempt (*pṭwr*).

> T. 1:7a (p. 229, ls. 25-28)
> (Cf. M. Pe'ah 1:6, 4:8,
> M. Hal. 3:4, y. Ma. 1:6[49b])

         T. is autonomous of M. It is placed within T.'s discussion
of M. 1:7 because it raises an issue relevant to completing the
manufacture of wine. The pericope consists of two apocopated
sentences, A-D and E-I, each of which is composed of a compound
protasis presenting a case (A-C, E-G) and an apodosis stating the
law (D, H-I). E's language assumes A and depends upon it for
context. The elements of the pericope are well balanced, with
B-C standing over against F-G, and D corresponding to I. H is
an explanatory interpolation.

         As they stand before us, A-D and E-I present two contradic-
tory views of the consequences of redeeming wine which has been
processed while consecrated to the Temple. In both cases a man
has made a gift of wine to the Temple. As Temple property, the
wine is now exempt from the laws of tithes, for the Priests and
Levites do not give themselves offerings. Now, while the wine is
in a state of consecration, either the donor (B) or the Temple
treasurer (F) completes the processing, and the wine is now ready
for priestly use. At this point, however, the donor decides to
redeem the wine. That is, he buys the wine back from the Temple,
exchanging a monetary gift for the original wine. D rules that
the wine, whose processing has been completed, becomes liable to
tithes upon return to the donor's possession. H-I, on the other
hand, explains that since the wine was not subject to the law at
the time of its processing, it remains exempt even upon return to
the original donor. The contradiction is that the conditions of
H satisfy the case of A-C as well as that of E-G, for in both
instances the wine was Temple property at the time of processing.
On what grounds, then, does D require the wine of A-C to be
tithed upon return to the donor's possession?

         I can make no sense of what is before us within the framework
of principles provided by M.-T.[108] The soundest exegetical path
has been suggested by GRA, who simply deletes B, the stich which
has the donor skimming the Temple's wine. While the observed

formal balance of our pericope would normally inhibit such a
maneuver, in this case there is much to recommend it. First of
all, the deletion makes sense of the pericope. Now A+C-D tells us
that a man who consecrates his wine and then redeems it *before
completing the processing* is responsible for removing tithes once
he completes the work. The point of the rule is now explicable
in terms of H. Since the wine has passed into and from the Temple
ownership without undergoing any acts of processing, its status
is identical to that which it had before being consecrated. It
is simply wine which has not yet been completely processed. Therefore, as soon as the donor completes the processing of the redeemed
wine, it becomes liable to tithes like anything else.

There are also formal grounds for accepting GRA's version of
the pericope. While his deletion of B is unsupported by any MS
evidence[109] and cannot explain why B was inserted into the pericope in the first place, there is a close formal and substantive
parallel between our pericope (minus B) and M. Pe'ah 4:8 (= M. Hal.
3:4).

A.   One who consecrates his fruits before they have reached their
       tithing season.
B.   and he redeemed them--
C.   [the fruits] are subject [to the law of tithes] (*ḥyybyn*).
D.   [If] he consecrated them after they have reached their tith-
       ing season,
E.   and he redeemed them--
F.   [the fruits] are subject [to the laws of tithes] (*ḥyybyn*).
G.   [If] he consecrated them before they were completely processed
       (*ᶜd šl' ngmrw*),
H.   and the Temple treasurer completed their processing.
I.   and afterwards the owner redeemed them--
J.   [the fruits] are exempt (*pṭwryn*),
K.   since at the moment [in which] their liability [to tithes]
       [should have been incurred] they were exempt (*šbšᶜt ḥwbtn hyw
       pṭwryn*

A-C above corresponds precisely to A+C-D of our pericope.
D-F, which simply provides a complement to *A-C* exemplifying the
same principle, is lacking in T. *G-K* corresponds almost exactly
to E-I, the sole difference being in the phrasing of the crucial
principle at *K* and H, which in any event leaves the principle
unaltered. Clearly, T. and M. Pe'ah 4:8 are alternate formula-
tions of the same principle. This is convincing evidence that B

is indeed a confusing and confused interpolation, and that GRA's deletion should be accepted.

H. *Wine--after he skims [the scum from the fermenting juice in*
    the receiving tank]. Even though he has skimmed, he collects
    [liquid] from the upper vat and from the duct and drinks
    [without tithing] [= M. 1:7W-Y].
    Oil--after it has flowed into the trough. Even though it
    has flowed, he takes [oil] from the pressing bale, from the
    press beam, and from between the boards [of the pressing vat],
    and places it into a plate or dish [= M. 1:7Z-BB].
J. But he may not gather it in a vessel [in sufficient quantity]
    to make [continual] use of it (*lhywt mštmš mmnw[whwlk]*).[110]

T. 1:7b (p. 229, ls. 28-31)

J ignores M. 1:7CC-EE entirely, appending its own gloss to M. 1:7Z-BB. The point is obvious. Placing the oil into a vessel for continuous use is tantamount to storing the produce, and therefore renders the oil, even though it is unprocessed, liable to the removal of tithes (cf. M. 4:1 G-I).

A. [If] he was eating [untithed produce as a random snack]
B. and left [some food] over (*whwtyr*),
C. and dusk fell on Sabbath Eve (*wḥšyky blyly šbt*)--
D. [he is] permitted [to continue eating the leftovers on the Sabbath].
E. Said R. Simeon b. Eleazar, "Under what circumstances?
F. "[Only] in the event that he was eating and left [some food] over, and dusk fell on Sabbath Eve.
G. "But he may not intentionally add (*l' ytkwyn wytn*) [the food] to [a bowl containing] much *anigaron*[111] in order to make a surplus (*bšbyl šywtyr*) and bring it into his home."

T. 1:8 (p. 229, ls. 31-33)
(A-D: cf. M. Ter. 8:3, y. Ma. 1:6
[49b])

T. is autonomous of M., and far more relevant to M. Ter. 8:1-3, where A-D is paralleled in a ruling attributed to Eliezer in dispute with Joshua.[112] At issue in A-D, as Peck points out,[113] is whether an individual can complete a forbidden act which, at its inception, was permitted. When the man began eating his untithed produce, he was fully within his rights. With the onset of the Sabbath, however, all eating is deemed a regular meal, in honor of the day of rest (see discussion to M. 4:2, pp. 125-126. Since it is forbidden to tithe on the Sabbath (M. 4:2), the

question is whether the man must cease eating. A-D permits him to
continue to eat, since he began his eating at a permissible time
(cf. y. Ma. 3:9[50d] and b. Bes. 35a). Simeon b. Eleazar (E-G)
adds that this rule applies only when the man does not intentionally plan to circumvent the law.

A. One who skims [wine]in a tub (*^{c}rybh*)
B. and one who skims [wine] in a vessel (*kly*)
C. puts [the skimmed wine] *into a small bowl or a plate*
   [= M. 1:7BB].
D. One who pours [hot food] from [one] cauldron into [another]
   cauldron, and from [one] stew-pot (*'lpś*) into [another]
   stew-pot, and from [one] pot into [another pot]
E. is permitted to put [untithed wine or oil] into the second
   [vessel],
F. and forbidden from putting [it] into the first [vessel].
G. One who squeezes (*ŚḤṬ*) [the juice of] grapes into his hand
   [is] exempt [from tithing the juice].
H. [One who squeezes the juice] into a cup--lo, this one is
   required [to tithe].

T. 1:9 (p. 230, ls. 34-36)
(D-F = T. Shab. 3(4):9;
G-H: cf. M. 4:1)

T. presents three cases, A-C, D-F, and G-H, sharing a common
formulary pattern: *h* + present participle + apodosis. The cases
refine M. 1:7's principle that wine and oil remain exempt from
the removal of tithes until their processing is complete.

A-C augments M. 1:7W-BB's demonstration that residual wine
or oil left in the press after processing is exempt from tithes.
T. shifts our attention to a case in which the actual processing
of the wine has no affect upon its prior status. The rule describes a situation in which someone has filled a container with
unskimmed wine directly from the receiving tank of the wine-press.
Should he then skim the wine in the container, A-B, the skimming
does not render the wine liable to tithes, as C, which permits
the wine to be placed in a bowl or plate, points out.[114]   In this
case, the act of skimming, which normally renders the wine in the
receiving tank liable to tithes, has not been done in the normal
fashion. Only a small portion of wine has been skimmed in a
container other than the tank. Therefore, the skimming does not
have its usual effect of rendering wine liable. Both the wine
still in the tank and that in the container retain their former
exempt status.

D-F augments M. 1:7CC-DD in light of M. Shab. 3:5. Here we
learn that while untithed wine or oil may not be poured into a
pot in which food is cooking, one may nevertheless place the untithed product into a vessel containing hot food which has been
removed from the fire. Since the food in the latter vessel is
not actually cooking, its heat is not considered sufficient to
cook the oil (y. Ma. 1:7[49b], s.v. $^c d$ $hykn$).

G-H extends M. 1:7's rule that products which require sophisticated manufacturing are not liable until that process is completed. Now we find that even the relatively simple process of
squeezing grape juice is considered a type of manufacturing which
is subject to specific regulations. The issue is whether or not
the grapes have been dealt with in a way which constitutes processing. Since crushing the grapes in one's hand is not a normal
way of obtaining juice, it is exempt even if drunk. However,
crushing the grapes into a cup prepares the juice for consumption,
and it must be tithed as a manufactured product. The principle
is identical to that of A-C. Only a normal method of manufacture
is sufficient to render the product liable.[115]

A. Oil pressers who take their lighting oil alternatively from
    one press and another (Jastrow's translation, p. 139 of:
    $hbddyn$ $hmdlyqyn$ mbd lbd)--
B. one does not suspect ('yn $ḥwššyn$) them of robbing the owner
    ($mšwm$ $gyzlw$ $šl$ $b^c l$ $hbyt$)
C. for this is customary behavior.

                              T. 1:10 (p. 230, ls. 37-38)

     The only apparent connection between T. and M. is interest
in oil. The point, according to Lieberman (TK, II:675,37), is
that since the owner would not want his workers to labor in the
dark, he gladly permits them to use the oil in order to aid them
in their work.

A. [If] he was pressing [them] into a jar or rolling [them] in a
    mold, [and] the jar broke or the mold opened, he shall not
    make of them a random snack. And R. Yose permits [him to make
    a random snack [= M. 1:8MM-PP],
B. because the [figs on the] bottom require the [figs on] top
    [in order to keep from falling apart without the mold to hold
    them together].

                              T. 1:11 (p. 230, ls. 38-39)
                              (B = y. Ma. 1:8[49b])

T. simply cites M. and provides a gloss at B which explains
Yose's reasoning. The dependency of the completely pressed lower
layer of figs upon the pressure exerted by the unpressed upper
layer indicates that the processing, while begun, has in fact not
been accomplished.[116]

X. On what basis [do I know] that a man tithes what he eats?
    Scripture says: "You shall tithe" (Dt. 14:22).

Y. Is it possible [to tithe produce] even though its processing
    is not completed in the field?

Z. Scripture says: "as the corn of the threshing floor"
    (Nu. 18:27)--lo, it [i.e., the threshing floor:Neṣib] is in
    the field[117] (whry hw' bsdh; V reads: whry hy' ksdh, "lo,
    it is like the field");

AA. "and as the fullness of the wine press" (Nu. 18:27)--[he is
    not required to tithe] until it [i.e., the wine] is in the
    wine press (ᶜd šhy' byqb; B and Neṣib read: ᶜd šhyqb bsdh,
    "until the wine press is in the field") [but he is *permitted*
    to tithe beforehand],

BB. Is it possible that a man make make a snack in the field [after
    processing is complete: R. Hillel]?[118] Scripture says: "You
    shall tithe" (Dt. 14:22).

CC. On what basis do I know that he must tithe what he sows?
    Scripture says: "what comes forth from the field" (Dt. 14:22).

EE. They said: They destroyed the stalls of the sons of Ḥanan
    (bny ḥnn; B and y. Pe'ah 1:6 read: byt ḥnn, "Beth Hanan")[119]
    three years before [the fall of] the Land of Israel [to the
    Romans] because they [i.e., the stall owners] would remove
    their produce from the scope of the tithing laws (mydy
    mᶜsrwt).

FF. For they would interpret [Scripture] to mean [the following]:
    "You shall tithe ... and *you* shall eat" (Dt. 14:22)-- [that
    is, the one who eats shall tithe,] but not the merchant.

GG. "the yield of your seed (Dt. 14:22)--[that is, the farmer
    shall tithe,] but not the buyer.

                          Sifre Dt. 105d (Finkelstein, p. 165,
                          ls. 9-15) (H-J: cf. b. B.M. 88a,
                          y. Pe'ah 1:6[16c])

    X-CC provide a series of exegeses establishing Scriptural
warrant for fundamental tithing rules. The whole is relevant to,
but exhibits no literary dependence upon, M. 1:5-8. X requires no
comment. Y-AA is obscure no matter which combinations of readings
we prefer. Y's question raises an issue which has elsewhere been

settled by T. 1:6A-C, which permits the tithing of produce which
is not completely processed. I do not understand the point of Z.
The answer to Y is at AA: even though wine--and presumably other
products--are not liable until completion of processing, one is
permitted to tithe them before that time just as we have learned
at T. 1:6A-C. BB-CC continue elementary exegesis. EE, glossed
by FF-GG, is autonomous of the foregoing, appended to it by
"they said." EE tells us that the greed of the stall-keepers of
Beth Ḥanan hastened their doom. FF-GG now ties EE into the
interests of CC. CC has established scriptural warrant for the
obligation of the farmer-owner to tithe. FF-GG bring Scripture
to bear upon the obligations of merchants and buyers, the next
logical step in the extent of the law's power. It says that the
stall-keepers of EE *misinterpreted* Scripture to exclude the
merchant and the buyer from the obligation to separate tithes,
while Scripture intends just the opposite (cf. M. Demai 2:2).

MAASEROT CHAPTER TWO

Chapter Two develops the thesis of M. 1:5-8, that the owner
of untithed produce incurs the obligation to tithe when he effects
acquisition of it. In the present chapter the focus merely shifts
from produce which the householder brings home from his own field
to produce which he acquires from another. Such acquisition may
occur either in the form of a gift or through financial transaction. Under either circumstance the recipient of produce incurs
the obligation to tithe it only when the transaction is complete
and he has actually claimed as his own the produce involved. This,
in fact, is the point of the entire chapter. The recipient of a
gift of untithed figs, for example (M. 2:1-2), may snack on the
produce until he brings it home. He must tithe it at that point
only, for as we recall, this is the point at which the produce
becomes his. Those who purchase produce in the market (M. 2:5-6),
however, or who exchange their labor (M. 2:7-8C) or their own
produce (M. 2:8D-J) for untithed produce, incur the obligation to
tithe as soon as they accept the produce for which they have
bargained. Since the transaction cannot be rescinded after a
buyer has taken his purchase (M. B.M. 4:2), he is deemed to have
effected acquisition immediately, even prior to bringing the
produce home.

The problem in each of the chapter's three primary units
(M. 2:1-2, M. 2:5-6, M. 2:7-8) is to distinguish cases in which
produce merely changes hands from genuine transactions in which
title to the untithed produce is actually transferred to a second
party. Only in the latter transactions does the second party
incur the obligation to tithe. The unit on gifts (M. 2:1-2) begins the discussion, for here matters are most clear-cut. M.
assumes that gifts remain the property of the donor until the
recipient brings them into his home. It follows that the recipient
of a gift of untithed produce shares the donor's privilege to
make a snack of it until he becomes the new owner. Within this
framework, M. raises two issues. First, if the recipient has
cause to assume that the donor himself has incurred the obligation
to tithe, the produce is forbidden to him as well (M. 2:1F-I). He
may, however, refrain from the produce until he brings it home, at
which point, as the owner of the produce, he tithes and eats it.
Secondly, if the recipient accepts untithed produce in his place

of business (deemed by M. to be analogous to his own home) he may
not eat the produce unless he tithes, for he has already become
the new owner (M. 2:2J-O).

M. 2:3 and M. 2:4, appended to M. 2:1-2, are out of phase
with the chapter's overall inquiry. M. 2:3 carries forward
M. 2:2J-O's interest in structures deemed analogous to a man's
own home. Travelers who carry untithed produce on a journey may
eat it without tithing until they enter a dwelling which serves
as their temporary home. Meir (M. 2:3E) holds that such a surrogate for the home must be a place in which the traveler is made
to feel like a guest, while Judah (M. 2:3H) holds that any dwelling
will do, even if the traveler just passes through it. At issue
in M. 2:4, a pair of disputes, is whether the removal of heave-
offering from unprocessed produce renders the remainder forbidden
until all other offerings have been removed as well. The pericope
is relevant to our chapter only insofar as the answer to its
question determines whether the householder may snack on the produce after the removal of the heave-offering. The true interest
of the disputes, however, lies in the nature of the tithing process itself, a matter we shall examine in detail in the commentary.
Here we simply observe that this potentially crucial matter is
never again addressed in M., and remains buried at the end of a
sub-unit on the privilege of making a snack of untithed produce.

At M. 2:5-6, the second of the chapter's three units, we
turn to what is perhaps the paradigmatic transfer of title, monetary purchases. According to Mishnah's general theory of purchases, such transactions are consummated as soon as the purchaser
takes possession of the product (M. B.M. 4:2). It follows that
until the purchaser of untithed produce accepts the produce for
which he has paid, no title has been transferred, and the purchaser assumes no obligation to tithe the produce. On this basis
Judah rules (M. 2:5C) that if a purchaser refrains from gathering
his stipulated purchase, he may eat at random one piece of produce at a time without tithing. Thus a man who stipulates a
purchase of five figs may, without obligation, eat one at a time
from the bin, for he is not deemed to have accepted the produce
until he gathers five figs at once. Despite the disagreement of
Meir (M. 2:5B), Judah's position serves as the foundation of two
further series of cases at M. 2:6E-I and J-O.

Investigation of transactions continues at M. 2:7, the chapter's final unit, which takes up the special problem of barter.
M. 2:7's triplet presents cases in which a field worker stipulates
that any produce he eats while on the job shall be deemed part

of his wage. Normally, we should expect such produce to be liable
to the removal of tithes, for the worker has acquired it by his
labor. In the present circumstances, however, there has been no
transfer of title over the produce. All field workers, as
M. 2:7L-M (cf. M. B.M. 7:2) points out, are entitled by the Torah
to eat produce which they are harvesting. Such produce, therefore,
is deemed the worker's, even though it grows in his employer's
field. It follows that despite the worker's stipulation there
has in fact been no transfer of title, for the produce belongs to
the worker in the first place. He therefore eats it while on the
job without obligation to tithe. If, however, he offers figs to
non-laboring dependents (M. 2:7D-G), or eats them himself after
he has finished his work (M. 2:7H-K), these are deemed his by
acquisition and must be tithed.

Following a minor gloss of M. 2:7 at M. 2:8A-C, M. 2:8D-J
concludes the chapter with a second case of barter, in which figs
are exchanged for other figs. The unit does not address the
chapter's central interest, but rather raises a secondary problem
in Judah's name. He points out that if one receives as barter unprocessed figs, they need not be tithed until the purchaser completes the processing. The point, which we have already encountered
in M. 1:5-6, is that produce is permitted even after formal acquisition until it is made desirable as food. M. 3:1A-B, as we shall
see, assumes this point as well, permitting us to view Judah's
discussion as a transition to M.'s third chapter.

T. for our chapter consists of only five pericopae. Its
observations are episodic and do not follow the order of M.'s
chapter. It is interesting to note that T.'s most carefully
constructed commentaries upon M., T. 2:1 and T. 2:2-3, do not
relate to the major issues of M.'s chapter, but rather concentrate
upon M. 2:3 and M. 2:4, the secondary materials appended to
M. 2:1-2.

                                2:1-2

A. (1) [If] one was passing through the market
B. and said, "Take figs for yourselves,"
C. [those who accept them] eat [the figs while they are in
    the market] and are exempt [from tithing] (*'wklyn wpṭwryn*).
D. Therefore, if they brought [the figs] into their homes
E. they tithe (*mtqnym*) [them as they would tithe figs which are]
    certainly untithed (*wd'y*) [*viz.*, they remove heave-offering,

first tithe and either second or poorman's tithe in the usual
manner].

F. (2) [If he said,] "Take [the figs] and bring [them] into
    your homes,"

G. [those who accept them] shall not make a random snack [of the
    figs while they are in the market].

H. Therefore, if they brought [the figs] into their homes

I. they tithe [them] only [as they would tithe figs which are]
    doubtfully tithed (dm'y) [viz., they remove only the heave-
    offering of the tithe, and consume the rest of the produce
    as if it was completely tithed].

                        M. 2:1

J. (3) [If] they were sitting in a doorway or stall,

K. and [the passer-by] said, "Take figs for yourselves,"

L. [those who accept them] eat [the figs in the doorway or stall]
    and are exempt [from tithing] ('wklyn wpṭwryn).

M. But (w-) the owner of the doorway or (w-) the owner of the
    stall are required [to tithe].

N. R. Judah exempts [the owner from tithing]

O. unless (ᶜd š-) he turns his face [away from the public] or
    unless he moves from where he is sitting [to a private part
    of the stall].

                        M. 2:1-2

    The present triplet assumes that the recipient of untithed
produce shares those privileges or restrictions regarding its
consumption which apply to the donor himself.[1] If the donor yet
enjoys the privilege of making a snack of his produce without
tithing (A-C, J-L: cf. M. 1:5L-M), the recipient shares his right.
If, on the other hand, the donor has already obliged himself to
tithe his produce, those to whom he offers such untithed produce
are likewise obliged to tithe it before eating (F-G). Materials
appended to the basic triplet, while falling into distinct formal
groups (D-E, H-I vs. M+N-O), all address a single secondary notion.
The recipient of the produce is obliged to tithe it as soon as he
effects appropriation of it, despite the fact that untithed produce remaining with the donor may still be exempt. In all, then,
M. must be regarded as an application of the principle informing
M. 1:5L-M, that produce is permitted as a snack until it is
appropriated by its owner for his personal use. Under discussion
now is the point at which the produce is deemed to have a new
owner. At this point the status of the produce vis a vis the law
is determined solely by the new owner's actions and intentions.

A provides the context for both B-C and F-G. The contrast
between the two rulings (C vs. G) is generated by the change in
locution at B and F ("take figs" vs. "take figs home"). The
problem is whether the recipient can assume that the figs are
permitted to the donor himself as a random snack. A-C is clear
that if a passer-by simply offers figs to his fellow in the market,
the latter may snack on them without tithing. Since the figs are
not offered for sale, we assume the donor is taking them home
(Maim., *Comm.*). As M. 1:5L-M points out, they may therefore be
eaten by their owner as a snack. A-C simply adds that they are
permitted as well to anyone to whom the owner offers his figs.
Matters change at F-G because the ambiguity of the donor's remark
casts doubt upon whether or not he himself has the privilege of
eating his figs. His stipulation that the recipient bring the
figs home may indicate that the figs are presently liable to the
removal of tithes, i.e., that they are intended for sale in the
market.[2] In light of this ambiguity the recipient refrains from
consuming the figs until he is certain of their status regarding
the law. That is, he waits until he brings them to his own home,
where they are clearly liable to tithes on his account.

This solution generates a new problem--how are such figs to
be tithed when the recipient brings them home? H-I assumes that
although the figs are certainly liable to the removal of tithes,
it is unclear whether the donor had removed any of the offerings
on his own behalf prior to offering the figs. The figs, therefore, are deemed *demai*-produce. That is, there is doubt whether,
and to what extent, agricultural offerings have been removed by
the original donor. In such circumstances we assume that heave-
offering, the priestly gift (and the smallest offering), has
already been removed.[3] The householder, therefore, removes only
the heave-offering of the tithe--the other sanctified priestly
offering--and consumes the rest of the produce as if it were fully
unconsecrated. Tithing of the produce at A-C, of course, requires
no such precautions, for we have no reason to assume that the
donor tithed his exempt figs in the first place. Therefore, as
D-E states, the recipient tithes them in the normal fashion when
he brings them home.

J-L, the third case, repeats B-C at K-L. The superscription
at J, however, changes the situation in an important respect,
preparing us for the amplifications at M+N-O. Now the recipients
accept the figs in a doorway or stall instead of in the open air
of the market (J). The problem is whether the structure functions
in a way which is analogous to the recipients' homes. If so, they

would be required to tithe the figs just as if they had taken them
home. K-L rules that the recipients may eat the figs without
tithing. The explanation comes at M, which stipulates that only
the *owner* of the structure must tithe his figs. The point is that
since the structure is his possession it is equivalent to his home.
The other recipients, however, who are merely guests or customers,
need not tithe, for they are not deemed at home.[4] Judah, N-O,
qualifies M. His point is that the stall or doorway, since it
affords no privacy, is not analogous to the home (cf. M. 3:5
below). The owner of such a structure, therefore, need not tithe
his figs unless he establishes for himself a private corner within
the structure. Only then is the space deemed *his* and, therefore,
analogous to his private home.

2:3

A. One who transports (*hm^{c}lh*) produce from Galilee to Judea,
B. or [who] goes up (*^{c}wlh*) [from a location in Judea: TYY] to
    Jerusalem,
C. eats of [his untithed produce] until he reaches his destina-
    tion (*lmqwm šhw' hwlk*) [at which point he must tithe before
    eating].
D. And [this is] also [the case] on the return trip (*wkn bhzrh*).[5]
E. R. Meir says, "[He eats] until he reaches the place [where he
    intends to] spend the Sabbath (*lmqwm hšbyth*: y. Ma. 2:3[49d])."
F. [Eleven MSS. omit *w-*, "And"] peddlars who circulate among [a
    number of] towns
G. eat [their untithed produce] until they reach their night's
    lodging (*lmqwm hlynh*) [at which point they must tithe before
    eating].
H. R. Judah says, "The first house [he enters] is [considered]
    his house [even should he lodge elsewhere]."

M. 2:3

The present pericope, like M. 2:1-2, carries forward the
consequences of M. 1:5L-M. As before, we assume that a man may
eat, as a random snack, untithed produce which he has not yet
brought into his own home. The present problem, for which
M. 2:2J-O has prepared us, is to determine what counts as a surrogate for a man's actual home, such that any produce he brings into
it is rendered liable to the removal of tithes. The matter is
examined in two glossed rulings (A+C+E and F-G+H) which discuss
individuals who carry untithed produce with them on a journey.

There are two basic positions concerning what constitutes such a
traveler's surrogate home. The first, assumed by both A+C and
Meir (E), is that such a surrogate is constituted by any house in
which a man is deemed at his ease. Meir's qualification of A+C
does not challenge this basic position. The same point informs
F-G as well, to which Judah (H) now objects. His position is that
any home is a surrogate for a man's actual dwelling, as long as he
has been granted access. Judah, it appears, holds a "formalist"
position:[6] the surrogate for a man's home is quite literally any
dwelling into which he enters. For Meir, A+C and F-G, however, a
surrogate for a man's home must *function* as his home. That is,
the owner of the dwelling must offer his guest the comforts of
home. Only then is the dwelling deemed equivalent to the guest's
actual home in such a way that he must tithe any untithed produce
he brings into it.

We turn now to the details. Disregarding for the moment the
interpolations at B and D, we see that A+C permits the transporter
of untithed produce to snack on it until he reaches his destination, i.e., the house where he will establish temporary domicile
while away from home (TYY). Any dwelling in which he takes shelter during the journey is deemed too temporary to function as a
surrogate for his own home. His produce, it follows, is not
rendered liable when he enters such dwellings, and remains permitted to him as a snack until he completes his journey (Maim.,
Tithes 4:11). Meir observes that if the Sabbath intervenes during
the journey, the place where the traveler takes his Sabbath rest
is deemed his temporary home (MR). It follows, for Meir, that the
produce must be tithed as soon as the traveler accepts Sabbath
hospitality, for it is as if the man has entered his own home
with the untithed produce.

The interpolations at B and D do not alter the point of A+C
in any way. B simply augments A's description of a journey covering some distance, claiming that even a journey from a locale in
Judea to Jerusalem requires the law's attention. D adds that the
rule of A-C holds true as well for the return trip. I can think
of no reason for stressing this point.[7]

F-G, the second ruling, assumes that peddlars pass through a
number of towns and therefore can be expected to enter many homes
in order to sell their wares.[8] The point of the ruling is that
these homes, like those in which the transporter takes shelter
(A+C), are not surrogates for the home of the peddlar. Any untithed produce he happens to bring into such homes, therefore, need
not be tithed. Rather, such a surrogate is constituted only by

the home in which he spends the night, i.e., where he is made to
feel at home (A+C+E). Judah, at H, objects, stating that the very
first home entered by the peddlar is considered "his" home, and
therefore renders the produce with him liable to the removal of
tithes. Judah's point must be that any dwelling renders liable
the produce of the person who enters it.[9]

A. Ass-drivers and householders ($b^c ly\ btym$; ed. princ.: $b^c ly$
   $hgtym$, "oil merchants") who were traveling from place to place
   ($mmqwm\ lmqwm$)

B. eat [untithed produce in their possession] and are exempt
   [from tithing it] ($'wklyn\ wptwryn$)

C. until they reach the specific place [they have in mind]
   ($l'wtw\ mqwm$) [cf. M. 2:3A-E].

D. Therefore, if a householder [at whose dwelling they arrive]
   designates a specific lodging-place for them--

E. if they spend the night there, they are required to tithe
   [untithed produce in their possession before eating it],

F. and if not, they are exempt from tithing.

G. $M^c sh\ \breve{s}$-: R. Joshua went to visit Rabban Yoḥanan b. Zakkai
   at Beror Ḥayil, and the townspeople brought figs out to them.
   They [i.e., those in Joshua's party.] said to him, "Must we
   tithe [the figs] ($mh\ 'nw\ l^c sr$)?"

H. He said to them, "If we are going to spend the night ($'m$
   $lnyn\ 'nw$) [we are] required to tithe, and if not, [we] are
   exempt from tithing."

I. [If] they arrived *at their night's lodging* [= M. 2:3G]--

J. even [if they remained only] two hours[10]--

K. they must tithe ($ṣrykyn\ l^c sr$).

L. R. Meir says, "[If] they arrived *at the place [where they*
   intended to] spend the Sabbath [= M. 2:3E]--

M. even [if they arrived] on the second day [of the week]--

N. he is required to tithe ($ḥyyb\ l^c sr$; E reads: $ptwryn\ ml^c sr$,
   "they are exempt from tithing").[11]

T. 2:1 (pp. 230-31, ls. 1-7)
(G-H: cf. y. Ma. 2:3[49d],
y. Dem. 3:1[23b])

    T. contains three independent units: A-C+D-F, G-H and I-N.
A-C, in accord with the "functionalist" position of M. 2:3A+C, E,
and F-G, permits ass-drivers, who transport grain over wide areas
(HY), and householders, who presumably make shorter journeys, to
snack on produce in their possession until they reach their final
destination. The rule is a substantial reformulation of M. 2:3A-C

and F-G. A, which includes the long-distance transporter (M. 2:3A)
and the local traveler (M. 2:3F) in a single category, claims that
one rule holds for all who carry untithed produce on a journey.
As B-C tells us, these travelers eat of their produce, for it does
not become liable until it is brought into the home-surrogate,
established by the owner at his destination. But, D-F adds, if
someone designates a lodging-place for the traveler, his produce
becomes liable to tithes unless he refuses the hospitality. The
point is that by accepting the householder's hospitality the
traveler makes the home of the householder his own. Thus it is
as if the traveler brought the produce into his own home, rendering it liable to tithes as produce which is going to be eaten at
the table.

The independent precedent at G-H demonstrates the point made
at D-F. Joshua (H) points out that the figs are liable only if
the travelers intend to sleep in their host's house. In light of
D-F, the redactor leads us to assume that if they have no such
intention, they may eat the figs as they please until they actually
decide to spend the night at someone's home.

I-N is separate from the foregoing materials, introducing
glosses into M.'s text. I-K defines the minimum amount of time
which is considered a night's lodging. If the travelers spend as
little as two hours of the night at a householder's home, they are
considered to have made his home their own, and must tithe their
produce before eating it. L-N expands Meir's opinion[12] to include
the notion that if the traveler reaches his Sabbath resting place
early in the week, his produce is immediately liable. The produce is liable as early as the second day of the week preceding
the Sabbath, for the traveler is already enjoying the privileges
which, on the Sabbath, render the home a surrogate for his own.

2:4

A. Produce from which one separated heave-offering before its
    processing was complete--

B. R. Eliezer prohibits making a random snack of it [from that
    moment on].

C. But Sages permit [a random snack until the processing is
    complete],

D. except [in the case of] a basket of figs.

E. A basket of [unprocessed] figs from which one separated
    heave-offering--

F.   R. Simeon permits [making a random snack of it].

G.   But Sages prohibit [making a random snack of it].

                         M. 2:4 (A-C = b. Bes. 35a, b)

At issue in the present pericope is the effect of removing
heave-offering from produce which the householder is not yet
obliged to tithe.[13] All would agree that produce removed as heave-
offering prior to the completion of processing may be used as
heave-offering, despite its premature removal (M. Ter. 1:10). Our
problem concerns the effects of this act on the householder's
right to use the remaining unprocessed produce. Quite simply, we
want to know whether the removal of heave-offering, an act normally
performed upon forbidden produce, requires us to impose a forbidden
status on produce which, for other reasons, is exempt from the
law. The matter is disputed twice, first at A-C, in regard to
produce in general, and again at E-G, regarding a basket of figs.
The substance of the disputes is identical, except that Sages of
A-C hold a position which contradicts Sages of E-G. D, which links
the two disputes, harmonizes the contradiction.[14] The pericope as
a whole is a singleton, bridging two larger independent units
(M. 2:1-3, M. 2:5-8) with an issue relevant to both--conditions
under which untithed produce may be eaten.

Underlying the two disputes are divergent theories of the
tithing process. For Eliezer[15] (= Sages, G) this process, which
brings the owner into contact with the sacred,[16] has a continuity
which cannot be interrupted. Once begun, the owner may not inter-
rupt his removal of offerings by making a snack from that very
produce. Now that part of the produce has been designated for a
sacred purpose, the remainder is taboo (ṭebel) until the deconsecration of the entire batch is completed. The fact that, in the
present circumstances, the owner is not yet obliged to tithe in
the first place, can therefore be of no concern to Eliezer. The
process of deconsecration, once begun, must be completed before
the produce may be eaten. Sages at C (= Simeon, F), however, hold
that designating part of the produce for a sacred purpose has no
affect upon the remainder, unless the produce as a whole has already been processed and is desirable as food. Prior to the point
at which a man is obliged to tithe, the removal of offerings is
viewed as a series of discrete, unconnected actions. While the
removal of the heave-offering itself is valid, the act of removal
imposes no special taboo upon the produce from which it is separated. Since the owner has incurred no obligation, his produce
remains permitted to him for snacking. It remains so until the

processing is complete and the produce, now desirable as food,
stands under God's claim (cf. pp. 25-26). At the completion of
processing, Sages will agree with Eliezer that all remaining
offerings must be removed before the produce is permitted to its
owner.

The juxtaposition of the two disputes places Sages of A-C
in opposition to the position attributed to Sages at E-G. At C
Sages appear to object to Eliezer (B) on grounds supplied by
Simeon (F), while at G Sages dispute with Simeon on the basis of
Eliezer's earlier position. The inconsistency is harmonized by
the linking of the two disputes at D. D points out that for most
types of unprocessed produce Sages permit a snack after the
removal of heave-offering, except when the heave-offering has been
removed from a basket of figs. In the latter case, they agree
with Eliezer that all eating must cease. M. provides no clue to
interpreting this distinction. T., however, will suggest that at
issue at E-G is whether a basket of figs are deemed to be processed
or unprocessed. In this case Sages, who at C permit a random
snack of unprocessed produce after the removal of heave-offering,
simply hold that a basket of figs is already deemed processed, and
therefore is forbidden even before the removal of the heave-
offering. This interpretation goes quite beyond the data of M.
and, as we shall see below, requires a most curious interpretation
of Simeon's reason for permitting a random snack of the figs.

A. One who separates heave-offering from 1) dried figs [which]
   are going to be pressed, [or from] 2) dates [which] are
   going to be mashed--

B. R. Eliezer says, "He shall not make a random snack of them
   [from that point on]."

C. But Sages say, "He makes a random snack of them [until the
   processing is complete]" [cf. M. 2:4A-C].

D. R. Eliezer concedes to Sages in the case of one who separates
   heave-offering from 1) grain [which] is going to be threshed,
   [or from] 2) grapes [which] are going to be made into wine,
   [or from] 3) olives [which] are going to be made into oil,
   that he shall make a random snack of them [until the grain is
   threshed and the grapes or olives are pressed].

E. And Sages concede to R. Eliezer in the case of a basket of
   fruit (klklh šl pyrwt: E reads klklt t'ynym, "a basket of
   figs") from which he separated heave-offering before its processing was complete, that he shall not make a random snack
   of them [from that point on] [cf. M. 2:4D].

F.   But R. *Simeon permits* [*making a random snack of them until
     their processing is complete*] [= M. 2:4F]

G.   on the basis of an argument *a minoris ad majus (mql whwmr)*:
     since he makes a random snack when there is an obligation to
     remove three tithes from it [viz. heave-offering, first tithe
     and either second tithe or poorman's tithe], it is logical
     that he shall make a random snack when there is an obligation
     to remove only two tithes.

                              T. 2:2

H.   One who purchases 1) dried figs [which] are going to be
     pressed, [or] 2) dates [which] are going to be pressed--

I.   R. Meir says, "He shall not make a random snack of them,

J.   "and he removes tithes [from them as he would for] doubtfully
     tithed produce."

K.   But Sages say, "He makes a random snack of them,

L.   "and he removes tithes [as he would for] doubtfully tithed
     produce" (*wm^{c}srn dmyy; ed. princ.* and y. Ma. 2:4 read:
     wm^{c}srn wdyy, "and he removes tithes as he would for certainly
     untithed produce").

M.   Yet (*w-*) R. Meir concedes to Sages in the case of one who
     purchases 1) grain [which]is going to be threshed [or] 2)
     grapes [which] are going to be made into wine, [or] 3) olives
     [which] are going to be made into oil, that he shall make a
     random snack of them.

N.   And Sages concede to R. Meir in the case of produce which does
     not require completion of processing [e.g., grapes or olives
     picked for immediate eating],[17] that he shall not make a
     random snack of it.

                              T. 2:3
                              T. 2:2-3 (pp. 231, ls. 7-19)
                              (A-C: cf. y. Ma. 2:4[49d];
                              F-G: *loc. cit.*; H-L: *loc. cit.*.
                              cf. b. Bes. 35b)

     The two primary units of T. are A-E and H-N, exhibiting care-
ful formal balance. Each unit begins with a dispute (A-C, H-L),
the protases of which differ only in the operative verbs (*twrm* vs.
lwqh). These protases, however, raise separate problems regarding
the disposition of the produce in question. Thus the additional
stichs, J and L, must be added at I-L to the otherwise identical
apodoses, B-C and I+K. In each unit the dispute is followed by
a description of exceptional cases (D-E, M-N) in which the disputants are said to agree with each other. In substance, the
pericope creates an excellent bridge between M. 2:4 and M. 2:5.

A-E amplifies the dispute at M. 2:4A-C (+ D-G), while H-N introduces the problem of the tithing of produce which has been sold,
the issue raised for the first time in M. at M. 2:5.

A-C offers a more detailed version of M. 2:4A-C, with Eliezer
and Sages holding their positions as before. The important amplification of M. is at D, which, by qualifying Eliezer's objection
to Sages, forces us to rethink the issue underlying the dispute.
At D Eliezer agrees that if heave-offering is separated from
totally unprocessed produce, the owner continues to snack on it.
The reason emerges from the contrast between the produce of A and
that of D. The former is in the midst of processing, while the
latter is entirely untouched. The point can only be that, in the
former case, the removal of heave-offering indicates that the
householder considers the processing complete and the produce
liable, while in the latter, the removal of heave-offering is obviously a matter of choice, for the produce can hardly be considered processed in its present condition. For T., then, the
dispute at M. 2:4A-C concerns whether the act of separating
heave-offering from unprocessed produce indicates that the owner
deems the processing complete and the produce liable. E-G now
takes up the problem of M. 2:4D+E-G. E, in conjunction with D,
indicates that the Sages hold a basket of figs to be completely
processed.[18] The figs, therefore, are liable whether or not
heave-offering has been removed. Simeon's objection, explained
at G, is most interesting. He, like Sages, considers the figs
processed and liable to the removal of tithes. Unlike Sages,
however, he argues that the removal of heave-offering, the most
holy of the offerings, actually decreases the power of the taboo
which applies to the remaining produce. This theory of tithes,
we must note, is attested nowhere else in M.

The second unit of the pericope, H-N, assumes that the sale
of processed produce renders it liable (cf. M. 1:5L). The question
at H-L concerns the disposition of produce which has been sold
before the completion of processing. The figs and dates of H-L
have been sold *after* drying but *before* pressing. There are two
problems to solve. First, since the owner will not be able to
process the produce any further after he sells it, do we therefore
consider the produce completely processed at the time of sale?
Second, can we assume that the owner has tithed the produce before
selling it, even though he had not completed the processing which
would make him responsible for tithing it? Meir (I) prohibits
the purchaser from making a snack on the grounds that the owner's
intentions to press the figs or dates are nullified by the sale.

In effect, the produce acquired by the purchaser is completely
processed in its dried condition, and rendered liable by the sale.
Yet (J), the purchaser tithes the produce under the assumption
that the owner might have separated the heave-offering before sale,
as A has indicated. Sages (K) permit the purchaser to make a
snack, applying the same reasoning which they employ at C. Since
the produce is intended for pressing, it remains in the category
of unfinished produce until it is actually pressed, despite any
intervening events. Thus the purchaser eats them until he himself
presses them. Thereafter, as we would expect, he tithes the
purchase as if it were certainly untithed.[19]

Turning to the familiar example of completely unprocessed
grain, grapes or olives (M), Meir agrees with Sages that sale of
such produce does not inhibit the purchaser's privilege of making
a chance meal. As at B, he holds that the owner's intentions to
process the produce are nullified by the sale. However, since the
produce at M is completely untouched, the purchaser has simply
acquired unprocessed produce. Therefore, he may continue to make
a random snack of it, since the sale cannot render unprocessed
produce liable. The concluding stich of the pericope (N) seems to
be tacked on to provide the required case in which Sages agree
with Meir, for it raises a non-issue. Produce which does not require completion of processing is simply ready for eating as soon
as it is picked. Naturally, when it is sold, no one would dispute
the fact that it is liable to the removal of all tithes before it
may be eaten.

A. One who harvests his vineyard for marketing,
B. [under the condition] that, if ($š'm$) he finds no customers
    ($l' m\d{s}' lhn šwq$), he shall return them [i.e., the grapes]
    to the press (lgt);
C. [or, one who harvests] his olives for marketing,
D. [under the condition] that, if he finds no customers, he
    shall return them to the press (lbd)--
E. [the purchaser of the grapes or olives] makes a random snack
    of them [without tithing],
F. but (w-) tithes them [as he would tithe] produce which is
    certainly-untithed.

                          T. 2:4 (p. 232, ls. 19-20)

The pericope is autonomous of both M. and T. 2:2-3. The
sentence has a double protasis, with C-D dependent upon A-B. E-F
completes the rule, with an apodosis familiar from M. 2:1 and
T. 2:3. T. employs principles already familiar to us. The owner

of the produce has harvested the crop and brought it to market,
under the condition that, if he cannot sell it, he will process
the produce further, i.e., press the grapes for wine or the olives
for oil. The question raised is whether the produce is rendered
liable by the owner's intention to sell it (as in M. 1:5L-M), or
conversely, whether the owner's intention to process whatever he
cannot sell exempts the entire batch from the removal of tithes
until the processing is complete. The ruling (E) is that the
purchaser of the produce may make a random snack. That is, the
owner's intention to process what he cannot sell determines the
status of that which he does sell. Whatever he sells is considered
incompletely processed; therefore, as in T. 2:3M, the buyer makes
a random snack. F assumes that the buyer knows the owner's plans
to process the produce which remains unsold, for the buyer is
required to tithe the produce as he would tithe produce which is
certainly untithed. Since the buyer knows that the owner intends
to press the grapes or olives, he assumes that the owner has not
tithed them (Liberman, *TK* II: 679.21).

2:5-6

A. "One who says to his fellow, 'Take (*hylk*) this *issar*[20] and
    give me five figs for it,'

B. "shall not eat [the figs] unless he tithes"--the words of
    R. Meir.

C. R. Judah says, "[If] he eats [the figs] one by one ('*ht* '*ht*),
    he is exempt [from tithing]; but if he gathers [them] together
    (*srp*), he is required [to tithe the figs before eating any of
    them]."

D. Said R. Judah, "*m*ᶜ*sh b*-: There was a rose garden in Jerusalem
    [where] figs were sold at three or four per *issar*, yet heave-
    offering and tithes were never removed from [the purchase]"
    (*mmnh*).

                    M. 2:5 (D: cf. T. Neg. 6:2,
                    b. B.Q. 82b)

E. One who says to his fellow, "Take this *issar* [in payment] for
    ten[21] figs which I shall choose (*š'bwr ly*),"

F. chooses and eats [each fig separately without tithing the
    batch as a whole] (*bwrr w'wkl*).

G. [One who says, "Take this *issar* in payment] for a cluster of
    grapes which I shall choose," plucks one grape at a time
    (*mgrgr*) and eats [each grape without tithing the cluster as
    a whole].

H. [One who says, "Take this *issar* in payment] for a pomegranate
    which I shall choose," splits it into segments (*pwrṭ*) and eats
    [each segment separately without tithing the pomegranate as
    a whole].

I. [One who says, "Take this *issar* in payment] for a melon which
    I shall choose," cuts it into slices (*šwpt*) and eats [each
    slice separately without tithing the melon as a whole].

J. But if he said to him, ["Take this *issar* in payment] for
    these twenty figs,"

K. [or] "for these two grape clusters,"

L. [or] "for these two pomegranates,"

M. [or] "for these two melons,"

N. he eats as he pleases and is exempt [from tithing the batch],

O. for he bought [them while they were still] attached to the
    ground (*mḥbr lqrqᶜ*) [*viz.*, before they were picked, when they
    were exempt from the removal of tithes].

M. 2:6

All purchases are deemed acts of appropriation by which the
purchaser makes his own that which formerly belonged to another.
The purchaser of untithed produce, therefore, must tithe it just
as if he had brought it into his home. The present pericope
offers an exemplification of this principle at A-B, and proceeds
to qualify it with glosses at C-D and a major expansion at E-I +
J-O. The point of Meir's ruling is that once money has changed
hands and the quantity of the purchase is specified, any produce
the buyer receives is deemed part of his purchase. It therefore
must be tithed. Judah (C), however, points out that as long as
the purchaser refrains from gathering the entire quantity into
his possession at one time the purchase is deemed unconsummated
(cf. M. B.M. 4:2).[22] The purchaser, therefore, may eat one piece
of produce at a time without incurring any obligation to tithe,
for in this manner he refrains from appropriating the produce.
Since it is at no point deemed a separate batch under his control,
he cannot be responsible for tithing it. D, also attributed to
Judah, is autonomous of the foregoing. I am unclear what the
precedent is intended to demonstrate. Perhaps it explains Meir's
stipulation that the sale include five figs. If so, Judah now
points out that purchases of fewer than five figs are too insig-
nificant to be tithed.[23]

E-I, a secondary development of A-C, depends upon A for its
language and C for its principle. In each of the four cases the
purchaser offers to select the produce he intends to purchase.

E-F, the model for G, H, and I, states that if a customer stipulates a purchase of ten figs, he may select and eat each one at a
time, and never be obliged to tithe. Since he has not gathered the
stipulated quantity into his possession, the figs he has chosen
are not deemed to belong to the batch he has bargained for. The
same logic is exhibited, in progressively more subtle cases, at
G-I. If a man purchases a cluster of grapes on the vine he must
tithe them as soon as he picks the cluster. At G such a customer
avoids this obligation by picking one grape at a time from the
cluster while it remains on the vine (Maim., *Comm.*). As at E-F,
he at no time has the stipulated purchase in his possession. The
purchase of a pomegranate (H) raises more complicated problems
for its segments are joined together into a single fruit. Once
the fruit is plucked, it is, naturally, liable to be tithed.
Nevertheless the purchaser, who has stipulated a purchase of the
entire pomegranate, may split individual sections from the fruit
and eat them without tithing, as long as the pomegranate itself
remains on the tree. The last problem, I's melon, demonstrates
the lengths to which E-F's logic may be pushed. The melon is
obviously a single, indivisible fruit, yet as long as the melon
is attached to the vine, the purchaser may cut slices of melon
and consume them without tithing. In all of these cases, Judah's
principle (C) clearly supersedes Meir's (A-B). If Meir had his
way the mere transfer of coins would oblige the purchaser to tithe
any part of the purchase he actually takes into his possession.

J-N, clearly formulated to balance E-I, is obscure. Now
the purchaser doubles the quantity of his purchase, but no longer
selects it himself (L-M). He merely indicates the produce he has
in mind. I cannot explain why these conditions of purchase permit
the buyer to eat as he pleases without tithing (N). O's explanation is hardly satisfactory. If the point is that the buyer paid
for the produce before it was picked (MR), this is clearly the
case at E-I as well. If, following Maimonides (*Comm.*), we understand O to indicate that the man has bought unripe produce growing on the vine, we are no nearer to a solution. While M. 5:1
certainly exempts such purchases from the removal of tithes,
there is no reason to believe that the case of J-N describes such
a purchase. I conclude that the glossator of J-N was as much
perplexed by it as I.

A. *One who says to his fellow, "Take this* issar *and give me five
    figs for it"* [= M. 2:5A],

B. *eats [the figs] one by one (ed. princ.* adds: *w-,* "*and*"*) is
    exempt [from tithing the purchase]. If he gathers [them]
    together, he is required [to tithe the figs before eating
    any of them]* [= M. 2:5C].

C. "If the owner brought (*hby'*) [the figs] out and hands (*nwtn*)
    [them] to him,

D. "he [i.e., the purchaser] eats and need not tithe" (*'wkl w'yn
    ṣryk l^c sr*; Lieberman emends: *'pylw 'ṣryk l^c sr*, "even [if
    he eats only] one [fig], he must tithe")[24]--the words of
    R. Meir.

E. R. Judah says, "In either case (*byn kk wbyn kk*), *he eats one
    by one (ed. princ.* adds: *w-,* "*and*"*) is exempt [from tithing
    the purchase]. If he gathers [them] together, he is required
    [to tithe the figs before eating any of them]*" [= M. 2:5C].
                                    T. 2:11 (p. 234, ls. 41-44)

A-B recasts M. 2:5A + C. Judah's gloss in M. now becomes
the apodosis of an anonymous rule, permitting a purchaser to pick
and eat one fig at a time without tithing. C-D (on the basis of
Lieberman's emendation) qualifies the foregoing. In Meir's view,
if the owner picks the figs himself and hands them to the purchaser, they are rendered liable by the sale. The owner has
gathered the figs together, requiring the purchaser, whose purchase
is now before him, to tithe. This understanding of Meir's ruling
at M. 2:5A-B suggests that, in T.'s view, Meir does not differ
with Judah over a case in which the purchaser himself picks the
figs (A-B; cf. y. Ma. 2:5[49d]). E glosses D in Judah's name,
adding that whether the purchaser picks the figs or receives them
from the owner's hand, the purchase is not complete (and the figs
are exempt) unless the purchaser actually gathers the figs into
his possession. If he does not do so, he may even eat one fig at
a time from the owner's hand without tithing (HY; MR, M. 2:5).

                                2:7

A. One who hires a worker to harvest (*lqṣwt*)[25] figs for him--

B. 1) [If the worker] said to him, "On condition that I eat
    figs [as part of my pay],"

C. he eats [figs during the harvest] and is exempt [from tithing
    them].

D. 2) [If the worker said to him,] "On condition that I and my
    dependents (*bny byty*; thirteen MSS. read: *bny*, "my son") eat
    [figs as part of my pay],"

E.   or [if he said, "On condition] that my son shall eat [figs]
     as [part of] my pay,"

F.   he [i.e., the worker] eats [figs during the harvest] and is
     exempt [from tithing them],

G.   while (w-) his son eats [figs during the harvest] but (w-) is
     required [to tithe them].

H.   3) [If the worker said,] "On condition that I eat [figs as
     part of my pay both] during and after the harvest"--

I.   during the harvest he eats and is exempt,

J.   while (w-) after the harvest he eats but is required [to
     tithe],

K.   for [in the latter case] he [is granted] no eating privileges
     by the Torah ('ynw 'wkl mn htwrh).

L.   This is the general principle:

M.   One who [is granted] eating privileges by the Torah is exempt
     [from tithing what he eats], while (w-) one who [is granted]
     no eating privileges by the Torah is required [to tithe what
     he eats].

> M. 2:7 (A-G: cf. b. B.M. 92a-b;
> M-N: cf. M. B.M. 7:2)

Not all purchases involve an exchange of money. Workers,
for example, who barter their labor for produce, are deemed to
have purchased that produce, just as if they had acquired it with
coins in a market. Consequently, they must tithe any untithed
produce acquired in payment for their labor. The present pericope
examines an important qualification of this assumed principle.
L-M, which glosses and explains the entire pericope, points out
that field-workers, who are granted by the Torah the right to eat
freely of produce during the harvest (M. B.M. 7:2),[26] need not
tithe such produce. Since it is theirs by right, it cannot be
deemed a purchase, and since they eat by right of Torah *only*
during their labor (M. B.M. 7:4),[27] whatever they eat is deemed a
random snack.

The cases themselves are straightforward. A sets the context
for the triplet (B-C, D-G, H-J + K), in which each case adjudicates
the tithing responsibilities of those who eat produce earned by
the worker's labor. The problem in each case is raised by the
worker's stipulation that produce to which he is entitled by the
Torah is to be included in his wage. At B-C the worker continues
to enjoy the privilege of eating the produce without tithing.
Even though he identifies the figs as his pay, his prior right to
eat them exempts him from tithing what he himself regards as a
purchase.[28] The privilege accorded by the Torah, in other words,

overrides any contractual obligations incurred by the worker. At
D-G we distinguish between the privileges of the worker himself,
and the privileges of those whom he stipulates shall eat in exchange
for his own labor. While the worker remains under the privilege
of the Torah, his non-laboring dependents do not, and therefore
must tithe whatever they eat. His contract is inapplicable to
the figs he eats, but applies to all figs eaten by his dependents.
As a purchase, such figs must be tithed. H-J, the third and final
case, assumes with M. B.M. 7:4 that the worker's privilege is
limited to produce eaten while he is actually working on the
harvest. Any produce eaten thereafter under the terms of the
contract is therefore deemed a purchase, for the Torah no longer
deems such produce to be his by right (K). All such produce,
consequently, must be tithed.

2:8

A. [If] he was working on [*hyh* ^{c}*wsh b-*) cooking-figs (*lbśym*);[29]
    he shall not eat white figs (*bnwt šb^c*)[30] [without tithing
    them: Maim., *Tithes* 5:12].

B. [If he was working on] white figs, he shall not eat cooking-
    figs [without tithing them].

C. To be sure (*'bl*), he [may] restrain himself [from eating
    altogether] until he reaches the area [in which] the high-
    quality [figs] grow, and [then may] eat.

D. One who exchanges [figs] with his fellow--

E. [If] his [figs] are for eating and his fellow's are for eat-
    ing,

F. [or if] his [figs] are to be dried and his fellow's are to be
    dried,

H. he is required [to tithe what he acquires].

I. R. Judah says, "One who exchanges [his figs for figs] which
    are for eating is required [to tithe],

J. "but (*w-*) [if he exchanges his figs for figs] which are to
    be dried, he is exempt [from tithing until the figs are dried]."

                              M. 2:8 (A-B = b. Ned. 50b;
                              A-C: cf. M. B.M. 7:4, Sifre Dt.
                              266; D-J = b. Bes. 35b)

    While independent of M. 2:7, A-B+C carries forward the
latter's thesis that a worker's privilege to eat produce he is
harvesting exempts him as well from the obligation to tithe what
he eats. A-B makes an important clarification. Should the worker
eat one type of produce while harvesting another, his privilege

no longer extends to the produce eaten. He must therefore remove
tithes from such produce, for it is deemed to have been acquired
in exchange for his labor. The gloss at C is irrelevant to the
issue of tithing. It simply adds that the worker may refrain from
eating poorer produce on which he happens to be working until he
begins work on the better produce. He may then eat his fill of
the latter without fear that he will be overstepping the privilege
accorded to him by the Torah.

The irrelevance of C to A-B is solely a function of the
context within which A-B+C has been redacted. In fact, the entire
unit appears, with minor changes, at M. B.M. 7:4,[31] where it qualifies a list of workers who are entitled by the Torah to eat produce with which they are engaged (M. B.M. 7:2). The point of
M. B.M. 7:4A-B (= M. 2:8A-B) is that the worker, entitled by the
Torah to eat produce which he is harvesting, may eat only that
produce. If he interrupts his labor to cross the field and eat
another type of produce, he is deemed responsible for reimbursement. C now adds a plausible, if obvious, afterthought. The
worker may refrain from eating poorer produce while he is harvesting it, and fill up on the finer once his work brings him into
that area of the field. The point is perfectly appropriate to
A-B in the context of M. B.M. 7:2ff., but is ill-suited to
M. 2:8A-B, once we have read into the ruling the contextually-
required issue of tithing.

D-H + I-J returns us to the basic task of the chapter, the
enumeration of transactions which impose upon the recipient of
untithed produce the obligation to tithe. Exchange of produce
for produce, like the exchange of produce for labor, involves the
actual transfer of ownership over the produce. It is therefore
equivalent to a monetary purchase, obliging the new owner to
tithe what he has received in exchange for his own produce. The
basic ruling is at D+H, into which E-G, which introduces a separate issue, has been interpolated. This interpolation then generates Judah's qualification at I-J. The point of E-G is that
barter, as an act of appropriation, obliges the recipient of
produce to tithe it, even if the produce requires further processing (F-G). This position is analogous to that established by
the glossator of M. 1:5-6. There, we recall, unprocessed produce
must be tithed if the owner stores it away, the act by which he
effects acquisition of the produce. Judah disagrees with this
general position. He holds that despite the appropriation of the
produce its unprocessed condition permits the assumption that it
is undesirable as food to its new owner. Since he is assumed to

desire it only after processing, it remains permitted to him as a
snack until that time. According to Judah, then, the simple fact
of appropriation is insufficient to oblige the owner to tithe.
The essential condition is that whatever has been appropriated is
first useful and desirable as food (cf. M. 3:1A-B).

A. 1) [If] he said to him, "Go pick figs for yourself from the
tree"--

B. [the one who picks] makes a random snack of them,

C. and tithes them [as he would tithe] produce which is certainly-
untithed [should he make a regular meal of them: cf. M. 2:1].

D. 2) [If] he said to him, "Go and fill this basket for yourself"--

E. [the one who fills his basket] makes a random snack of [the
figs],

F. and tithes them [as he would tithe] produce which is doubtfully-
tithed [should he make a regular meal of them].

G. "Under what circumstances [does he tithe them as he would
tithe produce which is doubtfully-tithed]? When [the owner
of the figs is an] ^{c}am ha'areṣ [i.e., someone who cannot be
trusted to keep the laws of uncleanness and tithing].

H. "But [if the owner is a] ḥaber [i.e., someone committed to
keeping the laws of uncleanness and tithing], he eats [freely]
and need not tithe"--the words of Rabbi.

I. Rabban Simeon ben Gamaliel says, "Under what circumstances
[does he tithe them as he would tithe produce which is
doubtfully-tithed]? When [the owner of the figs is an]
^{c}am ha'areṣ.

J. "But [if the owner is a] ḥaber, he shall not eat [at all] unless he tithes [the produce as if it were certainly untithed],

K. "for ḥaberim were not suspected of separating heave-offering
[from one batch of produce in the name of a second batch which
was] not in the same vicinity (šl' mn hmwqp)."

L. Said Rabbi, "I prefer my opinion to the opinion of Rabban
Simeon ben Gamaliel. It is preferable that ḥaberim separate
heave-offering [from one batch in the name of a second which
was] not in the same vicinity, for [thus] they do not supply
the ^{c}amei ha'areṣ with forbidden produce (ṭblym)."

T. 2:5

M. 3) [If] he said to him, "Go and pick figs for yourself[32] from
the tree"--

N. [the one who picks] eats [the figs]

O. and is not apprehensive [that the owner might consider his
eating] to be robbery (w'yn ḥwšš mšm gzl).

P. 4) [If he said to him,] "Go and fill this basket for your-
    self"--

Q. lo, this one is apprehensive [that the owner might consider
    his eating] to be robbery.

R. In either case, he removes, on their behalf, heave-offering
    and tithes from [other produce] belonging to the householder,

S. and is not apprehensive [that the householder might consider
    the act of removing heave-offering and tithes to be robbery].

T. 5) [If] he said to him, "Go and pick twenty figs for yourself
    from my [figs], and I shall eat my fill of yours"--

U. the one who picks a specified quantity (*bmnyyn*) is required
    [to tithe],

V. [but] the one who eats his fill is exempt [from tithing]
    [cf. M. 2:8D-H].

                          T. 2:6

W. R. Eleazar b. R. Ṣadoq (E reads: b. R. Simeon[33]) says, "One
    who combines (*hmṣrp*) three figs [together] in his mouth is
    exempt [from tithing],

X. [but if he combines] four, lo, this one is required [to tithe]
    [cf. M. 2:5C].

Y. [If] he said to him, "Go and pick a large basket [of figs]
    for yourself,"

Z. [the quantity he picks] is at least a *śe'ah*.[34]

AA. [If he said,] "a medium-sized [basket],"

BB. [the quantity he picks] is at least three *qabs*.

CC. [If he said,] "a small [basket],"

DD. [the quantity he picks] is at least two *qabs*.

                          T. 2:7
                          T. 2:5-7 (pp. 232-33, ls. 20-33)
                          (A-L = b. Erub. 32a; D-L: cf. y.
                          Ma. 2:1[49c]; K: cf. b. Erub. 30b,
                          b. Git. 30b, b. Hul. 7a; M-Q: cf.
                          y. Ma. 2:1[49c]; T-V = y. Ma. 2:1
                          [49c]; W-X: cf. y. Ma. 3:8[50d]

     T. concludes its discussion of M. Chapter Two with an auton-
omous formulation consisting of five substantially glossed cases.
Each case--and the final gloss at Y-DD--is built upon the identical protasis, *'mr lw ṣ' wlqṭ/wml' lk*.

     A-C and D-F return us to the problem of M. 2:1, determining
the status of a gift of produce, the growth and processing of
which one has not personally supervised.[35] In the first case,
the owner of a fig tree gives a friend permission to eat figs from
his tree. The recipient makes a random snack, as he does at
M. 2:1A-C, for the figs have been picked right from the tree and

clearly have not been rendered liable by processing, passage
through the donor's home, or sale. It follows that, should the
recipient take the figs home or make a regular meal of them elsewhere, he tithes the figs in the certainty that the owner had
removed none of the required offerings (M. 2:1D-E). Since the
figs have come directly from the tree, the owner had neither reason
nor opportunity to tithe them. D-F offers a complementary case
in which the friend is now told to fill a basket of figs for himself, presumably from figs which are harvested. The man makes a
random snack under these circumstances as well, for even if the
processing is complete, the figs have not been rendered liable
either by passage through the donor's home or by sale. This time,
however, if he himself renders the figs liable, he tithes them as
if they were doubtfully tithed. Since he filled his basket from
figs which were already harvested, the possibility exists that the
owner might have already tithed them before giving them to his
friend.

     G-L glosses F with a debate concerning the tithing procedures
likely to be practiced by ḥaberim. Rabbi (G-H) says that the
recipient of a basket of figs tithes them as doubtfully-tithed
only if the owner of the figs is an ᶜam ha'areṣ, who is expected
to be careless about proper tithing. However, if the owner is a
ḥaber, the recipient assumes that the figs are already fully
tithed, and eats them freely. The assumption is that a ḥaber
will not permit any of his produce to be eaten unless he has properly tithed it, whether or not it is liable (b. Erub. 32a, s.v.,
d'mr rb ḥnyn' ḥwz'h). Simeon b. Gamaliel agrees with Rabbi that
the case of F must refer to an owner who is an ᶜam ha'areṣ, but
differs concerning the disposition of the produce should the owner
be a ḥaber. In the latter case, the recipient assumes that the
figs are fully liable and have yet to be tithed. As K suggests,
the owner is not expected to have tithed the figs before they become liable, nor is he expected to remove tithes from another
batch of produce outside the immediate vicinity on behalf of those
which he has just given away (M. Bik. 2:5, cf. b. Erub. 32b, s.v.,
bm'y qmplgy). Rabbi (L) is given the victory in the debate. He
reasons that a ḥaber is likely to separate heave-offering (and
tithes) from a separate batch of produce for that which he has
given away, rather than risk the possibility that one who is not
scrupulous about tithing might acquire the produce and eat it
before it is tithed.[36]

     M-O and P-Q share the protases of A-C and D-F, but discuss an
issue tangential to M. The rulings are, in fact, more appropriate

to M. B.M. 7:2-4, the source of M. 2:7-8's discussion of the
rights of the worker to eat produce without being accused of theft.
If a man receives permission to pick figs from someone's tree,
he may eat as many figs as he pleases without fear that the owner
will accuse him of robbery (M-O; cf. T. Ter. 1:5). Since the
owner did not specify a particular amount, he has indicated that
the man is free to eat an unlimited quantity (MB). However, if
the owner specifies a particular amount, such as a basketful, as
his gift, matters change (P-Q). Now, should the recipient eat any
figs other than those in the basket, he may be suspected of robbery, for the owner has specified that he may eat only what he can
fit into the basket. Judah (R-S) glosses M-Q, returning us to the
theme of M. If the recipient removes offerings from a separate
batch of the owner's produce on behalf of those which he has been
given, he need not fear that the owner will consider the offerings
to have been stolen. MB, HY and Lieberman (*TK*, II: 681.29) explain that the owner would not want to diminish his gift by
requiring the recipient to remove the offerings from the gift itself. Therefore, he intends the recipient to remove the offerings
from other produce in his possession on behalf of the gift.

The last case, T-V, qualifies M. 2:8E-H's ruling that an exchange of produce is considered a sale, rendering the produce
liable. Now we are told that only exchanges which involve specific
quantities are considered purchases. A man gives twenty figs of
his own for the right to eat as many of his friend's figs as he
pleases. The man who accepts the twenty figs must tithe them,
for they are rendered liable by the exchange, as M. 2:8E-H would
lead us to expect. However, the one who receives the right to
eat as much as he wants need not tithe. He has not received a
specific quantity, and further, at no point has his purchase
before him, for he has agreed to purchase only what he has already
eaten. In effect, he has made no purchase at all.[37]

W-X breaks the formal unity of the pericope, and is clearly
an interpolation. The rule states that the purchaser may place
as many as three figs in his mouth without tithing them, a significant rejection of the idea that he may only eat one at a time
(M. 2:5C). Y-DD returns to the formal traits of the preceding
cases, but changes the topic to a definition of the capacities of
various sizes of baskets. Presumably the information would be
important in a case such as P-Q, where one who is told to fill a
small basket, for example, might be suspected of robbery if he
placed three *qabs* or more in the basket.

CHAPTER THREE

MAASEROT CHAPTER THREE

The first unit of Chapter Three, M. 3:1-4, continues and
brings to a close Chapter Two's discussion of transactions involving untithed produce. Of interest are further problems regarding
produce eaten in exchange for labor, a topic familiar from
M. 2:7-8C. M. 3:5-10, the chapter's second unit, stands entirely
on its own. Although it is clearly a composite construction, the
unit as a whole offers a coherent and thorough discussion of a
single thesis--that the courtyard surrounding a home is deemed
to be an extension of that home. It follows that produce brought
into such a courtyard, like produce brought into the home, is
immediately rendered liable to tithing. While the chapter's units
are thematically unrelated, each performs a similar task--the
application of familiar principles to new cases.

M. 3:1-3, a unitary construction of five cases, is conceptually dependent upon M. 2:7's notion that workers in the course
of their harvesting are entitled by the Torah to eat the harvested
produce. M. now inquires about produce eaten by workers who are
not engaged in harvesting. We recall that such workers have no
special privilege to the untithed produce. The problem now is
to determine whether produce eaten by such workers has been taken
in exchange for their labor, and, therefore, ought to be tithed.
If, as in M. 2:7, the employees receive board as part of their
wage, they indeed must tithe what they eat, for their labor is
the medium of exchange by which the produce becomes theirs. Workers
earning a cash wage, however, are permitted to snack on produce
during their labor without tithing. We assume that it is in the
employer's interest to be generous with the workers, and that
whatever they eat will be written off as a gift. Since gifts are
not deemed to have undergone transfer of ownership until the
recipient brings them home (M. 2:1), produce eaten by cash earners
during their labor remains exempt from the law. M.'s entire unit
on the transfer of title over untithed produce, begun at M. 2:1,
concludes at M. 3:4, a pericope only tangentially relevant to the
unit as a whole. The heavily glossed triplet is concerned with
the tithing of abandoned produce. While such produce is normally
exempt from the law (y. Ma. 1:1[48d]), M. argues that if the produce was processed before being abandoned, the finder must take
upon himself the loser's obligation to tithe.

     An entirely fresh topic, the tithing of produce brought into
the courtyard of a private home, occupies M. 3:5-10. The basic
principle informing the unit has already been anticipated by
M. 2:3. There, we recall, it is argued that any dwelling in which
a traveller is made to feel at home is deemed a surrogate for his
own home. Untithed produce which he brings into such a dwelling
is therefore rendered liable to the removal of tithes. The present unit assumes and develops this principle in regard to the
domestic courtyard, an extension of (rather than a surrogate for)
the home itself. M. 3:5 introduces the unit with a fundamental
conception. The five authorities cited in M. 3:5 all agree that,
insofar as a courtyard affords the sense of privacy characteristic
of the home, such a courtyard is considered an extension of the
boundaries of the home. All produce brought into such a courtyard,
it follows, is rendered liable to tithing. The notion that
privacy is defined by analogy to the home is further investigated
at M. 3:6. Its two rulings define areas within the courtyard itself to which the analogy of the home, and therefore the liability
of produce stored there, is problematic. Rooftops (M. 3:6A), for
example, are above the space of the courtyard and are deemed a
domain separate from the courtyard itself (M. Erub. 9:1). Produce
placed on the rooftop in order to dry is therefore exempt even
after it has dried, for while processed, it is outside the con-
fines of the courtyard. Produce placed in the courtyard's gate-
house or portico, on the other hand, need be tithed only if the
courtyard itself affords privacy (M. 3:6B-D). These structures,
unlike houses, are not independent dwellings, but rather serve
the courtyard itself and are deemed part of it. Thus they share
its status regarding the law (cf. M. Erub. 8:4).

     After a brief digression concerning the suitability as
surrogates for the home of other non-domestic structures--such as
field-sheds (M. 3:7)--M. returns to the law of the courtyard. A
triplet at M. 3:8-9 demonstrates that principles of acquisition,
familiar from M. 2:5-6's discussion of commercial transactions,
apply as well in the quite different setting of the courtyard.
M. 2:5-6, we recall, argues that a purchase of untithed produce
need be tithed only after the purchaser gathers the produce into
his possession. Prior to the gathering, the purchaser may eat
single pieces of fruit without tithing, for he is not yet deemed
to be in possession of the produce. This logic is applied, at
M. 3:8-9, to the problem posed by a tree or vine growing within
a domestic courtyard. Clearly, as soon as the householder harvests the produce, he must tithe it before making any use of it.

The reason is that since the produce is in the courtyard it is
deemed appropriated the moment it has been harvested. M. points
out, however, that as long as the produce is unharvested, it may
be eaten without the removal of tithes. The fruit on the tree,
like the fruit in the purveyor's bin, is not yet the possession
of the householder, even though it is technically within his domain (or, in the case of the customer, is already paid for). Like
the purchaser, therefore, the householder may pick and eat a single
piece of fruit from the tree without tithing. Neither the customer
nor the householder need tithe produce which is not yet his own.

M. 3:10A-G adds a fourth case to M. 3:8-9, but indeed addresses a different problem. The question is whether the liability
of produce is determined by the laws applicable to the place in
which it grows or by those which apply to the place in which it is
actually picked. We have a tree growing in a courtyard, with a
branch extending beyond the courtyard into the neutral area of the
garden (A-C), and a matching case (D-G) in which the location of
tree and branch are reversed (i.e., tree/courtyard + branch/garden
vs. tree/garden + branch/courtyard). The principle is that the
status of the produce *vis a vis* the law of tithes is determined
by the laws of the place in which the produce is actually harvested.
The problem of M. 3:10A-G, but not its substantive concerns, is
carried forward by the chapter's concluding set of materials, a
series of four formally unitary cases at M. 3:10H-P. A tree grows
in one legal domain, while its branch extends into a second domain
within which different laws apply. The problem, as above, is
whether in adjudicating the diverse legal issues raised in the
cases, the location of the roots or the branch is the key factor
in determining the status of the tree or its fruit.

T. to Chapter Three requires little comment. Although T.
provides a relatively large amount of materials to M.--fourteen
pericopae in all--these materials offer no unified perspective
upon M.'s law, and simply offer random observations and clarifications of relatively minor points.

                                3:1-3

A.   1) One who brings (*hm^c byr*) figs through his courtyard in
     order to spread them out for drying (*lqṣwt*)[1]--
B.   his sons and his dependents eat them and are exempt [from
     tithing].
C.   2) [As for] the workers who are [working] for him--

D. should (*bzmn š-*) they have no claim upon him for their
    board (*'yn lhm ^clyw mzwnwt*),[2] they eat and are exempt from
    tithing .

E. But (*'bl*) if they have a claim upon him for their board
    (*yš lhm ^clyw mzwnwt*), lo, these shall not eat without first
    removing tithes .

                                    M. 3:1 (A-B: cf. b. Bes. 34b,
                                          35b)

F. 3) One who brings (*hmwṣy'*) his workers out to the field--

G. should they have no [claim] upon him [for their] board, they
    eat and are exempt [from tithing].

H. But (*w-*) if they have [a claim] upon him [for their] board,
    they eat one by one from the tree (*t'nh*),

I. but (*'bl*) not from the basket, or the bin, or from the pile
    in which the figs are being dried (*mwqṣh*).[3]

                                    M. 3:2

J. 4) One who hires (*hśwkr*) a worker to work among olives [but
    not to harvest them: y. Ma. 3:3 (50c)]--

K. [if the worker stipulated,] "On condition that I eat olives
    [as part of my pay]," he eats one by one [from the tree], and
    is exempt [from tithing].

L. But if he gathered [them] together, he is required [to tithe].

M. 5) [One who hires a worker] to weed among onions--

N. [if the worker] stipulated (*'mr lw*), "On condition that I
    eat shoots (*yrq*) [as part of my pay]," he plucks (*mqrṭm*) a
    leaf at a time (*^clh ^clh*) and eats [without tithing].

O. But if he gathers [the leaves] together, he is required [to
    tithe].

                                    M. 3:3

     The five rulings before us resume M. 2:7's discussion of
produce eaten by workers. The rulings fall into two formal groups,
identified by the formulaic peculiarities of their apodoses. In
the first group (A-B+C-E, F-I), the apodoses depend upon the *'yn/*
yš contrast (D-E, G-I) while the apodoses of the second group (J-L
+ M-O) repeat the direct discourse familiar from M. 2:7 (*^cl mnt...*).
The whole is unified by the protases at A, F and J, which establish the identical formulary pattern for all cases (*h* + participle).
The imposition of a single pattern upon the diverse materials
stresses the fact that a single theme is addressed in all five
cases. As the contrast between A-B and C-E makes clear, at issue
is the distinction between the tithing obligations of a householder's dependents, who share his food by right, and his hired

hands, who may establish by contract their dependence upon his
board. Only untithed produce eaten by the latter need be tithed,
for the workers' contract defines produce eaten by them as a purchase. Assumed at C-E, F-I, J-L, and M-O is the fact that the
workers in question, who are not engaged in the actual harvesting
or processing of the produce, are accorded by the Torah no special
privileges to eat the produce (see p. 185, n.26). Their obligation to tithe, therefore, is determined solely by whether or not
their contract stipulates board as part of their wage.

     While the courtyard of A-B is considered part of a person's
home (M. 3:5), unprocessed figs brought into it are not rendered
liable to the removal of tithes. Since the figs are not yet desirable to the owner, he may continue to make a snack of them without
tithing, despite having brought them home (cf. Judah, M. 2:8J).
The householder's dependents, who share all the householder's
privileges regarding the consumption of untithed produce, may
also eat the untithed figs until the processing has been completed.
Matters are more complicated regarding the workers who actually
bring the figs into the courtyard (C-E). We assume that some have
contracted with the householder to eat at his table in exchange
for their labor, while others simply earn a cash wage. The latter
(D) need not tithe any snack they take from the produce, for they
are understood to benefit from the householder's generosity
(T. 2:10b, T. 2:13). Whatever they eat, in other words, is deemed
a gift (cf. M. 2:1), and is not liable to the removal of tithes.
The former (E), however, who have a contract for board, are deemed
to have purchased the produce, and must therefore tithe even a
snack (MR).[4]

     At F-I, the concluding case of the first group of rulings,
workers are brought out for field work. The principles of C-E
apply as well to produce eaten by these workers. Those with no
contract for board snack with the permission of the householder,
while those with such a contract must tithe. H-I, which varies
the formulary pattern of its formal mate at E, makes a point
familiar from M. 2:5-6. As in more conventional purchases, produce eaten in exchange for labor is exempt from tithes if the
worker picks and eats one piece of produce at a time. If, on the
other hand, the produce is already gathered before him, e.g., in
a basket, his purchase is already deemed to be consummated. Any
produce he removes from the basket, even one by one, is therefore
liable to the removal of tithes. The final two cases (J-L, M-O)
make the same point. Since olives or onions eaten by the workers

certainly stand under the terms of his contract, they are tithable
purchases, subject to all rules governing such purchases.

A. One who brings figs from the field
B. in order to eat them in a courtyard which is exempt from [the
    law of] tithes [e.g., it is not a private courtyard; cf.
    M. 3:5]--
C. [if] he was careless (*škḥ*) [5]
D. and brought them into his house,
E. he removes them [from the house] to the courtyard,
F. and makes a random snack of them.

                        T. 2:8 (A-F: cf. y. Ma. 3:1
                        [50 b-c])

G. One who brings figs from the field
H. in order to eat them in a courtyard which is exempt from [the
    law of] tithes--
I. [if] he was careless
J. and brought them up to the roof [in order to dry them]--
K. even [while the figs are] within his house [prior to bringing
    them up to the roof],
L. he makes a random snack of them.

                        T. 2:9

M. One who brings figs from the field
N. in order to eat them on the roof--
O. [if] he was careless
P. and brought them into another courtyard (*lḥṣr 'ḥrt; ed. princ.*
    and E read: *ltwk/lḥṣr ḥbrw*, "into the courtyard of his fel-
    low") [prior to bringing them up to the roof],
Q. he shall not eat unless he tithes.
R. R. Yose b. R. Judah says, "He brings them up to the roof and
    eats."

                        T. 2:10a (pp. 238-39, ls. 33-39)
                        (M-R: cf. y. Ma. 3:1[50b-c])

    T. offers an important complement to M. 3:1A-B, investigating
the relationship between actions and intentions with regard to
the appropriation of untithed produce. The issue emerges from
M. 3:1A-B, which has pointed out that the act of bringing produce
into the courtyard reveals the intention to consume it *only* if the
produce itself is processed, i.e., ready for consumption (cf.
M. 4:1-5D).

    The point of A-F, the first case of the triplet, is that an
unintended act of appropriation may be reversed without imposing

liability to tithing upon the produce. A farmer who has uninten-
tionally brought untithed produce into his home is indeed forbidden
from eating them there unless he tithes. He may, however, remove
them from the house and make a snack of them without tithing, just
as if he had never brought them home in the first place. G-L is
similar in its basic point. Since the farmer intends to bring
his produce to the roof, a place in which produce is not made
liable to the removal of tithes (cf. M. 3:6A), passage through
the house is deemed of no effect. The man may even snack upon
his untithed produce within the house since he intends to store
them elsewhere. M-Q, the conclusion of the triplet, presents a
case in which the man clearly demonstrates that he intends to
appropriate the produce. He has gone out of his way by passing
through his neighbor's courtyard prior to bringing his produce
home (KM, *Tithes* 4:13; PM, y. Ma. 3:1, s.v., *hby' t'nym*).[6] We
assume therefore that there is no inadvertance at all, but rather
that the householder intended to bring the produce to a location
where they would become liable. He may not eat the produce,
therefore, unless he tithes. Yose b. Judah (R) argues that the
case is no different from the others. The man's original intention prevails despite his suspect action.

A. *One who brings his workers out to* his *field* [= M. 3:2F]

B. may not (*'yn rsyy*) feed them [in exchange for their labor]

C. unless he has indeed tithed [the produce which he gives
    them].

D. And they may not eat [in exchange for their labor]

E. unless they have indeed tithed [the produce which they re-
    ceive].

F. If the householder brought [produce] out and placed it before
    them as a gesture of generosity (*b^c yn yph*),

G. they eat and need not tithe.

                    T. 2:10b (p. 234, ls. 39-41)

     T. cites M. 3:2F at A and then proceeds to supplement M. by
providing rulings relevant to the employer rather than to the
employees. B-C prohibits the employer from providing the workers
with untithed produce in exchange for their labor. Since the exchange of produce for labor is regarded as a sale, the owner
must tithe that which he sells to the worker (cf. M. Dem. 2:2).[7]
D-E is the same law stated from the point of view of the worker.
Since he purchases the produce with his labor, he must tithe this
purchase as he would any other. F-G brings us outside the

framework of the above cases. Now the employer simply places the
produce at the disposal of the workers as a gift. Since no sale
is involved, the workers share the owner's right to make a chance
meal, for he has offered them what is his.

A. "One who purchases (*lwqḥ*) dried figs [directly] from the
    pile in which they are being dried (*mn hmwqṣh*),
B. "shall not eat unless he tithes"--the words of R. Meir.
C. Said R. Judah, "Under what circumstances [is this the case]?
    When he takes (*lwqṭ*) [figs] from his own [pile].
D. "But when he takes [figs] from his fellow's [pile],
E. "he eats and need not tithe."

                              T. 2:12 (p. 234, ls. 44-47)

     T. is autonomous of M., placed here because of M. 3:2I, which
forbids workers to eat figs from the drying-pile. Meir says that
if one purchases figs while they are drying, i.e., before their
processing is complete, they are rendered liable. He has given a
comparable ruling at T. 2:3 (cf. M. 2:5). Alternatively, the figs
are liable because, having been purchased from the pile, they are
already gathered into a batch before the purchaser (M. 3:2I). On
either reading of Meir's reasoning, Judah's gloss is obvious. He
states that Meir's ruling holds only for the figs in the pile
which has been purchased. The purchaser may, however, eat other
figs freely, for he has not purchased them (cf. Lieberman, *TK*
II:685.44-45).

A. Workers who were weeding (*mnkšyn*) in the field,
B. or hoeing (*m^c dryn*)[8] in the field,
C. shall not eat [olives] from the olive tree or [figs] from
    the fig tree,
D. unless the employer (*b^c l hbyt*) has given them the right
    ntn lhn ... ršwt).
E. Therefore, if the employer has given them the right,
F. they eat, and gather [more than one olive or fig] together
    [at a time], and are exempt [from tithing](*wpṭwryn*; E reads:
    whyybyn, "and are required [to tithe]").
G. Under what circumstances [is this the case]? *In a case in
    which they have no [claim] upon him [for their] board*
    [= M. 3:2G].
H. *If they have [a claim] upon him [for their] board* [= M. 3:2H],
I. they eat [one by one] and are exempt [from tithing].
J. But if they gathered them together (*ṣyrpw*, following E),
    they are required [to tithe].

                              T. 2:13

K. Workers who were hoeing (‛wdryn; Lieberman emends to:
    'wryn, "who were picking") figs,

L. or cutting down (gwdryn) dates,

M. or harvesting (mwšqyn) olives,

N. eat [while they work] and are exempt [from tithing],

O. for the Torah has given them the right (ršwt) [cf. M. 2:7].

P. He [i.e., the worker] shall not take a slice (yšpyt) [of
    fruit dipped] in salt, and eat [without tithing],

Q. unless the employer has indeed given him the right [to do so].

R. And he shall not eat his bread (ptw) with them [i.e., the
    fruit],

S. unless the employer has indeed given him the right [to do so].

                              T. 2:14 (K-S: cf. b. B.M. 89b)

T. *One who hires a worker to weed among onions--*

U. *[the worker] plucks one leaf at a time and eats [without
    tithing]* [= M. 3:3M-N].

V. He shall not grab an [entire] shoot (qlḥ) in his hand and
    eat [it].

W. Rather ('bl), he plucks [single leaves] while [the onion
    itself] is joined to the ground, and eats [one by one].

                              T. 2:15

X. Workers who were digging up (‛wqryn) onions,

Y. or tying [bunches] ('wgdym) of onions,

Z. eat [while working], and are exempt [from tithing],

AA. for the Torah has given them [ed. princ. adds: ršwt, "the
    right"] [cf. M. B.M. 7:2].

                              T. 2:16 (pp. 234-35, ls. 47-56)

     T. is an extended commentary to M. 3:2-3, exploring the
worker's tithing obligations in relation to variable factors such
as the type of work he is performing and the conditions of payment
established by the employer. There are four distinct cases, A-D
+ E-F (glossed by G-J), K-O (glossed by P-Q + R-S), T-W and X-AA.
     The workers at A-D are not involved in harvesting or pro-
cessing the produce. Thus they have no right to eat produce with
which they are working unless the employer specifically grants it
to them. In that case (E-F), they gather the produce in convenient quantities and make a snack of it without tithing, for, as
we know from M., the owner's permission is like a gift which
extends his rights of eating to those whom he designates as
recipients. G-J clarifies the case, in light of the specific
conditions established at M. 3:2.

K-O's workers are in the field harvesting produce.[9] The rule
repeats what we already know from M. 2:7 and M. B.M. 7:2--that
the Torah grants workers the right to eat produce which they are
harvesting. Important qualifications, however, are introduced at
P-Q + R-S. While the worker is permitted by the Torah to eat produce he is harvesting, he may do so only if he eats it in its
natural condition, without the accompaniment of salt (P) or bread
(R).[10] The use of either salt or bread removes the repast from
the category of a "snack," and indicates that the worker is making
a regular meal (cf. M. 4:1, 3). This is forbidden in all circumstances unless tithes are removed. If, however, the owner express-
ly consents to either of these modes of eating (Q, S), we assume
that he will have tithed the produce before offering it to the
workers (cf. T. 2:10b).

T-U repeats M. 3:3M + O, excluding M.'s establishment of
specific contractual conditions. Since the worker is not harvesting, whatever he gathers together is a purchase which is liable
to tithes. V-W explain the precise meaning of this "gathering
together" (M. 3:3O) which renders the produce liable. The worker
may not take the entire onion shoot in his hand and pick the leaves
off, for their attachment to the uprooted shoot combines them into
one batch in his hand. Rather he must pick one leaf at a time
from the shoot while it is still attached to the ground (cf. M.
3:2H-I, M. 2:6). X-AA tells us nothing new. The workers are
either harvesting the onions (X) or completing the processing (Y),
both of which activities place the worker under the category of
those to whom the Torah has extended the right to eat.

3:4

A. 1) [If he] found harvested figs (qṣyṣwt)[11] in the road--
B. even [if they were found] beside a field [full of] harvested
    figs--
C. and [this] also [holds true for] (wkn)
D. a fig tree which over-arches the road, and he found figs
    beneath it--
E. [the figs] are permitted under the law [which defines] stolen
    property (mwtrwt mšm gzl),
F. and they are exempt from [the law of] tithes (wpṭwrwt mn
    hm^{c}srwt).
G. But (w-) [in similar cases] concerning olives or carobs,
    they are subject [to the law of tithes] (ḥybym).

H. 2) [If he] found dried figs--

I. if most people had pressed [their figs by that time],

J. he is required [to tithe those he found] (ḥyb);

K. and if not [i.e., if most people had not pressed their figs],

L. he is exempt [from tithing those he found].

M. 3) [If he] found sections of a fig-cake (plḥy dbylh),

N. he is required [to tithe them] (ḥyb),

O. since they obviously (šydwᶜ) come from a finished product
    (mdbr gmwr).

P. And [as for] carobs--

Q. as long as he has not piled them on top of the roof, he brings
    [some] of them down for the cattle (nine MSS. add w-, "and")
    is exempt [from tithing it],

R. for he returns the surplus.

> M. 3:4 (A-F: cf. b. B.M. 21b;
> P-Q: cf. y. Ma. 3:1[50b])

The pericope consists of two autonomous units. The triplet
at A-O concludes M.'s discussion of the liability of untithed
produce which undergoes a change of ownership (M. 2:1-3:4), while
P-R provides a transition to M. 3:5-10's discussion of untithed
produce brought from a public place onto the householder's private
property. If there is a redactional reason for juxtaposing the
units, it is a superficial similarity of substance; i.e., the
produce in each unit is exempt from the law because of its location in what M. deems to be a public place--a road or rooftop.
Problems arise only after someone takes possession of it, by either
picking up the lost produce (A-O) or by bringing the produce into
a space analogous to his own home (P-R).

Informing each case of A-O is the principle that produce
which is irretrievably lost is deemed to be abandoned (cf.
M. B.Q. 10:2, M. B.M. 2:1-2).[12] As such it is exempt from the
law of tithes (cf. M. 1:1B). The problem before us is to determine whether the lost produce is likely to have been processed by
the owner prior to his losing it. If so, the produce is liable
to the removal of tithes despite the fact that it is ownerless,
for it became liable before it was lost. The intervening period
of ownerlessness is disregarded, and the finder incurs all obligations presumed applicable to the loser.

The first case, A-F+G, is formally the most difficult and
substantively the most interesting. The basic ruling is at A+E-F,
which assumes that harvested figs found in the road are deemed
abandoned. The finder may therefore carry the figs off, without

fear of prosecution by the original owner (E), and, accordingly,
need not tithe (F). B glosses A, stressing the fact that the
location of the figs in the road is the salient consideration in
determining that they are abandoned.[13] Even if the figs were
found next to a field of harvested figs, there is no assumption
that those in the road belong to the owner of the field. C-D,
an interpolation, depends upon the point stressed at B. Even if
we can assume that the figs fell from the tree of a known farmer,
the fact that they are in the road permits the supposition that
the owner has given up hope of retrieving them. Thus E-F applies
to C-D as well. Such figs may be taken without fear of accusa-
tion, and may be eaten as ownerless property without the removal
of tithes. The foregoing offers little guidance for the interpretation of G, which states that olives or carobs lying in the road
remain subject to the law of tithes, and presumably are to be
considered stolen property if carried off by the finder.[14] As
the Amora, Raba, sees matters (b. B.M. 21b), interpretation of G
depends upon E. Carobs and olives are hard and unlikely to be
crushed in the road. For this reason the owner of the tree is
not likely to have written the fallen produce off as a loss.
Since it is not yet considered ownerless, it remains subject to
laws concerning theft and tithing.

The problem of H-L, the triplet's second case, is to determine whether or not the figs, which have already been dried prior
to loss, have also been pressed (i.e., processed). Two contrastive
apodoses (I-J, K-L)[15] provide the alternatives, both of which
depend upon the practice of local farmers. If the figs are found
after the local farmers have pressed their dried figs, those
found in the road are assumed to be fully processed as well, and
liable to the removal of tithes. If, on the other hand, the
majority of the farmers have yet to process their figs, those in
the road are deemed unprocessed as well. As ownerless property
they are permitted for use without tithing. M-N, a simple declarative sentence, concludes the unit with an obvious third case.
Anyone finding fig-cakes must tithe them without question, for
as O explains, fig-cakes are clearly fully processed produce.

The w- at P suggests that it is intended to carry forward
the problems of A-O. Nevertheless, Q-R addresses entirely new
matters. The ruling assumes two principles: 1) untithed produce
on a rooftop is deemed to be outside the householder's home, and
is therefore not yet liable to the removal of tithes (M. 3:6); and
2) a householder's courtyard is deemed part of his home, such that

produce brought into it is rendered liable to the removal of
tithes (M. 3:5). At P-Q a farmer has brought carobs up to his
roof and spread them out for drying. Before piling them up, i.e.,
before the processing is complete (M. 1:6N), he brings some down
to his courtyard to feed his cattle. We have no reason to expect
the carobs to be liable to the removal of tithes (Q). In the
first place, unprocessed produce is not made liable in the courtyard (M. 3:1A-B). Secondly, the carobs are to be eaten by cattle,
not human beings. Since the law of tithes applies only to human
food (M. 1:1B), there should be no question about tithing the
carobs fed to cattle. The addition of R, however, presents a
problem.[16] It assumes that if the householder does not return
part of the carobs to the rooftop for further drying, that which
he has brought into the courtyard is liable to the removal of
tithes. The reason must be that if the householder keeps the
uneaten portion of the carobs inside the courtyard, we assume he
intends to use it himself at some later date. Although it is
technically unprocessed, we assume that it is desirable to him in
its present condition. It therefore must be tithed before the
householder may make any further use of it (cf. M. 4:3).

A.   1) [If he] found small sheaves (*krykwt*) [of grain lying] in
     the private domain (*ršwt hyḥyd*),[17]

B.   it is forbidden ('*šwr*) under the law [which defines] stolen
     property,

C.   and they are subject to [the law of] tithes (*ḥyybwt bm^{c}srwt*).

D.   2) [If he found them] in the public domain (*ršwt hrbym*),

E.   *they are permitted under the law [which defines] stolen
     property,*

F.   *and they are exempt from the [law of] tithes* [= M. 3:4E-F].

G.   3) But large sheaves ('*lwmwt*),

H.   whether [they are found lying] in the private domain or in
     the public domain,

I.   are forbidden under the law [which defines] stolen property,

J.   and they are subject to [the law of] tithes.

K.   4) [If he] found grain [which had been] smoothed over--

L.   that which is piled up (*h^{c}syh kry*) is forbidden under the
     law [which defines] stolen property.

M.   [That which has become] strewn about is permitted under the
     law [which defines] stolen property.

N.   In either case, he designates it (^{c}*wsh 'wth*; Lieberman,
     following E, emends: *mwṣy' ^{c}lyhn*, "he removes on their

behalf") heave-offering and tithes for (^{c}l; E reads: $m\breve{s}l$,
"from") produce belonging to the householder,

O.   and need not be apprehensive [that he be considered a thief].

P.   5) [If he] found a covered basket,

Q.   it is forbidden under the law [which defines] stolen property,

R.   and it [i.e., its contents] is subject to [the law] of tithes.

S.   How does he proceed [when tithing the fruit in the basket]?

T.   He reckons the cash value [of the produce and pays the owner
     the entire amount, minus the value of the produce removed as
     tithe] (^{c}wsh $'wth$ $dmym$).

> T. 2:17 (p. 235, ls. 57-63)
> (A-N; cf. T. B.M. 2:5-6,
> b. B.M. 22b-23a; K-N: cf. y. Ma.
> 3:3[50c]; P-T: cf. y. Ma. 3:3
> [50c])

The five cases of our pericope, each of which is modeled upon
M. 3:4A-B + E-F, fall into three groups, A-J, K-O and P-R. The
operative principle in each case is identical to that of M.: if
produce appears to be abandoned it is exempt from the law of
tithes. The finder may, in addition, make free use of it without
being liable to any indemnity should the owner return and make a
claim against the finder.

Each case within A-J is dependent for its sense upon A,
which sets the context. A man has found small sheaves lying in
the private domain; that is, an enclosure at least ten hand-
breadths high and four square (T. Shab. 1:1). All objects found
within such an enclosure are considered private property insofar
as they may not be moved outside of the private domain on the
Sabbath (M. Shab. 1:1-3; T. Shab. 1:3-5). It follows that the
sheaves found within the private domain are assumed to belong to
someone. Thus if the finder consumes the grain, he will be liable
to the owner's claim for compensation (B). Since the grain is
assumed to be under someone's ownership, it is also subject to
the law of tithes, as we would expect (C). If, however, the
sheaves are found in the public domain (D), such as an encampment
or other large enclosure (T. Shab. 1:2), they are considered ownerless goods. As M. has already told us, use of such property is
not considered robbery, and the produce itself is exempt from the
law of tithes (E-F).[18] Matters change if one finds large sheaves,
for in either domain they are considered private property (G-J),
and are subject to all restrictions appropriate to such property.
b. B.M. 23a (s.v., rb' $mtr\d{s}$ $lt^{c}myh$) explains that large sheaves
are heavy and remain where they fall. Thus the owner will not

despair of recovering them until he returns to the place where he
lost them and confirms that they have been carted away.[19]

The issue of ownership is also at the heart of K-O. A man
has come across grain which has been smoothed over, i.e., completely processed (M. 1:6Q) and subject in principle to the law
of tithes. If the grain remains stacked up after smoothing, the
assumption is that the owner intends to return for the stack, for
its neat condition indicates that it has not been abandoned. Thus,
one who uses it is liable to pay reimbursement (K-L). But if the
grain has become strewn about, this indicates that no one intends
to retrieve it. The finder, therefore, is not required to reim-
burse the owner who returns for the stack (M: cf. M. B.M. 2:1-2).
The introductory formula of N ("in either case") prepares us for
a ruling applicable to both K-L and M. In fact, N ignores M
entirely,[20] for if the property is ownerless, there is no reason
to require the finder to offer the produce as heave-offering and
tithes on behalf of produce belonging to the householder (N). Nor
is there any reason for the finder to be worried that his actions
be misinterpreted as robbery (O). The point of N-O, then, is
that the finder (K-L) may offer the piled-up produce as heave-
offering or tithes on behalf of other produce belonging to the
householder. In this way the finder gains no benefit from his
disposition of the other man's produce. It should be noted that
M. Ter. 1:1 denies that one may offer heave-offering from another's
produce. Such heave-offering is deemed to be of no consequence,
and the produce remains forbidden until heave-offering is properly removed.[21]

P-R is clear. The covering on the basket indicates ownership
(y. Ma. 3:3[50c]), for we assume that the owner has intentionally
avoided leaving the basket open to the public. Thus it is within
the category of things which may be considered stolen property,
and is subject to the law of tithes. The gloss of S-T provides a
loophole for the finder who wishes to make use of produce which
is not technically his. He fixes the market value of the produce
and then separates the required offerings, using the remainder as
he wishes. Should the rightful owner return and make a claim,
the finder returns the cash, less the value of the produce removed
as heave-offering and tithes.

A. [If] he found harvested figs [= M. 3:4A],
B. he shall not grab (qwṣṣ) [some] and continue [on his way]
   (whwlk) with them,

C.   for most people are suspected [of petty-theft] regarding
     them.

                              T. 2:18 (p. 235-36, ls. 63-64)

     A's incomplete citation of M. is meant to signify the entire
case presented at M. 3:4A-B, i.e., a man has found figs in the
road next to a field of figs. T. stipulates the conditions under
which M.'s ruling--that the figs are not stolen goods--is applicable. The finder must not take these figs from the spot where he
finds them, for such an act may be interpreted to mean that he
stole the figs from the field itself and is now making off with
them. Rather, he eats in the road next to the field, demonstrating
by his proximity to the field that he has nothing to hide, for he
is merely eating what he found in the road (cf. Lieberman, *TK*,
II.689.63 and HD against GRA).

A.   [If] he had a stack
B.   of onions,
C.   or of dried figs,
D.   or of carobs
E.   on top of his roof,
F.   he selects [onions from the stack] and eats [without
     tithing];
G.   he selects [dried figs from the stack] and places them on
     the table [without tithing];
H.   he selects [carobs from the stack] and throws [them into
     the courtyard] for his cattle [without tithing][cf.
     M. 3:4P-Q].
I.   R. Simeon b. Eleazar says, "Cattle do not make a random snack
     [of processed produce] in the courtyard [unless the owner has
     tithed it]."
J.   And any of these which he brought from the field into town
     [without tithing]--
K.   he shall not make a random snack of it,
L.   for he does not finally return the surplus [to the field]
     [cf. M. 3:4R].
                              T. 2:19 (p. 236, ls. 64-67)
                              (J-L: cf. y. Ma. 3:1[50b])

     T. supplements M. 3:4P-R with independent materials appro-
priate to M.'s theme. A-H, however, flatly contradicts M., which
has told us that unstacked produce may be brought from roof to
courtyard as cattle fodder, without incurring liability to tithes,
as long as the owner intends to return the unused carobs to the
roof. The items of A-D have all been stacked, at which point

their processing is complete (cf. M. 1:6/O). On the basis of
M., we would now expect them to be rendered liable if brought
into the house or courtyard. F does not address this issue, for
it merely permits the owner to take some items from the stack and
eat them on the roof. Since roof-tops are an exempt area (M. 3:6A),
the produce, eaten as a snack, is not rendered liable. G-H, however, permits the owner to bring the produce to his table, or to
his cattle in the courtyard, without incurring liability. This,
as we have seen, is prohibited by M. Apparently, T. assumes that
the owner intends to return the surplus to the roof (M. 3:4R).
If so, T.'s theory is that, since the larger quantity of processed
produce remains in an exempt area, the portion removed shares its
status, *unless* the owner intends to use all he has removed. At
this point it becomes a separate quantity of produce in its own
right (cf. M. 4:3). Since it is processed, it is rendered liable
in the owner's courtyard (for differing views see Lieberman, *TK*,
II:689.69 and KM, *Tithes* 3:20).

     I is an independent ruling which the redactor has introduced
as a gloss of H. The point of stating that cattle may not eat
untithed produce in the courtyard after processing is to argue
that the tithing laws appropriate to human food apply as well to
cattle fodder (cf. T. 2:20a). If we read I as the framer of the
unit intends us to read it, the ruling disputes A-D + H. Cattle
may not eat processed produce in the courtyard whether or not the
principle is in an exempt area.

     J-L refers us back to A-D. It confirms our inference that
A-H assumes the owner's intention to return the surplus to the
roof, for now we have a case which specifies that no such intention
is operative. If the owner brings a portion of his stacked produce from the field to town, he may not make a snack prior to
tithing, for he is not expected to return the surplus such a great
distance.

A. Under any circumstances ($l^c wlm$) he may feed [his cattle]
    bunches of sheaves ($pqy^c y \ ^c myr$: so Jastrow, p. 1209, s.v.
    PQY^c)
B. unless he ties them into bales.
                              T. 2:20a (p. 236, ls. 67-68)

     T. assumes that, should cattle be fed produce which is suit-
able for human consumption, such produce remains subject to all
laws regarding proper tithing. The man need not tithe bunches of
sheaves which he feeds his cattle, for their processing is not complete until he ties the bunches into bales.

3:5

A. What type of courtyard is subject to [the law of] tithes
   (*ḥybt bm*^c*srwt*) [i.e., what kind of courtyard renders liable
   to tithes produce brought within it]?
B. R. Ishmael says, "A Tyrian courtyard,
C. "for household wares are kept [safely] within it."
D. R. Aqiba says, "Any [courtyard] (*kl š-*) which one [house-
   holder] opens, but another locks up is exempt [from the law
   of tithes]."
E. R. Nehemiah says, "Any [courtyard] in which a man eats unself-
   consciously (*š'yn 'dm bwš ml'kl btwkh*) is subject [to the law
   of tithes]."
F. R. Yose says, "Any [courtyard] into which [one] enters and
   no one inquires, 'What do you want?', is exempt [from the
   law of tithes]."
G. R. Judah says, "[If there are] two courtyards, one within
   the other,
H. "the inner [courtyard] is subject [to the law],
I. "while (*w-*) the outer [courtyard] is exempt [from the law]."

                        M. 3:5 (A-I: cf. b. Nid. 47b;
                        E = y. Ma. 2:1[49c]; G-I: cf.
                        y. A.Z. 1:10[40b])

     M. begins a new unit, M. 3:5-10, which refines and applies
the principle that courtyards are deemed to be extensions of the
home. M. 3:1A-B and M. 3:4P-R, we recall, have already assumed
the possibility that produce which a householder brings into his
courtyard has been appropriated thereby and, it follows, is liable
to the removal of tithes. Of concern at A is to define which
kinds of courtyards are deemed to be extensions of the home such
that the householder must tithe what he brings into them. All
authorities cited at B-F assume that, in order to be considered
an extension of the home, a courtyard must be analogous to the
home in some concrete way. The fundamental analogy, upon which
all rulings depend, is privacy, i.e., control over one's personal
space (cf. Maim., *Comm.*, *et al.*). A courtyard renders produce
brought within it liable to the removal of tithes if it exhibits
those characteristics which, in the home, ensure the householder's
privacy and security. While all parties accept this fundamental
analogy, the pericope itself appears to be a composite of three
formally distinct units (B-C, D-F, G-I) brought together under the
organizing rubric of A.[22] Only B-C, a verbless clause, is appro-
priately formulated in answer to A, or even depends upon A for its
sense. The lemmae at D-F, sharing a common formulary pattern

($k\ell$ $\check{s}$- ... $\dot{h}ybt/p\dot{t}wrh$), simply offer three distinct rulings regarding different types of courtyards. G-I as well could certainly stand alone (cf. MS, citing Joseph Ashkenazi).

The pericope's unity of principle is apparent in all lemmae, with the possible exception of Ishmael's (B-C). B stands on its own as an adequate, if terse, answer to A. C's gloss, which explains the relevant characteristic of the Tyrian courtyard, can have been added in order to bring Ishmael in line with the authorities with whom his saying has been redacted.[23] Archaeological knowledge concerning Tyrian courtyards is insufficient to determine whether they in fact are distinguished by the protection they afford to utensils or other items stored within them.[24] In contrast to B-C, all lemmae at D-F are manifestly dependent upon the analogy of privacy. For Aqiba (D), if more than one householder of a shared courtyard has control of access, the courtyard affords absolute privacy to neither.[25] Either householder, therefore, may bring untithed produce into the courtyard without obligation to tithe until he enters his home, which is accessible to him alone. Privacy is the main concern of Nehemiah (E) as well. He argues that the courtyard is like the home only if the householder is comfortable eating within it (cf. Judah, M. 2:2N-O). Laws, therefore, which apply to the place where a man eats his meals (i.e., to the home), apply as well only to a courtyard which affords the same domestic privacy. The principle of home-like privacy appears again in Yose's lemma (F). If no one requires an intruder into the courtyard to state his business, the courtyard is deemed a public place, and fundamentally unlike the home. Naturally, such a courtyard is of no interest to the law of tithes.

Judah's case (G-I) concludes matters by applying M.'s amply stated principle to a problematic example. Presumably, we have a house which opens into a courtyard, which itself opens into a fore-court in the following way:

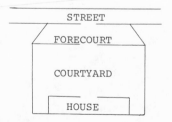

The fore-court leading into the public thoroughfare is easily accessible to passers-by, who may enter and leave without the knowledge or consent of the householder. The fore-court, therefore,

is considered part of the public thoroughfare, and is of no account
regarding the law of tithes.[26] Matters are different with the
courtyard adjacent to the house. We assume that the owner of the
house will take pains to ensure that those entering the forecourt
will not enter his own courtyard without permission (TYY). Since
he considers this area his private property, any produce he brings
within it is rendered liable to the removal of tithes.

A.   R. Simeon b. Eleazar says in the name of R. Aqiba,
B.   *"Any [courtyard] which one [householder] opens but another
     locks up* [= M. 3:5D]--
C.   "for example (*kgwn*), [either] two neighbors owning homes
     which share the same courtyard (*šwtpyn*)[27]
D.   "[or] two tenants [who do not own the homes which share the
     same courtyard] (*dywryn*)."

                              T. 2:20b (p. 236, ls. 68-69)
                              (Cf. y. Ma. 3:6[50d])

     Simeon b. Eleazar cites and glosses M. 3:5D. We originally
assumed that the ruling referred only to two householders who hold
the keys to a common courtyard. Since neither has absolute control of access, the courtyard affords privacy to neither party,
and does not render produce liable. C confirms this conception,
but D states that the ruling holds even if neither inhabitant owns
his home. This addresses a very different issue, for now the
courtyard remains under the jurisdiction of a single landlord, and
may be thought to constitute his private space. However, since
people with no property rights over the courtyard have access to
it, the courtyard no longer affords privacy to the landlord alone,
even though it remains his property. Such a courtyard does not
render produce liable.

                              3:6

A.   Roofs are exempt [from the law of tithes], even though
     [the houses upon which they are constructed] are situated
     in a courtyard which is subject [to the law of tithes].
B.   A gate-house (*byt šᶜr*),[28] a portico ('*kšdrh*),[29] or a balcony
     (*mrpšt*)[30]--
C.   lo, these [share the status] of the courtyard [in which they
     are situated].
D.   If [the courtyard] is subject [to the law], they are subject
     [to the law], but if [the courtyard] is exempt, they are exempt.
                              M. 3:6

M. 3:6 further refines the principle that, in regard to the
obligation to tithe produce, courtyards are deemed extensions of
the home. The topic now is areas within the courtyard which appear
to constitute domains independent of it. A's discussion of roof-
tops is relevant to any area above the surface of the courtyard
(cf. M. 3:8E), while B-D, a formally independent ruling, discusses
enclosed structures found within the courtyard. To be determined
is whether produce placed in elevated or partitioned areas is
governed by the rules which apply to produce placed anywhere else
in the courtyard.

A argues that roof-tops are in principle exempt from laws
applicable to houses and courtyards. The analogy of privacy,
which unites houses and courtyards into a single legal domain,
breaks down in the case of roof-tops, for the householder has no
direct control over that space. It is outside the walls of his
home and above those of his courtyard.[31] It follows that produce
stored on the roof is not rendered liable to the removal of tithes
until the householder brings it down into his house or courtyard
(cf. M. 3:4P-R, T. 2:9-10, 2:19).

B-D addresses a separate but related issue. While all the
structures named at B are within the space of the courtyard, each
is distinct from that space by virtue of some kind of permanent
enclosure. Should these structures, therefore, constitute domains
within which laws governing the courtyard do not apply? C-D
assumes that walls, in and of themselves, do not transform the
space contained within them into a separate domain. Since all
structures at B are structurally integral to the courtyard, they
share whatever status the courtyard itself enjoys, as this status
is established by the relative privacy afforded by the courtyard.[32]
Produce brought into such structures, therefore, is rendered
liable only if the courtyard itself is of the type deemed analogous to the home (M. 3:5). If not, these structures themselves
are of no consequence in determining the liability of produce
found within them.

A. *Roofs are exempt [from the law of tithes].*
B. *Even though [the houses upon which they are constructed]*
   are situated in a courtyard which is subject [to the law]
   [= M. 3:6A-B],
C. he carries them [e.g., his carobs, etc.] to the rooftop and
   eats [without tithing].

                          T. 2:20c (p. 236, ls. 69-70)

T. is composed of two citations--A-B, which cites M. 3:6A-B,
and C, which cites Yose b. Judah's opinion at T. 2:10a(R). Here
C glosses A-B, forcing us to read T. as two sentences, A and B-C.
The resulting rule tells us that the intention to bring one's
produce up to the exempt area of the roof permits one to bring it
through a private courtyard without rendering the produce liable.
The case is substantially identical to that upon which Yose b.
Judah rules at T. 2:10a.

3:7

A.   Storage huts (*grypyn*),[33] watch-turrets (*bwrgnyn*),[34] and field-
     sheds ('*lqtywt*)[35] are exempt [from the law of tithes].
B.   A hut [such as those used in the area of] Gennesar (*śwkt
     gnwśr*).[36]
C.   even though it contains millstones and poultry,
D.   is exempt [from the law of tithes].
E.   A potter's hut--
F.   the inner part is subject [to the law]
G.   and the outer part is exempt.
H.   R. Yose says, "Any [structure] which does not [serve] as
     [both] a summer dwelling and a winter dwelling (*dyrt ḥmh wdyrt
     gśmym*)[37] is exempt.
I.   A festival hut (*śwkt ḥhg*) during [the week of] the Festival
     [of Tabernacles]--
J.   R. Judah declares it subject [to the law during that week],
K.   but Sages declare it exempt [for that week].

M. 3:7 (E-G: cf. b. Suk. 8b;
I-K = b. Yom. 10a)

We have learned at M. 3:6B-D that walls are not sufficient to
transform an enclosed space into a home. The present pericope,
while independent of M. 3:6B-D, simply adds that it is the function of that enclosed space which determines whether it is deemed
a home. The important principle is attributed to Yose (H): in
order to be deemed a dwelling of consequence for the law of tithes,
a structure must serve as a dwelling the year round. Produce
brought into a building which serves only as an occasional dwelling,
therefore, is not rendered liable to the removal of tithes, even
if it is presently in use as a home.

     Yose's principle explains both A and B-D. Storage huts,
watch-towers and field-sheds (A) are designed for non-domestic
purposes, and are unsuited for use as permanent dwellings. The

owner of the hut or shed, or the soldier in the tower, may therefore eat untithed produce in these buildings without incurring
liability for eating *tebel*. Owners of Gennesar huts (B-D) enjoy
the same privilege. According to Maimonides (*Comm.*), such huts
are used by the residents of the area during the harvest months
alone. Even though accoutrements of home-steading, such as milling
stones and poultry, are found within the hut, its temporary nature
prevents it from entering the category of "home." Inhabitants of
such huts, it follows, eat untithed produce within them, even
during the season in which the huts are in use.

Although Yose's lemma immediately follows E-G, the principle
is hardly relevant to the case of the potter's hut. Such huts are
divided into two sections, the potter's permanent living quarters,
and a storage area for the display of finished work.[38] Untithed
produce brought into the inner living area is rendered liable to
tithes, while that brought into the display area is exempt. The
reason, despite Yose, has nothing to do with the permanence of
either area as a dwelling. The logic, rather, follows that of
M. 3:5G-I, a formally identical ruling which discusses the case of
two courtyards, one within the other. Since the public has access
to the outer area of the hut in order to view the potter's wares,
it is not considered his private space, and, like the forecourt
of M. 3:5G-I, is of no account in rendering produce liable to the
removal of tithes. The inner living quarters, to the contrary,
like the inner courtyard, are deemed private and fall within the
scope of the law. The exemption of the display area would surprise M. 2:2J-L, which assumes that places of business are deemed
analogous to the businessman's own home. One may argue, therefore,
that Yose's gloss at H is intended to harmonize M. 2:2J-L and F-G
by imposing a different principle upon the latter. Now the display
area is exempt because it does not serve as a shelter.

In the concluding dispute at I-K Sages stand with Yose
against Judah, who claims that a temporary shelter renders produce
within it liable to tithes as long as it is in use as a home. The
disputants take up the case of huts erected for use as dwellings
during the week of Sukkot, the Festival of Tabernacles (M. Suk.
1:9). Since such huts are used for eating and sleeping during the
Festival, Judah argues that produce brought within them during
this period is rendered liable to the removal of tithes. Although
temporary, they are deemed homes. Sages concur with Yose's principle. Since the hut serves as a home only during the Festival,
it is of no concern to the law of tithes.

A.   A house of assembly (*byt hknśt*) or a house of study (*byt htlmwd*)--

B.   if they include living quarters, one does not make a random snack [of untithed produce] within [the entire building].

C.   But if not [i.e., if there is no dwelling], one makes a random snack [of untithed produce] within them.

D.   Feed-sheds and granaries which are in the field:

E.   those utilized for storage--one makes a random snack within them.

F.   [Those which serve] as living quarters--one does not make a random snack within them.

                              T. 2:20d (p. 236, ls. 70-73)
                              (A-C: cf. y. Ma. 3:7[50d])

     A-C and D-F supplement M.'s examples, but Yose's principle is of no interest here. The house of assembly and the house of study are not used as dwellings, and there is therefore no reason to expect that produce brought into either building is rendered liable. If living quarters have been designated, however, the produce of those living within the building is rendered liable (y. Ma. 3:7, s.v., *dtny byt śpr*).[39] Feed-sheds and granaries do not render produce liable as long as they serve their normal function as storage areas (D-E). However, contrary to M. 3:7A, if someone does establish a dwelling within them, his produce is rendered liable upon entry (F).

A.   *A potter's hut--*

B.   others say in the name of R. Nathan,

C.   "*the inner part is subject [to the law]*

D.   "*and the outer part is exempt*" [= M. 3:7E-G].

                              T. 2:21 (p. 236, ls. 74-75)

     T. attributes M. 3:7E-G to R. Nathan, a contemporary of Rabbi Judah the Prince, of the last generation of Mishnaic authorities.

                              3:8-9

A.   1) A fig tree which is standing in a courtyard--

B.   [the householder] eats [the figs] one by one [from the tree], and is exempt [from tithing].

C.   But if he gathers [figs] together [before eating], he is required [to tithe them].

D.   R. Simeon says, "[If he has] one in his right hand, and one in his left hand, and one in his mouth [he is exempt from tithing]."

E. [If] he climbed to the top [of the tree], he stuffs his
    pocket [with figs] (mml' ḥyqw), and eats .[without incurring
    the obligation to tithe].

                          M. 3:8 (D: cf. y. Ma. 3:8[50d])

F. 2) A grapevine which is planted in a courtyard--

G. "[the householder] takes the entire cluster of grapes [from
    the vine, and incurs no obligation to tithe].

H. "And [this is] also [the case] (wkn) with a pomegranate [picked
    from a tree growing in a courtyard],

I. "as well as (wkn) a melon [picked from a vine growing in a
    courtyard]"--the words of R. Tarfon.

J. R. Aqiba says, "[The householder] takes one grape at a time
    (mgrgr) from the cluster [while it is on the vine, and incurs
    no obligation to tithe],

K. "or splits a segment (pwrt) from the pomegranate [while it is
    on the tree],

L. "or cuts a slice (śwpt) of the melon [while it is on the vine],
    [but if he takes an entire cluster, and so on, he incurs the
    obligation to tithe]."

M. 3) Coriander (kśbr)[40] which is sown in a courtyard--

N. [the householder] plucks one leaf at a time and eats [without
    incurring the obligation to tithe].

O. But if he gathers [the plucked leaves] together, he is required
    [to tithe them].

P. Savory, or sweet majoram or thyme which are [growing] in a
    courtyard--
       if they were being cultivated (nšmrym),[41] they are subject [to
    the law of tithes] (ḥybyn).

                          M. 3:9 (F-I = y. Ter. 8:3[45b];
                          P = b. Nid. 51a)

     The foundation of the pericope is the triplet at A-C, F-L, and
M-O, into which rulings at D and E have been interpolated. P is a
singleton, similar in form to the rulings of the triplet, but independent in substance. The triplet, for its part, skillfully
weaves two separate but related issues into a single discussion.
The primary issue, which accounts for the redaction of the pericope
in M.'s unit on the courtyard, is the liability of produce picked
from a tree growing in the midst of a courtyard (A-C). It would
appear that produce picked within a courtyard must immediately be
rendered liable to the removal of tithes, as would be any other
harvested produce found within its walls.[42] As C points out, however, produce picked within the courtyard is rendered liable only

if a batch is actually gathered together (i.e., harvested). If,
on the other hand, the householder picks a single piece of fruit
from the tree and eats it before picking another, he need not
tithe (B). A single plucked fig, for example, is deemed part of
the unharvested batch of figs remaining on the tree. Like that
batch itself, the single fig is deemed unharvested and is therefore
exempt from tithes (cf. M. 2:6/0). This resolution of the pericope's primary issue is itself the subject of a second inquiry,
carried forward at F-L and M-O, the second and third cases of the
triplet. If the householder picks and eats one piece of produce
at a time without tithing, it becomes necessary to ask how the law
applies to produce which is naturally divided into numerous edible
segments. A-C, F-L, and M-O, therefore, define a progressively
more subtle series of cases regarding the application of the
pericope's basic principle.

A-C begins discussion with the simple case of figs. The fig
is an indivisible piece of fruit, normally eaten whole in a single
mouthful. In the case of figs, then, the householder conforms to
the limitation of eating "one by one" if he picks and eats no more
than one fig at a time. Application of this stricture to the produce under discussion at F-L is more problematic, for grape-
clusters, pomegranates and melons are all large items divisible
into conveniently eaten sections (cf. M. 2:6E-I). At issue between
Tarfon and Aqiba is whether the privilege of eating such produce
"one by one" extends to the entire fruit (Tarfon) or merely to that
part of the fruit normally considered to be a single piece or
section (Aqiba).[43] In regard to grape-clusters, for example,
Tarfon permits the householder to pick the entire cluster from the
vine and munch on the grapes without removing tithes, for he deems
the entire cluster to constitute a single item of produce. Aqiba,
on the other hand, restricts the householder to eating a single
grape at a time while the cluster itself is attached to the vine.
If the householder takes two grapes at once from a cluster on the
vine, or plucks the entire cluster at once, he is deemed to have
gathered a batch of produce before him, and must therefore tithe.[44]
M-O's example of coriander, which concludes the triplet, is one
with which both Tarfon and Aqiba will agree, although for different reasons. Coriander leaves grow in individual shoots from a
central leaf.[45] The problem is whether one is restricted to
picking a single shoot off the leaf, on the model of Aqiba's
grapecluster, or whether one may pick the leaf in its entirety,
following the reasoning of Tarfon. The ruling, which permits the
householder to pick one whole leaf at a time, is calculated to

satisfy both parties. A single leaf of coriander is small enough
to constitute a single portion, the matter of utmost concern to
Aqiba, and is at the same time a single whole unit of produce,
the unit to which Tarfon holds the law to apply.

The interpolations at D and E, to which we now turn, do not
advance the discussion. Simeon (D) offers his own definition of
the maximum quantity of figs one may have in his possession and
still be free of the obligation to tithe. The point of E is that
as long as the householder remains in the tree any produce on his
person is deemed outside the courtyard and is therefore exempt
from the removal of tithes. The concluding ruling at P is also
tangential to the concerns of the triplet, but makes an important
point regarding produce grown in a courtyard. Produce which is
not intentionally sown and cultivated is considered a wild growth,
and is exempt from the law of tithes (M. 1:1B), even if it happens
to grow in a courtyard. Such produce is subject to restrictions
appropriate to cultivated produce only if the householder actually
tends the plant.

                              3:10

A.   A fig tree which is standing in a courtyard,

B.   but (w-) [one of its boughs] extends into the garden [beyond
     the courtyard's walls]--

C.   [a person standing in the garden] eats as he pleases [from
     that bough], and is exempt [from tithing].

D.   [If the tree] is standing in the garden,

E.   but [one of its boughs] extends into a courtyard--

F.   [a person standing in the courtyard] eats one by one [from that
     bough], and is exempt [from tithing].

G.   But if he gathers [figs] together, he is required [to tithe
     them].

H.   [A tree] standing in the Land [of Israel] with (w-) [its bough]
     extending outside the Land [of Israel, e.g., in Syria],

I.   [or one standing] outside the Land [of Israel] with [its bough]
     extending into the Land [of Israel]--

J.   [the status of] all [fruit on the tree] is governed by [the
     laws which apply to] the place in which the roots are located
     ($hkl\ hwlk\ 'hr\ h^{c}qr$).

K.   And concerning [the sale of trees belonging to] houses within
     walled cities--

L.   all [matters regarding the re-purchase of such trees by their

original owner] are governed by [the laws which apply to] the
place in which the roots are located [i.e., trees sold with the
houses of walled cities may be re-purchased along with the
houses within twelve months, as long as the trees are rooted
inside the wall].

M. And concerning [trees in or near] cities of refuge--

N. all [matters regarding the legitimacy of the tree itself as a
place of refuge] are governed by [the laws which apply to]
the place into which the bough extends (hkl hwlk 'ḥr hnwp)
[i.e., one guilty of involuntary manslaughter finds refuge at
the root of the tree even if only the bough extends into the
city of refuge].

O. And concerning [trees growing] in Jerusalem [the fruit of which
is designated as second tithe-produce]--

P. all [matters concerning the sale of such produce] are governed
by [the laws which apply to] the place into which the bough
extends [i.e., if only the bough extends inside the city, the
fruit of the entire tree must be eaten within Jerusalem, and
may not be redeemed for coins outside of it: T. M.S. 2:12].

> M. 3:10 (D-E = b. B.M. 88a;
> K-N = b. Mak. 12b: cf. M. Mak.
> 2:7; O-P: cf. M. M.S. 3:7,
> T. M.S. 2:12, T. Arakh. 5:14)

The pericope concludes the discussion, begun at M. 3:5, of
laws applicable to produce brought within a courtyard or specific
locations therein. The contrasting doublet of A-C+D-G carries
forward the interests and language of M. 3:8-9, applying an obvious
principle to a complication in M. 3:8-9's case. We are well aware
that a batch of produce picked from a tree growing in a courtyard
is deemed to have been brought into the courtyard, and is therefore rendered liable to tithes. The point of A-G is that the
location of the tree itself has no bearing upon the liability of
its fruit; rather, all depends upon the location in which the fruit
is actually picked. The fruit of a tree growing within the courtyard remains exempt from the removal of tithes if the householder
can pick the fruit while standing in the garden, an area beyond
the courtyard wall which is deemed no different from an open field
(A-C). While the tree is rooted in a "liable" domain, its fruit
has been picked in an area outside the farmer's home, and therefore has not been rendered liable. If, however, a bough of such
a tree extends into the courtyard, and the householder picks the
fruit while standing beneath the bough (i.e., within the courtyard), all laws applicable to the produce of M. 3:8-9 apply to

the present produce as well. The householder must tithe it unless
he picks and eats one piece of produce at a time (D-G).

The problem of the foregoing, the status of produce growing
from a tree which extends into legally distinct domains, is superficially carried forward at H-P--an entirely independent unit of
four formally identical rulings. At issue in each case is whether
the legal status of a tree is determined by the laws applicable to
the place in which it is rooted or whether, to the contrary, its
status is determined by the place into which its bough extends.
The problem, of course, is different from that of A-G, for in the
latter the law depends only upon the location of the person who
makes use of the tree, the location of the tree or its parts being
immaterial in determining the status of its fruit. In theme, as
well as in principle, the present unit is somewhat out of phase
with its context. Only the first (M-J) and last (O-P) rulings
are at all relevant to tithing issues. K-L and M-N, on the other
hand, are interested in matters more appropriate to the orders of
Holy Things and Damages, within which laws bearing upon their
interpretation are to be found. On the whole, H-P must be termed
a redactional conclusion to M. 3:5-10, signalling by its formal
and conceptual independence of context the end of a distinct
thematic unit.

H-J is the only ruling which addresses an issue of crucial
importance to the topic of our tractate. Despite the importance
of the issue, however, it is never discussed in the remainder of
M. The ruling assumes that produce grown in the Land of Israel
is subject to the law of tithes by virtue of the holiness of the
land from which it grows. Produce grown from a tree standing
across the border of the Land is exempt from the removal of
tithes, therefore, even if a bough extends into the Land and its
fruit is picked within the Land. Fruit, in other words, shares
the character of the soil from which it draws its nourishment.
If that soil is holy, the produce can become holy; if the soil
is profane, the produce can never become holy (cf. T. 2:22).[46]

K-L, the second in the present series, shares the apodosis of
H-J: *hkl hwlk 'ḥr hᶜqr*. The ruling itself presupposes Lv. 25:29:
*"If a man sells a dwelling house in a walled city, he may redeem
it [i.e., re-purchase it] within a whole year after its sale; for
a full year he shall have the right of redemption* (cf. M. Arakh.
9:3). K-L simply adjudicates the status of trees sold along with
the house. If they are rooted within the walls of the city, any
boughs extending over the wall do not affect the right of the
seller to repurchase the tree within a year. The tree is deemed

to share the status of the house, and is subject to all rules
governing the house itself. The ruling accords with M. Arakh.
9:5, which states that any real estate within the walls of the city
is deemed to be like a house with regard to re-purchase within the
year (see Neusner, *Holy Things* IV). Presumably, if the tree were
rooted beyond the wall, one who re-purchases his house would have
no ownership over boughs extending over the wall onto his property.

The location of the bough of the tree, rather than that of
the roots, determines matters in M-N and O-P, the remaining rulings
of the unit. The cities of refuge referred to at M-N are established by Mosaic legislation (Nu. 35:9-28; cf. M. Mak. 2:4-8) as
legal refuges for persons who, through carelessness, are responsible
for the death of another. While in such a city, the guilty party
is protected from the blood vengeance of the deceased's relatives.
The problem before us is whether a tree growing outside the limits
of such a city, of which a bough extends into the city, offers
refuge to the manslaughterer. M-N rules that, in such a case, the
entire tree, by virtue of its bough, is deemed to be within the
city limits. A manslaughterer reaching the trunk of the tree,
therefore, is protected from vengeance, even though he is technically outside the city limits.[47]

O-P, which concludes matters, assumes knowledge of the basic
strictures regulating the disposition of produce designated as
second tithe.[48] Such produce is to be taken by the farmer to
Jerusalem, where he is commanded to eat it as an offering to God
(Dt. 14:22ff.). In order to spare the expense and inconvenience
of transporting his produce to Jerusalem, however, the farmer may
instead bring to Jerusalem currency equal in value to the produce
designated as second tithe. Once in the holy city, he then purchases produce with this money and eats the produce as second
tithe, in place of the produce he originally designated as the
offering. The problem of O-P is the disposition of produce
designated as second tithe, which happens to be growing on a tree
near the wall of Jerusalem. We learn that if only as little as a
single bough is within the wall the entire tree is considered to
be within the city. Once the fruit of such a tree is designated
as second tithe, therefore, it cannot be exchanged for coins outside of Jerusalem, where the tree is actually growing. Even
though the produce may have been picked outside the city, it is
deemed to have grown within the city, and may not be "removed"
from within its walls (cf. M. M.S. 3:5). All such produce must
be brought into Jerusalem and eaten there.[49]

A. R. Nehemiah says, "A hoed courtyard--lo, it is considered to
    be a garden, in that [he] (*w-*) makes a random snack [of pro-
    cessed produce] within it [and need not tithe]."

                              T. 2:20e (p. 236, l. 73)
                              (= y. Ma. 3:10[50d-51a])

    T. supplements M. 3:10A-G. Hoeing a courtyard turns it into
a garden (y. Ma. 3:10 51a , s.v., *whhy' ylp' mn hd'*). Gardens,
like fields in general, do not render liable produce brought
within them. Therefore, just as the farmer may make a snack of
processed produce in the field until he enters his courtyard, so
may he do so in his own courtyard once it has been turned into a
garden. His privilege continues, presumably, until he enters his
home.

A. A fig tree which *is standing in a garden,*
B. *but [one of its boughs] extends* through a window [cf. M.
    3:10D-E]--
C. he eats as he pleases [from the bough], and is exempt [from
    tithing].
D. If he plucked [figs] and placed [them] on the table, even one
    [fig placed on the table] is liable.
E. A tree, part of which is rooted in the Land [of Israel], and
    part of which is rooted outside the Land [of Israel]--
F. "since part of it is rooted in the Land [of Israel], it is as
    if all of it is rooted in the Land [of Israel]"-- these are
    the words of Rabbi.
G. Rabban Simeon b. Gamaliel says, "The side (*hṣd*, following
    Lieberman's emendation of V's *hṣr*, "a courtyard") rooted in
    the Land of Israel--lo, it [i.e., the produce] is deemed
    [produce of] the Land of Israel; the side rooted outside the
    Land of Israel--lo, it is deemed [produce grown] outside the
    Land of Israel" [cf. M. 3:10H-J].

                              T. 2:22 (pp. 236-37, ls. 75-79)
                              (E-G: cf. y. COrl. 1:1[60d],
                              b. Git. 22a, b. B.B. 27b)

    A-D is modeled upon M. 3:10D-E, but contradicts its principle,
applying instead the ruling of M. 3:10H-J.[50] The status of produce picked from a bough which extends from the garden into a
window is determined according to the location of the tree's roots.
At C, therefore, we disregard the fact that the man has picked
the produce while standing in his house. Since the tree itself
grows in the exempt area of the garden, the householder may eat
as he pleases without the removal of tithes. D adds that if the

householder places even one piece of fruit on his table, it may not
be eaten unless tithes are removed. The householder, by placing
the produce on the table, indicates his intention to make a regular
meal of it, an intention which imposes upon the householder to
tithe his produce whether or not it has been rendered liable in
some other fashion (cf. M. 4:1).[51]

E-G, a dispute, presents a second application of the principle
behind M. 3:10H-J. Now the roots themselves extend into each
side of the border of the Land of Israel. Rabbi says that in this
case the entire tree is considered to be growing inside the Land
of Israel. y. Orl. 1:1's gloss of the rule, in the name of Rabbi,
explains that the roots draw nourishment from each other. It follows that even the roots outside the Land are sustained by the
holy soil. According to M.'s principle, therefore, all the fruit
of the tree--no matter where it is picked--is subject to the law,
and must be tithed before one eats the processed product at home.
Simeon b. Gamaliel objects to Rabbi's botanical theory, not M.'s
principle. He denies that roots draw nourishment from each other.
Rather, each side of the tree is independent of the other, and
only produce of the side growing in the Land is subject to the
law of tithes.[52]

Chapter Four offers a sustained discussion of a problem which
thus far has received only episodic attention in M., namely, the
role played by human intention in establishing the liability of
produce to the removal of tithes (cf. M. 1:1D-F, 1:5L-M, 2:2,
3:1A-B). The chapter's primary datum is the familiar notion that
untithed produce may be eaten as a snack without the removal of
tithes, but is rendered liable to tithing if its owner appropriates
the produce for his daily use, e.g., in a meal (M. 1:5-8). To this
M. now adds a simple but far-reaching proposition. If we can
establish that a householder has decided to use a specific batch
of produce for use in a meal, that produce may no longer be used
even as a snack unless it is first tithed. In other words, once
the intention to make a meal of produce has been formulated, we
interpret all subsequent acts of eating as expressions of that
original intention. The produce, now deemed to have been appropriated by the householder, must be tithed before it is consumed.
The task of Chapter Four is to introduce and apply this single
conception through a series of cases and problems. The coherence
of the chapter's discussion is remarkable in light of the fact
that each of its six pericopae is formally and substantively
autonomous of the others. It is the skill of the redactor alone
which binds these diverse materials into a single inquiry into
the logic and purpose underlying human actions.

The issue is cogently drawn at the very first pericope.
Untithed produce which is subjected to boiling, pickling or other
procedures normally associated with the preparation of a meal is
rendered liable by those procedures to the removal of tithes, even
if the produce is still lying unprocessed in the field (M. 4:1).
We assume that the produce, prepared as if it were to be part of
a meal, will indeed be so used. The householder's actions, which
permit reasonable access to his actual intentions, therefore
serve as a reliable guide in determining whether he has imposed
upon himself the obligation to tithe. The relationship between
intentions and actions is subject to more subtle scrutiny by the
Houses, in a dispute at M. 4:2D-F. Produce which is set aside
for a future meal, but which has not as yet been subject to preparation (e.g., produce designated during the week to be eaten on the
Sabbath), is declared by the Hillelites to be liable the moment

121

the owner designates its intended use. Consequently, according
to the Hillelites, produce is forbidden for consumption during
the entire period between its designation for use as a meal and
the actual time of the meal--unless, of course, it is tithed. The
point is that the formulation of the intention itself effects the
liability of the produce, independent of any actions on the part
of the householder. What he actually does, i.e., making a snack,
is no longer of consequence once he has intended to do otherwise.

Reflection on the role of actions as signals for underlying
intentions is resumed at M. 4:3-5D. We are offered a general
criterion for determining a person's intentions in cases where his
actions are ambiguous. If a householder, for example, removes a
small quantity of untithed produce from a larger batch, and offers
no indication as to how he intends to use it, we are apparently at
a loss to determine whether he must tithe. According to Eliezer
(M. 4:3D-F) and Sages (M. 4:4E), however, the person's intentions
may be inferred from the likelihood that he will return any leftovers to the original batch. If he alters the condition of the
produce so as to make it impossible to return it, e.g., by rendering unclean a batch of olives removed from a bin of clean olives,
we assume that he intends to remove the produce permanently. His
original purpose, then, was to make a meal of it. The produce,
obviously, must be tithed.

M. 4:5E-6, the final unit of the chapter, approaches the issue
of intention from an entirely fresh perspective, and indeed seems
to introduce M. 5:1-2's discussion of produce harvested before its
time. The power of a person's intention to determine the liability
of his produce is not limited to produce which has already been
harvested. Rather, from the moment the crop is sown the householder's intentions determine whether it shall be deemed a food at
its harvest. If, for example, an edible crop such as coriander
is sown not for its leaves, but for its agriculturally useful seeds,
the entire crop--inedible seeds as well as edible leaves--is
exempt from the removal of tithes (M. 4:5E-F). A related issue is
raised by Eliezer, Gamaliel, and Aqiba (M. 4:5G-6L). Assuming
that a plant yielding edible fruit or leaves in addition to rarely-
eaten stalks or flowers is sown for food, our authorities wish to
know which parts of the plant must be tithed as food. Eliezer and
Gameliel argue that since the householder intends the crop to be
harvested as food, even the rarely-eaten portions are deemed food
as well. Aqiba, however, is given the last word. Only the fruit,
i.e., the part normally used as food, is subject to the law.
Thus Aqiba challenges the main thrust of the unit, arguing that

the householder's intention has no power to contravene customary
distinctions between the edible and the undesirable.

4:1

A. 1) One who pickles, boils, [or] salts [produce] in the field[1]
    is required [to tithe].
B. 2) One who buries [produce] in the ground is exempt [from
    tithing].
C. 3) One who seasons[2] [produce] in the field is exempt [from
    tithing].
D. 4) One who crushes olives so that the bitterness will exude
    is exempt [from tithing].
E. 5) One who squeezes [the oil of] olives onto his body is exempt
    [from tithing].
F. If he squeezed [the oil] and placed it in [the palm of] his
    hand, he is required [to tithe].
G. 6) One who skims [a ladle of wine for use][3] in a stew is exempt
    [from tithing].
H. [If he poured the ladle of wine] into a pot [and then skimmed
    the wine], he is required [to tithe],
I. since it is like a small vat.

M. 4:1

The pericope is in two parts, the four rulings at A-D and the
formally related, but substantively distinct, couplet at E-H (+I).
Uniting the two parts is a common interest in the intentions presumed to inform a person's consumption of untithed produce. We
recall (M. 1:5ff.) that untithed produce is permitted for consumption as a snack only. If a householder, therefore, indicates by
his actions a desire to use his untithed produce in a meal, he must
tithe the produce forthwith. The basic agreement between A-D and
E-H on this point obscures the fact that rather separate problems
are addressed by each unit. At A-D the salient issue is whether
the householder has prepared the produce in a manner normally
employed in the preparation of a meal. E-H, on the other hand, is
interested primarily in whether the liquid, at the moment it is
consumed, can be deemed by the householder to be a food.[4]
    Exegesis of A-D proceeds from the contrast between the apodo-
sis of A (ḥyb: liable) and those of B-D (pṭwr: exempt). The
procedures enumerated at A and B-D differ primarily in that the
former--pickling, drying and boiling--are normally part of the
preparation of produce for use in a meal, while the latter are at

best methods of improving the palatability of fresh produce. The
point of the contrast, then, is that once a person's intentions to
use the produce in a meal are clearly expressed, e.g., when he
boils it, all further consumption of the produce is forbidden
unless it is tithed. The householder incurs no obligation, however, if his preparation of the produce reveals no particular
intentions one way or the other, e.g., if he buries produce to
hasten its ripening (Maim., *Comm.*). Unless we have concrete
evidence, we assume that the householder intends to eat the produce
as a snack.

   The exegetical route into E-H, as at A-D, lies in the analysis
of contrasts--in this case, those at E vs. F and G vs. H. The
only difference between the oil at E and that at F is that the
former has clearly been squeezed for use as an ointment, while
the latter, having been gathered in a cupped hand, is now capable
of being used as food in its own right. Since the man has gathered
the oil in his hand, we assume that he intends to use it for some
purpose other than anointing, i.e., in some kind of dish. The oil,
consequently, is forbidden for use unless it is tithed. Similar
logic informs G-H. If a man takes a ladle of unskimmed grape
juice from a vat and skims the juice in the ladle, he need not
tithe whatever he pours into his stew.[5] The liquid, which has not
been skimmed in a fashion suitable for wine production, is not
deemed wine, and is therefore permitted for use without tithing
(cf. M. 1:7W-Y and discussion, pp. 47-48, and T. 1:9, pp. 58-59).
Should the man pour the juice into a pot, however, and then skim
it, he must tithe whatever he uses in his stew. As I points out,
the skimming has now been performed in a proper vessel. The
liquid, now deemed wine, must therefore be tithed before its owner
uses it in a meal.

A.   R. Simeon b. Judah says in the name of R. Simeon,

B.   "One who parches [grain over a fire: y. Ma. 4:1] in the field--

C.   "lo, this one is required [to tithe]."

                              T. 3:1 (cf. y. Ma. 4:1[51a])

D.   "One who mashes garlic or cress in the field--

E.   "lo, this one is required [to tithe]."

                              T. 3:2a (p. 237, ls. 1-2)
                              (cf. y. Ma. 4:1[51b])

   T. supplements M. 4:1A-B with two further acts deemed to
constitute preparation of produce for use in a meal.

4:2

A.   Children who hid [untithed] figs away [intending to eat them
     on] the Sabbath,

B.   but forgot to tithe them [by Sabbath Eve],

C.   shall not eat [the figs] at the close of the Sabbath unless
     they tithe.

D.   A basket [of untithed produce designated for] the Sabbath
     (klklt šbt)--

E.   the House of Shammai declare it exempt [from the removal of
     tithes] [i.e., one who snacks on the produce prior to the
     Sabbath need not tithe].

F.   But the House of Hillel declare it liable [to the removal of
     tithes] [i.e., one who snacks on the produce prior to the
     Sabbath must tithe].

G.   R. Judah says, "Also ('p): one who gathers a basket [of
     produce] to send to his fellow [for the Sabbath] shall not
     eat [any of the produce] unless he tithes."

                              M. 4:2 (A-C = b. Bes. 34b,
                              y. Ma. 4:2[51b]; D-F = M. Ed. 4:10,
                              T. Ed. 2:4; G: cf. T. Ed. 2:4)

     The point of the pericope follows neatly from M. 4:1. Once
the intention to use produce in a meal has been formulated--in
the present case, the moment during the week at which the untithed
produce is designated for use on the Sabbath--the produce is
liable to the removal of tithes regardless of when or how it is
eventually consumed. The issue is framed most simply at A-C.
Prior to the Sabbath, children have hidden figs and forgotten to
tithe them. Certainly the figs may not be eaten on the Sabbath,
for tithing of produce is forbidden on the day of rest.[6] One
might expect, however, that after the Sabbath the children may
make a snack of the figs without removing tithes. Since the figs
were designated to be eaten only on the Sabbath, it is plausible
that with the passing of the Sabbath the original intention has
been nullified by the failure to eat them at the appointed time.
The failure, that is, to confirm the intention by the appropriate
act, might lead us to regard the intention as non-existent. The
figs, consequently, might return to the exempt status they enjoyed
prior to being designated for the Sabbath. C clearly rejects this
conclusion. Once the intention to make a meal of the figs has
been formulated, the owner must tithe them even after his original
intention can no longer be fulfilled. Thus one who wishes even a
snack of the figs after the Sabbath must tithe them, for the
original intention to use them in a meal is deemed binding.

The issue is carried forward by the Houses at D-F,[7] although
the brevity of the protasis of this dispute makes interpretation
difficult. The Houses appear to go over the ground of A-C.[8] If
a basket of produce is designated for the Sabbath, but does untithed prior to that day, the Shammaites permit the householder to
snack on the produce following the Sabbath, while the Hillelites
require him to tithe before he takes so much as a bite. The
Hillelite ruling thus accords with A-C, and appears to offer the
latter the prestige of Hillelite precedent (cf. T. 3:2b-4).
Judah's gloss at G, however, requires us to view the dispute from
a different perspective (reflected in the bracketed portion of my
translation of D-F). Judah argues that a farmer who sends a
basket of Sabbath fruit[9] to his neighbor must tithe the produce if
he himself wishes to partake of it prior to sending the gift. The
point is that the farmer's designation of the produce for the
Sabbath immediately imposes upon it the status of food which has
been set aside for a meal. The produce is liable to the removal
of tithes from that moment on, no matter how it is used.

The connective '*p*, which links G to D-F, proposes that the
principle of G is at work in D-F as well. That is, the Houses
dispute the point at which the designation of produce for the
Sabbath first imposes upon it the status of *ṭebel*. The Shammaites
hold that since the produce is intended for use on the Sabbath
only, it remains exempt from the removal of tithes until then,
and may therefore be eaten as a snack during the week without
removing tithes. Any tithing during the week is solely to prepare
the produce for the Sabbath. The Hillelites, however, argue that
the designation of the produce for use on the Sabbath imposes
liability upon the produce immediately. Once the owner designates
produce for a meal all use of the produce is deemed for that purpose, regardless of the fact that the appointed time for the meal
has not yet arrived. From this perspective, the Hillelite position
appears to be an application of A-C rather than a precedent for it.
Once we conclude that no actions are required to confirm a person's intention to make a meal of produce (A-C), it is a small
step to conclude that such intention imposes liability upon the
produce as soon as the intention is formulated.[10]

A. *Children who hid* [*untithed*] *figs away* [*intending to eat them
    on*] *the Sabbath* [= M. 4:2A]--
B. [if they hid] black [figs for the Sabbath], but found white
    [figs in their place after the Sabbath],

C. [or if they hid] white [figs before the Sabbath], but found
    black [figs in their place after the Sabbath],

D. doubt [concerning the identity of the figs renders them]
    forbidden [as a Sabbath meal],

E. on the grounds that doubt [concerning] the preparation [of
    the figs specifically for the Sabbath renders them] forbidden
    (*špyqn 'šwr mpny ššpq mwkn 'šwr*)[11] [i.e., since the identity
    of the figs is in question, there is doubt as to whether they
    have indeed been set aside for the Sabbath].

F. *A basket [of untithed produce designated for] the Sabbath--*

G. *the house of Shammai declare it exempt [from the removal of*
    tithes].

H. *But the House of Hillel declare it liable [to the removal of*
    tithes] [= M. 4:2D-F].

I. R. Judah says, "Hillel himself used to forbid it."

                          T. 3:2b (B-C = M. Bes. 1:4;
                          F-H = M. Ed. 4:10)

J. *One who gathers a basket [of produce] to send to his fellow*
    [for the Sabbath], shall not eat [any of the produce] unless
    he tithes [= M. 4:2G].

K. R. Judah says, "Hillel himself used to forbid it."

                          T. 3:3

L. One who transports [untithed] figs from place to place [before
    they are rendered liable] [cf. M. 2:3A, T. 2:1A],

M. and the Sabbath occurred [before the end of the journey]
    (*w^c brh ^c lyhn šbt*)--

N. at the close of the Sabbath, he shall not eat [even a snack]
    unless he tithes [cf. M. 4:2C].

O. R. Judah says, "Hillel himself used to forbid it."

                          T. 3:4 (pp. 237-38, ls. 2-8)
                          (F-O = T. Ed. 2:4,
                          L-N: cf. b. Bes. 35a)

    Two autonomous units, A-E and F-O, have been joined together
so that their individual citations of M. 4:2 (at A, F-H and J)
follow the sequence in which these appear in M. This gives the
impression of a running commentary to M.--but the impression is
false. Although A cites M., the case presented at B-E has little
bearing on the problem of tithes.[12] Similarly, F-O's citations of
M. are not intended to instruct us further in the logic or scope
of M.'s law. T.'s only concern is to identify Hillel as the
authority behind M. Thus, while T. cites M., it is completely uninterested in contributing to the analysis of M.'s problem.

A-F shows that the rules regarding the preparation and eating
of produce on the Sabbath are identical to those governing Festival
Days. On both days, it is forbidden to eat what has not already
been set aside in preparation for that day (cf. Maimonides, *Comm.*,
M. Bes. 1:1). The model for T.'s case appears at M. Bes. 1:4:

A. [If before the Festival Day] he designated (*zmn*) black [pigeons
    as his Festival meal], but [on the Festival Day] he found white
    [pigeons in their place];
B. [or if beforehand he designated] white [pigeons], but [after-
    ward] he found black [pigeons in their place];
C. [or if beforehand he designated] two [pigeons], but [after-
    ward] he found three [pigeons in their place]--
D. [those which he found on the Festival Day] are forbidden
    [for the Festival meal].

Aside from the operative verbs (*zmn* vs. *tmnw*), and the language I
have interpolated in brackets, M. Bes. 1:4A-B = A-C.[13] In both
pericopae, white food items have been set aside in one place,
while black food items have been set aside in another (so b. Bes.
5a, s.v., '*mr rb'*). On the Sabbath or Festival Day it is discovered that there has been a switch--black food items occupy the
place formerly containing the white, while white food items are
found where the black once stood. It is possible that someone
has merely switched the two, setting white where the black were
and *vice versa*. In this case, both sets of food items would be
permitted on the Sabbath or Festival, since both were properly
designated beforehand. Only their location has changed. However,
it is also possible that entirely undesignated white food items
have been substituted for the black, and so on. For this reason,
M. Bes. 1:4D prohibits its pigeons for consumption on the Festival
Day, for there is doubt as to whether they have been properly
designated. Similarly, D of our pericope rules that the doubt
regarding the identity of the figs prevents their preparation for
use in the Sabbath meal. E, despite the uncertainty of its textual
tradition, glosses D with the observation that since the identity
of the figs is in doubt, there is doubt as to whether they have
indeed been set aside for the Sabbath. The point appears redundant,
and supports Lieberman's suggestion that D and E are conflations
of two independent apodoses to A-C.

F-O is independent from the foregoing in both form and substance. The unit is composed of three elements: two citations
of M. (E-H, J) and one case (L-N) employing a variant of M. 4:2C's
apodosis. The whole is knit together by Judah's identical glosses

at I, K and O. The polemical character of the unit is evident in
these glosses, which are uninterested in the substance of M., but
rather seek to show that its laws derive from Hillel himself.[14]
T. argues that M.'s rulings are ancient--hence unchallengeable--
positions. This polemic confirms our suspicion that the material
in M. as well is hardly ancient at all, but rather is at issue
among Ushan circles at the time of M.'s formulation and redaction.[15]

A. Branches of a fig-tree with figs on them (*wbhn t'nym*),
B. [or] fronds of a date palm with dates on them (*wbhn tmrym*)--
C. [if] children or workers brought them [into the house],
    [the produce on the branches or fronds] is exempt;
D. [if] the householder brought them [into the house],
    [the produce on the branches or fronds] is liable.

T. 3:5a (p. 238, ls. 8-9)
(cf. T. Y.T. 4:2)

T. is formally independent of M., but assumes M.'s principle
that intention to make a meal of unprocessed produce renders it
liable. Branches with fruit attached to them have been brought
into the house (A-B). M. 3:1A-B, which permits dependents and
employees to make a snack of produce brought into the householder's
courtyard for further processing, would lead us to expect that the
fruit on these branches is also exempt from the law, until some
form of processing takes place. C-D, however, does not address
the issue of processing at all. It merely states that the produce
is liable if the householder himself brings it into his house,
but it is exempt if children or workers do so. The point can only
be that the act of bringing the produce into the house demonstrates
intention to make a meal of it, despite its crude condition. T.,
in this regard following M. 3:1A-B, claims that affective intention
belongs to the owner of the produce alone. Children and workers,
since their right of possession derives solely from their relationship to the householder, cannot render liable produce which still
belongs to him (cf. M. 2:2). Therefore their intention to make a
formal meal is null.[16]

4:3

A. One who picks olives out of the softening-bin
B. dips [them] one by one in salt, and eats [without tithing].
C. If he salted [them] and placed [them] before him, he is re-
    quired [to tithe].
D. R. Eliezer says, "[If he picked them] from a bin [of olives

which were preserved in] cleanness (mn $hm^c tn$ $hthrh$), he is
required [to tithe],

E.   "but [if he picked them] from [a bin of olives which had been
     rendered] unclean (mn htm'), he is exempt [from tithing],

F.   "because he returns the surplus [to the bin of unclean
     olives]."

                         M. 4:3 (A = y. Ned. 2:4, 6:3;
                         A-F = b. Bes. 35a)

A-C continues the unit's interest in explaining how a person's
intended use of produce affects his obligation to tithe it. The
olives in the bin are awaiting pressing for their oil. Since the
owner views the olives primarily as a source of oil, they are not
yet regarded desirable as food. As a non-food, therefore, they
need not be tithed if a snack is made of some of them prior to the
pressing of the remainder. Problems arise only if the owner of
the olives removes some of them from the bin and salts them (C),
for the salting prepares the olives for use as food in their own
right. These olives, consequently, must be tithed, for they have
been separated from the batch and prepared for a purpose other than
pressing for oil (MR).[17] A single olive removed from the bin,
however, is permitted, even if it is salted (B). Like the fig
plucked in a courtyard (M. 3:8A-C), the single olive continues to
enjoy the status of its original batch, and may be eaten without
the removal of tithes, regardless of further preparation.

     Eliezer's gloss at D-E, explained at F, refines the problem
of A-C.[18] A person who simply picks olives out of the softening
bin gives no indication of his intended use of them. On the basis
of his actions alone, therefore, it is impossible to determine
whether olives he eats must be tithed. Eliezer's point is that the
householder's intentions may be inferred from factors which have
little to do with the actions of removal and consumption. If, for
example, the householder has prepared olives in strict observance
of the laws of cleanness, we may assume that he has no intention
of returning to the batch any olives he may remove. As he removes
them, the olives are made unclean by his hands and if returned,
will render unclean the entire batch in the bin.[19] We may safely
assume, then, that the householder has no desire to waste, by a
single careless act, all the trouble he has invested in preserving
the cleanness of the olives during their harvest and processing.
Since the olives are removed permanently, we are therefore entitled
to assume that they are no longer intended for use as oil, but
instead are deemed set aside, e.g., for use in a meal. As such,
they are liable to the removal of tithes before they may be eaten.

If, on the other hand, the olives in the bin are already unclean,
we learn nothing about the householder's intentions when he removes
a batch of them. Since they may be returned to the batch without
waste, we must wait for some further action on the householder's
part before the liability of the olives can be determined. Presumably, they remain permitted as a snack unless the householder
salts them (A-C) or in some other way prepares them for use as a
meal.

A.   They said before R. Eliezer, "Even though he does not (š'yn,
     following E) return them [i.e., the olives of M. 4:3A] to this
     bin, lo, he returns them to another bin."[20]

T. 3:7a (p. 238, ls. 12-13)

T. glosses Eliezer's ruling at M. 4:3D-F. Sages point out
that, according to Eliezer's own logic, it is impossible to determine the householder's intentions as he removes a batch of clean
olives from the bin. Even though he will not return the now unclean olives to the bin from which he has removed them, he may
nevertheless return them to another bin of unclean olives. Thus
Sages argue that, in the case presented by Eliezer, the householder's actions remain ambiguous and offer no clue as to his
intentions. The produce, therefore, remains permitted as a snack
until the householder's intentions are clarified.

A.   Pits [filled with] arum--
B.   [and] he selects the thick [stalks] while permitting the thin
     [stalks] to remain [in the pit]--
C.   [if he keeps the stalks] in his hand (btwk ydw, following E,
     G), lo, this one is exempt [from tithing the stalks].
D.   [But if he places the stalks] on the ground or in a container,
     lo, this one is required [to tithe the stalks].
E.   Said R. Simeon b. Eleazar, "The House of Shammai and the House
     of Hillel did not dispute that one who selects [arum from the
     pit and places it] on the ground is exempt [from tithing], and
     that one who selects [the arum and places it] in a container
     is required to tithe.
F.   "Concerning what did they dispute? Concerning one who selects
     [arum from the pit and keeps it] in his hand, for
G.   "the House of Shammai require [him to tithe], but the House of
     Hillel exempts [him from tithing]."

T. 3:10 (p. 239-40, ls. 28-32)
(F-H: cf. M. Bes. 1:8)

While the pericope has been redacted within T.'s discussion
of M. 5:1-2, it clearly presents a case dependent upon the issues
of M. 4:3. Arum, like the olives of M. 4:3A, has been left in
pits to soften, but its processing remains incomplete, for some
stalks remain hard and thin. The problem is to determine whether
the householder, who removes the softened (i.e., thick) stalks,
intends to use them in a meal. As M. 4:3B-C suggests, we assume
he intends a snack as long as he eats only what his hand can hold.
But if he places the stalks before him on the ground or in a
container, he is required to tithe. By creating a separate batch
of produce, the householder indicates intention to make a meal.

Simeon b. Eleazar, at E-G, revises an assumed Houses-dispute,
which is not before us. He argues that the Houses differ concerning the arum which the man has kept in his hand. The Shammaites
require the man to tithe, while the Hillelites exempt him from
tithing. Apparently, the Shammaites consider the softened arum to
be completely processed, regardless of the fact that the entire
batch is not yet ready for use. Since the processing of the arum
in hand is complete, even a snack is forbidden unless tithes are
removed. The Hillelites, however, stand within the presuppositions
of M. 4:3A-C. they hold that the processing of the entire batch
is incomplete. Therefore, by taking one stalk, the man has not
displayed intention to make a meal, and is therefore exempt from
tithing until he actually appropriates the produce for that
purpose.[21]

4:4

A.   "One drinks [wine] at the press ($\check{s}wtym$ ^{c}l hgt)[22]--

B.   "whether [it is mixed] with hot water or cold water--

C.   "(six MSS. add: w-, "and") he is exempt [from removing the
     tithes]"--the words of R. Meir.

D.   R. Eleazar bar Sadoq declares [him] liable [to removing the
     tithes].

E.   But Sages say, "Concerning [the wine mixed with] hot water,
     he is liable [to removing the tithes], but concerning [the
     wine mixed with] cold water, he is exempt [from removing the
     tithes]."

                         M. 4:4 (A-E = b. Shab. 11b,
                         b. Erub 99b; cf. M. Erub. 10:6)

Meir and Eleazar bar Sadoq dispute an issue far removed from
the problem of intention (A + C-D). At issue is whether wine

drunk at the vat is processed, and therefore liable to the removal
of tithes before it may be drunk (cf. M. 1:7W-Y). Only Sages'
gloss at E, and the accompanying interpolation at B, brings the
pericope within the wider range of M. 4:1-5D's interests. Now,
as at M. 4:3F, at issue is whether the wine, once removed from the
vat and mixed with water, is intended to be used as a separate
batch of wine.[23]

A-C's dispute concerns a matter already settled at M. 1:7W-Y
which states that wine is liable to the removal of tithes when it
is skimmed at the vat, for at this point its processing is complete.
This is the position of Eleazar bar Sadoq (C), who forbids the
owner to take a cup of wine as a snack from the skimmed vat unless
he tithes the wine remaining in the vat. Meir, who objects, must
hold that the skimming of wine is not its point of liability to
the law of tithes. Wine, rather, becomes liable at some later
point (e.g., when it is stored away in jars).[24] Wine drunk at
the vat, therefore, remains permitted as a snack without the
removal of tithes.

Sages (E) carry forward the position of Meir, for they assume
that, all things being equal, one is permitted to sample untithed
wine at the vat. Sages, due to the skill of our unit's redactor,
simply point out that Meir's position must be modified in view of
the householder's intended use of the wine. It is customary, for
example, to thin wine with water before drinking (e.g., M. Ber.
8:2). According to Sages, who in this regard are precise followers
of Eliezer (M. 4:3D-F: cf. b. Shab. 11b), the liability of the
thinned wine to the removal of tithes depends entirely upon whether,
after having been mixed, it can be returned to the vat without
damaging the rest of the wine. As at M. 4:3, therefore, we assume
that the householder intends his drink to be no more than a snack,
after which he shall return to the vat whatever remains in the cup.
The wine, it follows, need not be tithed. Wine mixed with hot
water, however, cannot be returned to the vat without killing
bacteria necessary for the fermentation of the wine. Since the
householder has made it impossible to return the wine, we assume
that he never intended to snack on it at all, but rather has a
meal in mind. As we would expect, he is now required to tithe the
wine before he uses it.[25]

4:5-6

A. One who husks barley (*hmqlp bs^cwrym*) removes the husks (*mqlp*)
    [from the kernels] one by one, and eats [without tithing].

B. But if he husked [a few kernels] and placed [them] in his
    hand, he is required [to tithe].

C. One who husks parched kernels of wheat (*hmwll mlylwt*)[26] sifts
    [the kernels] from hand to hand, and eats [without tithing].

D. But if he sifted [the kernels] and placed [them] inside his
    shirt, he is required [to tithe].

E. Coriander which [the farmer] sowed [in order to harvest its]
    seed [for future sowing] (*zr^ch lzr^c*)--its leaves are exempt
    [from the removal of tithes if they are eaten] (*yrqh ptwr*)

F. [If he] sowed it [in order to harvest its] leaves [for use as
    an herb] (*zr^ch lyrq*)--[both] the seeds and the leaves are
    subject to the law of tithes (*mt^csrt zr^c wyrq*).

G. R. Eleazar[27] says, "Dill is subject to the law of tithes [in
    regard to its] seeds, leaves and pods" (*mt^csrt zr^c wyrq
    wzyryn*).

H. But Sages say, "Nothing is subject to the law of tithes [in
    regard to both its] seeds and leaves save cress and field-
    rocket[28] alone" (*'ynw mt^csrt ... 'l' ... blbd*).

>   M. 4:5 (A-D = b. Bes. 13b;
>   E-F = y. Kil. 3:6[28d],
>   y. Orl. 1:1[60c]; H = b. A.Z. 7b,
>   cf. T. Sheb. 2:7)

I. Rabban Gamaliel[29] says, "Stalks of fenugreek, mustard plants,
    and fava plants (*pwl hlbn*)[30] are subject to [the law of]
    tithes" (*hybt bm^csr*).

J. R. Eliezer says, "The caper-bush (*slp*)[31] is subject to the law
    of tithes [in regard to its] stalks, berries and blossoms"
    (*mt^csrt tmrwt w'bywnwt wqprś*).

K. R. Aqiba says, "No [part of the caper-bush] is subject to the
    law of tithes except the berries (*'yn mt^csr 'l' 'bywnwt*),

L. "for they are the fruit [i.e., the part normally harvested for
    use as food]."

>   M. 4:6 (I = y. Ma. 1:1[48d];
>   J-K = b. Ber. 36a)

    The present division of the pericope into A-H and I-L has been
incorrectly imposed upon the text by copyists and is followed un-
critically by subsequent printers.[32] The natural divisions are
the doublet at A-D, which continues the theme of M. 4:1ff., and
E-L, a formally autonomous pericope which addresses a fresh issue
entirely. Since formal difficulties internal to E-L require us

to have all of its elements before us, I have presented the two pericopae as a single unit. Discussion of its major parts, however, will proceed independently.

A-D concludes M.'s discussion of criteria for determining whether a householder intends to use untithed produce in a meal. While the formal balance of the doublet is an aesthetically satisfying conclusion to a thematic unit, the substance of the rulings offers little that is new or challenging. The point in both cases is that a man's consumption of untithed produce is deemed a snack, and is exempt from the removal of tithes, only if he removes whatever he eats directly from the unprocessed batch itself. At A-B, for example, the husker may remove an unhusked kernel from the batch, husk it and eat it without tithing. Should he husk a few kernels and set them aside, however, he must tithe that batch before eating a single kernel. These are deemed to have been designated for a specific use and are as a consequence liable to the removal of tithes (cf. M. 3:8A-C). C-D is slightly more sophisticated. The householder is winnowing the husks from the wheat by sifting the kernels from hand to hand. While sifting, he may eat one kernel at a time, for at no point are the kernels ever gathered into a separate container (i.e., his hand; cf. M. 4:1I). Should he collect some inside his shirt, however, he must tithe them before eating, for the husked kernels have been gathered into a distinct batch, separate from the kernels which remain in the midst of their processing (M. 4:3A-C).

The issue which we have identified as so crucial to M. 4:1-5D, the affect of a person's intentions, is carried into a new range of problems by E-L, an entirely autonomous set of materials. The primary assumption of E-L is that a farmer's intended disposition of his crop when he sows it determines whether or not it shall be subject to the law of tithes when he harvests it. Thus a crop shall be deemed food, and shall be subject to the law of tithes (M. 1:1), only if the farmer sowed the crop for food in the first place. Our pericope presents two conflicting applications of this assumption. E-J, while hardly a unitary set of materials, nevertheless proposes a single thesis, that all edible parts of a plant sown for food are subject to the law, even if some parts of the plant are not usually desired for their food value.[33] K-L, on the other hand, argues that the intention to use a crop for food subsumes under the law of tithes only that part of the plant which is normally eaten. Underlying these conflicting views is disagreement as to whether an individual's private intentions, on the one

hand, or normal public custom, on the other, determine the fact
that a plant is a food.

Before proceeding to the details of E-L's two positions, a
number of literary problems require our attention. On the surface,
E-L is composed of two basic units, the paired rulings at E-F, and
the formally identical disputes at G-H and J-K (+L), separated by
a singleton at I. These materials are arranged according to the
relevant realia, with E-H discussing, in general, seeds and leaves,
and I + J-L concerned for the most part with stalks and berries.
This evident concern for organizing materials according to realia,
however, has created literary problems which substantially affect
the sense of the pericope. We may begin with G-H, the dispute
between Eleazar and Sages. Sages, we note, are not in conversation with Eleazar at all, for while he presents a thesis regarding
"seeds, leaves and pods," Sages know only "seeds and leaves."
Indeed, Sages' lemma (H) is a cogent response to E-F, which is
likewise concerned only with seeds and leaves. H, then, appears
to gloss E-F, and offers no dispute to Eleazar.[34] If so, the
interpolation of G requires explanation. Such explanation emerges
from the observation that J, attributed to Eliezer, is formally
identical to G: X $mt^{c}sr/t$ A + B + C. The formal identity and
substantive similarity of the lemmae suggests that prior to
redaction in the present context G + J comprised a matched pair,
probably in Eliezer's name.[35] The pair, we may suppose, has been
separated to conform to the substantive framework of the present
pericope: seeds vs. leaves + stalks vs. berries. G has been
interpolated between F and H to form a dispute with Sages,[36]
while Aqiba's gloss to J (K-L) has been formulated in the pattern
of H ('yn $mt^{c}sr$ 'l'). The redactional work now gives us two
formally identical "disputes," G-H and J-K + L. The singleton at
I, in turn, establishes the thematic separation desired by the
redactor. Relevant to J-L alone, I distinguishes the disputes
from one another and establishes I + J-L as its own substantive
unit. As we turn now to the interpretation of E-L's law, our
exposition will necessarily follow the proposed reconstruction of
its constituent parts: E-F + H, I, G + J-L.

The issue is set at E-F. A farmer sows a crop which may be
used either for its agricultural value as a seed-bearing plant,
or for its food-value as an herb. According to E-F the inclusion
of the crop under the category of tithable produce depends entirely
upon the intentions of the farmer when he sows the seed for the
new crop. If his intention is primarily to collect seed for
future sowing, even the edible leaves are exempt from the removal

of tithes, for the plant itself is destined for use as a non-
food (E). Should the farmer sow his seed in order to harvest the
crop for its leaves, however, even the seeds must be tithed (F).
Since these can be eaten, they share the status of the desired
leaves, and are subject to all laws applicable to food crops. The
Sages' objection at H concerns F's notion of the value of coriander
seed, rather than the general principle, with which they agree.
Sages assume that coriander seed is useless as food, and therefore
can never be subject to the law. They argue that only the seeds
of cress and field-rocket are edible and, therefore, tithable if
the herbs are used for food.

     Gamaliel (I) follows the principle of E-F as well. He holds
that the stalks of fenugreek, mustard and fava plants may be useful as food if pickled (T. 3:7c) or boiled (y. Ma. 1:1[48d]).
If such plants are grown for their berries, seeds or beans, it
follows that their stalks as well are subject to the law.[37] The
same point, of course, informs Eleazar/Eliezer at G + J. If dill
is sown for its spicy leaves, all parts of the plant which carry
that flavor must also be tithed (G). Matters are the same with
caper, also used to spice food (J). Only Aqiba (K-L) stands
against the prevailing theory of the pericope. He argues that no
part of the caper-plant need be tithed except the berries themselves, for these alone are normally used for food.[38] The point
must apply as well to dill, fenugreek, etc. Only that part of the
plant which normally serves as food is subject to the law of
tithes, even if the farmer chooses to eat a part of the plant
which is normally uneaten. For Aqiba, then, food is decidedly
not in the eye of the beholder. Only that which is normally
desirable as food is deemed to be actually desired in all concrete
circumstances. Caprice or perverse appetite have no bearing on
the application of the law of tithes.

A.   [If the householder] brought kernels of grain into his house
     in order to process them into dough, he is exempt [from
     tithing].
B.   [If he brought them into his house] in order to eat them [as]
     parched grain (*mlylwt*),
C.   Rabbi (Lieberman deletes "Meir") requires [him to tithe].
C.   R. Yose b. R. Judah exempts [him from tithing].

                              T. 3:5b (p. 238, ls. 10-11)
                              (Cf. T. Ter. 3:18, y. Ma. 4:1[51a],
                              b. Bes. 13a)

T. is hardly relevant to M. 4:5A-D, but finds its place here
because it discusses grain. The point of A is that the householder
intends to eat the kernels as bread, not as nuts. Therefore, he
need not tithe whatever kernels he may eat as nuts. The ruling
may be interpreted either within the principles of M. 3:1A-B or
those of M. 4:3A-C. If the former, the point is that the house,
like the courtyard of M. 3:1A-B, does not render liable produce
which is not yet desirable for consumption. If the latter, we
rule that, since the householder wants as food the finished produce (bread, oil), we assume that the raw produce (grain, olives)
is not deemed desirable for its food value in and of itself.

Under dispute at B-C is whether parching is necessary for
the desirability of the grain. For Rabbi, who declares the grain
liable upon entry into the house, the grain is perfectly palatable
whether or not it is parched. He therefore obliges the householder
to tithe it immediately. Yose b. Judah, on the other hand, claims
that the produce need not be tithed until the intended processing
is actually completed.

A. *One who husks barley* [= M. 4:5A]--
B. [if he husked] two [kernels at a time], he is exempt [from
    tithing],
C. [but if he husked] three [kernels at a time], he is required
    [to tithe].
D. But (*w-*) in [the case of] wheat [kernels]--
E. [if he husked] three [kernels at a time], he is exempt [from
    tithing],
F. [but if he husked] four [kernels at a time], he is required
    [to tithe].

                    T. 3:6 (p. 238, ls. 11-12)
                    (A-C: cf. y. Ma. 4:5)

T. cites M. at A, but then goes on to disagree with M. at
B-C and D-F. A separate batch of grain, contrary to M. is con-
stituted by three kernels of barley (C) and four of wheat (F).
A person collecting fewer kernels at one time need not tithe them.
I cannot explain why the quantities differ for barley and wheat.[39]

A. *Coriander which he sowed* [*in order to harvest its*] *seed* [*for
    future sowing*] [= M. 4:5E],
B. but [before harvesting the seed] he decided [to harvest] the
    leaves (*hšb* *ᶜlyh lyrq*)--
C. [*both*] *the seeds and the leaves are subject to the law of tithes*
    [= M. 4:5F].

D. Mustard which he sowed [in order to harvest its] seed [for use
    as a condiment],

E. but [before harvesting the seed] he decided [to harvest] the
    leaves--

F. [both] the seeds and the leaves are subject to the law of
    tithes.

G. "[In the case of mustard] they [i.e., Sages] treated its leaves
    as permissible" (*nhgw byrqw htyr*, following Lieberman's
    emendation)--the words of R. Eliezer.

> T. 3:7b (p. 238, ls. 13-15)
> (A-F: cf. T. Sheb. 2:7;
> G: cf. y. Ma. 4:6[51c])

A-C and D-F form a doublet, with G glossing D-F. T. adds an
important qualification to M. 4:5E-F's theory of intention. As
A-C points out, if the householder does in fact harvest the edible
coriander leaves prior to the harvest of the seeds, the entire
plant--leaves and seeds--becomes subject to the law of tithes.
Once the intention to use part of the plant as food is made clear,
the entire plant becomes subject to the law, as if the plant had
originally been sown for food (M. 4:5I-J). This, clearly, would
surprise the authorities behind M. 4:1-5D, who assume that an
intention, once formulated, governs the interpretation of all
subsequent actions.

The formal similarity of A-C and D-F obscures the fact that
D-F stakes out a very different case, based upon the ruling of
Eleazar at M. 4:5G. Eleazar suggests that even if the householder
intends to use only one part of a plant as food, other edible
parts are subject to the law. This is precisely the point of D-F.
Since one part of the plant is considered useful as food, all other
edible parts are subsumed under the law whether or not they are
actually destined to be harvested. The gloss at G dismisses D-F
entirely, for it claims that the leaves are exempt from the law
once the householder sows the mustard for the seeds. Eliezer's
point must be that once the householder determines to harvest a
particular part of the crop, other edible parts are no longer subject to the law even if they are harvested. T., then, brings
Eliezer into harmony with Aqiba, M. 4:6K-L.

A. Said R. Joshua ben Qebusa:[40] "Never in my life did I presume
    (*mymy l' gś lyby*) to tell a man, 'Go and pick mustard stalks
    and pickle [them], and you shall be exempt from [removing]
    tithes.'"

B. *Hemtalia* (*hmṭly'*)[41] was not treated by Sages as permissible
    (*l' nhgw bh ḥkmym hyṭyr*)--
    neither [in regard to the removal of] tithes, nor [in regard
    to harvesting it] in the Sabbatical year.
C. When he [i.e., the householder] separates heave-offering [from
    produce derived from any plant having two or more edible parts],
    he separates heave-offering from each [distinct part as heave-
    offering on behalf of other similar parts] (*twrm mkl 'ḥd w'ḥd*),
    for *they do not separate heave-offering from one kind* [*of
    produce*] *on behalf of a different kind* (*'yn twrmyn mmyn* ᶜ*l
    š'ynw mynw*) [= M. Ter. 2:4].[42]

                        T. 3:7c (p. 238-39, ls. 15-19)
                        (A: cf. y. Ma. 1:1[48d])

    T. concludes its discussion of M. 4:5-6 with three miscellane-
ous units. A, an independent lemma, is cited in support of
Gamaliel's ruling (M. 4:6I) that mustard stalks are liable to
tithes.[43] B is relevant to M. 4:5E-F's discussion of conditions
under which seeds are subject to the law of tithes. According to
b. A.Z. 38b,[44] *hemtalia* is a medicinal mixture of various seeds.
Since the mixture is consumed, it may not be used unless it is
tithed, and the seeds from which it is concocted may not be harvested in the Sabbatical year.

    C makes an important contribution to M.'s discussion of
plants having two or more edible parts. If one removes heave-
offering (and tithes) from, e.g., the caper-berry, he is not
permitted to eat from a separate part of the plant, e.g., the
caper-blossom, unless he tithes the blossoms as well.[45] The
point is that each separate part of the plant is regarded as a
distinct kind of produce, even though the entire plant becomes
subject to the law once a single part is designated as the intended
food harvest (cf. M. 5:8H).

MAASEROT CHAPTER FIVE

Chapter Five consists of three basic units, each of which is
thematically linked, in inverse order, to a corresponding unit of
Chapter One. The opening unit of the chapter, M. 5:1-2, addresses
the basic contention of Chapter One's closing unit (M. 1:5-8),[1]
that produce becomes *liable* to the removal of tithes only after it
is harvested and appropriated by the householder. The basic proposition of M. 5:3-6 (+7), the chapter's second unit, is that of the
second unit of Chapter One, M. 1:2-4, which rules that produce becomes *subject* to the law of tithes when it ripens and becomes
edible. The final unit of the chapter, M. 5:8, which offers lists
of produce exempt from the law of tithes, depends for its criteria
upon those presented at M. 1:1, the opening pericope of the tractate. The chapter, obviously, is an excellent conclusion to M.,
balancing Chapter One's thematic sequence (a-b-c) with a complementary one of its own (c-b-a).

The chapter's law, as I have indicated, is largely derivative
of and secondary to that of Chapter One. The primary point of
M. 5:1-2 is made in its opening triplet (A-F). Actions which normally indicate the appropriation of produce, and which therefore
render it liable to the removal of tithes, have no effect prior to
the harvest of the crop. Shoots, therefore, which are uprooted
prior to the normal harvest period, and unharvested produce which
is sold or given away, remain exempt from the law of tithes, even
though under normal circumstances produce subjected to such procedures would be deemed liable.

Central to M. 5:3-6 (+7) is the familiar notion that produce
becomes subject to the law of tithes only when it is ripe or
edible. M. 5:3-4, amplified at M. 5:6, prohibits the sale of
ripened produce or other edible products to persons known to vio-
late M.'s tithing regulations. Prior to the ripening, however, or
if the products are inedible, there is no restriction on the sale.
The reason is that the commodity is not deemed food and, by definition, is exempt from the law of tithes. M. 5:5 approaches the same
problem from a different perspective. An Israelite who acquires a
Syrian field need tithe that field's produce only if it ripens
after he becomes the field's owner. The point is that the Israelite
is responsible for tithing only that produce which becomes subject
to the law under his jurisdiction.

The basic issue of the unit is augmented by a series of
glosses at M. 5:3C, 5:4C-D, 5:5D+I and 5:6 F-H, which consistently
introduce a single point. A mixture of exempt produce and produce
subject to the law of tithes must be tithed according to the
percentage of tithable produce present in the mixture. The assumption is that what is exempt from the law cannot be used to meet
the requirements of the law (cf. M. Ter. 1:10). M. 5:7, which
stands outside the main thematic concerns of its unit, complements
the above series of glosses. It rules that produce, the liability
of which is in doubt, must be tithed if it is adjacent to a batch
of the same type of produce which is certainly untithed.

The chapter concludes, at M. 5:8, with lists of items which
are exempt from the law either because they do not grow in the soil
of the Land of Israel or because they are inedible (M. 1:1A-B).
A gloss adds that the inedible seeds of produce which is declared
heave-offering do not themselves enjoy the status of heave-offering.
They may therefore be eaten by any non-priests who desire them.
The point, superficially related to the glosses of M. 5:3-6, is
that mixtures of edible and inedible produce are taboo as heave-
offering with regard to the edible portion of the mixture alone.

The complementarity of Chapters Five and One consists of more
than thematic interests and redactional structure. Fundamentally,
Chapter Five completes Chapter One's partially-drawn description
of the shared rights of God and the farmer to the produce of the
land. Chapter One, we recall, portrays God and the farmer as
joint-holders of a common stock of produce, with God entitled to
his just share, the tithes, and the farmer entitled to his, the
rest of the harvest. According to Chapter Five, however, the
farmer is not simply the joint-holder of the produce with God.
He is as well the custodian of God's share until such time as this
share is properly removed from the produce held in common. The
point emerges from the central unit of the chapter, M. 5:3-6 (+7).
We are told in a variety of ways that produce which becomes subject
to the law of tithes while under the ownership of the farmer must
be protected from misappropriation until the tithes are removed.
M. 5:3-4 + 6, for example, points out that the farmer must make
sure that tithable produce which leaves his possession will be
tithed by whomever eventually consumes it. The farmer, in other
words, is responsible for ensuring that whatever comes under God's
claim while under his proprietorship is eventually given over to
God. Similarly, at M. 5:5, only that Syrian produce which ripens
under Israelite ownership is deemed under God's ownership as well.
Only such produce, therefore, must be reserved by the farmer for

the removal of tithes. In both instances, the point is clear: an
Israelite who comes to possess produce which is in part owned by
God, must preserve for God that portion which is due him.

T., for the most part, is unremarkable, except for T. 3:8.
The pericope points out that M. 5:3-5 (+7)'s interest in the
farmer's proprietary responsibilities may be read into M. 5:1-2
as well. While M. 5:1A-B permits a farmer to uproot shoots and
transplant them without removing tithes, T. argues that this is the
case only if the farmer transplants the shoots onto his own
property. If the farmer, however, transplants the shoots to
another's property, or transplants them outside the Land of Israel,
or in any other way jeopardizes the eventual removal of tithes
from the matured produce, he must tithe the shoots prior to transplanting. T., therefore, not only supports the conception of
M. 5:3-6 (+7), but argues that it informs the entire chapter, a
proposition which the thematic and redactional traits of Chapter
Five certainly justify.

5:1-2

A.   1) One who uproots shoots from his own [field] and transplants
     [them] within his own [field]

B.   is exempt [from tithing the shoots before replanting them].

C.   2) [If] he purchased [produce] which [was still] attached to
     the ground,

D.   [the produce] is exempt [from the law of tithes until the har-
     vest].

E.   3) [If] he picked (lqt)^{2} [produce] to send to his fellow [prior
     to the harvest],

F.   [the produce] is exempt [from the removal of tithes until the
     recipient processes it for his own use].

G.   R. Eleazar b. Azariah says, "If such as these are for sale in
     the market [at the time the produce is picked],

H.   lo, these are liable [to the removal of tithes before the
     donor sends them to his fellow].

M. 5:1

I.   One who uproots turnips or radishes from his own [field], and
     replants [them] within his own [field]

J.   in order [to harvest] the seeds [for planting],

K.   is required [to tithe the produce before transplanting],

L.   for this [uprooting] is their harvest ($grnn$)^{3}

M. Onions which have taken root ($b\varrho lym\ \check{s}h\check{s}ry\check{s}w$)[4] in the attic are
    insusceptible to uncleanness ($\underline{t}hrw\ ml\underline{t}m'$).
N. [But if] debris [from fallen beams] collapsed about them, and
    they were exposed [to the sky],
O. lo, these are deemed planted in the field [and are therefore
    subject to the law of tithes].

                              M. 5:2 (M: cf. M. Ter. 9:7)

     The pericope's two units, A-L and M-O, are in fact independent
pericopae, and must therefore be discussed separately.[5] A-L is
composed of a couplet, A-B + I-L, into which has been interpolated
a second couplet, C-D + E-F, the latter bearing a gloss at G-H.
Both couplets identify and adjudicate ambiguities in the application of generally-accepted principles. At issue in A-B + I-L are
the conditions under which agriculturally necessary transplanting
is deemed to constitute a harvest, i.e., an act of acquisition
which renders the produce liable to the removal of tithes (cf.
M. 1:5ff.). The problem of C-D + E-F is quite separate, for at
issue here is the liability of produce which is subjected to an
act of acquisition (sale, plucking) prior to the general harvest
of the field in which the produce grows (cf. M. 2:5-6). The fact
that each couplet is concerned with produce which is taken before
its proper harvest explains the redactor's interest in bringing
them together into a single pericope. He has done so, however,
in a way which obscures their formal and substantive differences,
while stressing what is common to both. A-B, C-D and E-F now
constitute a triplet exemplifying the simple proposition that
unharvested produce cannot become liable to the removal of tithes.
I-L, concerned with harvested produce, now appears to gloss the
completed triplet with a complementary clarification. M-O,
formally and substantively autonomous of the foregoing, is tacked
on. It adds to A-B and I-L yet a third case in which we must
determine the liability of uprooted produce which has been returned
to the field.

     Once the pericope's formal units are sorted out, its sub-
stance presents few difficulties. The interpretive crux of A-B +
I-L is the contrast between shoots, which are inedible, and
radishes and turnips, which may serve as food. Since the shoots
are of no value unless replanted for further growth,[6] their uprooting is not deemed a harvest. As unharvested produce, no tithes
need be removed from them (even, one supposes, if the farmer nibbles
on them). The uprooted radishes and turnips (I-K), on the other
hand, must be tithed before transplanting, for the period during

which they are uprooted is the only point in their growth at which
they are both edible and available for use as food. The uprooting,
in other words, is the only harvest the roots will undergo. Even
though the farmer has no plans to eat them, he must tithe them before transplanting, just as if the roots were harvested as a food
crop.[7]

Despite the formal identity of the stichs of the second couplet, C-D and E-F, each ruling makes its own independent point.
C-D states that produce purchased while it is still growing is
exempt from the law of tithes. This is obvious, for an assumed
datum of M. is that the purchaser of untithed produce need not
tithe it until he takes possession of it (cf. M. 2:5-6). Since
the purchaser cannot do so until after the harvest, the produce
remains exempt until that time. The couplet's second ruling, E-F,
illustrates a problem relevant to the laws concerning *demai*-
produce, i.e., produce concerning which there is doubt as to
whether or not the tithes have been removed.[8] The farmer has
picked some of his pre-harvest produce (MR) as a gift for a
friend. Normally, produce sent as a gift must be tithed by the
sender, as a precaution on behalf of the recipient. The latter,
thinking the produce has been tithed, might unwittingly consume
produce which is indeed *ṭebel* (cf. M. Dem. 3:3, T. Dem. 3:14).
Produce taken from an unharvested field, however, requires no such
precautions. We assume that the recipient, who knows the harvest
is not yet in, will presume the produce to be untithed. The
sender, therefore, need not tithe the gift, for he can expect the
recipient to do so before he consumes the produce. Eleazar b.
Azariah adds a useful observation at G-H.[9] He points out that if
produce of the type sent as a gift is already being marketed,
then the gift must be tithed by the farmer before he sends it
off. The recipient, Eleazar argues, is likely to assume that the
gift has been purchased and, like all purchases, has already been
tithed. In order to prevent the recipient from mistakenly eating
the produce without tithing, the donor must remove the tithes on
his friend's behalf.

The autonomous pericope at M-O is hardly appropriate to our
tractate, but, as I said, is intended to offer yet a third rule
regarding uprooted produce which has been returned to the earth.
The pericope provides two different kinds of "replanting," each
with appropriate consequences for the produce involved. The onions
of M have been harvested, presumably tithed, and then stored away.
If they resume their growth in the dirt floor of the attic, they
are deemed to be attached to the ground, and like all produce

attached to the ground, are insusceptible to receiving uncleanness
(cf. M. Uqs. 2:9-10, M. Ter. 9:7). The important point for the
present context is made at N-O, which assumes that the law of
tithes applies only to field-planted produce. If the roof of the
attic caves in and the sprouts of the onions are exposed, the
onions are now treated as if they are planted in a field, with the
earth of the attic beneath them and the open sky above. The point,
unstated in M., is that the onions once again become subject to
the law of tithes as if they had been replanted as a new crop. If
the householder goes up into his attic to get some onions for
dinner, he must tithe them before eating, for his uprooting of the
onions is now deemed a new harvest.

A. *One who uproots shoots from his own [field]* [= M. 5:1A]
B. in order to plant them
    1) outside the Land [of Israel] or
    2) as a seed crop (lzr^c),
C. or in order to
    1) declare [the uprooted shoots] ownerless, or
    2) to sell [the uprooted shoots] to a Gentile--
D. lo, this one [i.e., the farmer] is required [to tithe the
    uprooted shoots],
E. for [by his act] he removes them from the category of [produce
    subject to the law of] tithes (*mwṣy' mydy m^{c}srwt*).
F. R. Judah said in the name of R. Eleazar b. Azariah, "One who
    sends his fellow shoots, softened olives (reading with HD,
    Lieberman: ^{c}*tynyn*), or uncrushed flax (*hwṣny pštn*)--
G. "[the recipient] tithes them [as he would tithe] produce which
    is certainly untithed (*wdyy*),
H. "for most people are suspect concerning [the proper tithing]
    of these [types of produce, since their processing is not
    complete]."
I. But Sages say, "Lo, these are considered [in the same category]
    as all [other] produce, and [the recipient] need tithe them
    only as produce which is doubtfully tithed."

                         T. 3:8 (p. 239, ls. 19-23)
                         (F-H: cf. y. Ma. 5:1[51c])

    A-E, an important supplement to M. 5:1A-B, makes its point
at E. Once produce has become subject to the law of tithes, the
householder must see to it that it will eventually be tithed. If,
therefore, he uproots shoots from his land, he may neither transplant (B) nor relinquish ownership of them (C) if this entails the
possibility that the produce will be consumed in an untithed

condition. T.'s point, as we shall see, is basic to our interpretation of M. 5:3ff.

In the dispute at F-I, Judah assigns to Eleazar the logical consequence of the latter's position at M. 5:1G-H. That is, if a gift of produce is obviously unmarketable, the recipient must assume that the sender has not removed the tithes (= M. 5:1E-F). Sages (I), to the contrary, hold that the condition of the produce allows us to assume nothing regarding its tithing status. The produce, therefore, is tithed in the manner prescribed for doubtfully-tithed produce (cf. T. Dem. 3:14).

A. *Onions which have taken root* among each other in a bin [cf. M. 5:2M]--
B. lo, they are in their [prior] status (*bḥzqtn*) regarding [the removal of] tithes and [laws restricting the use of produce grown in] the Seventh Year.
C. If they were unclean, they have not left their unclean status (reading with E, *ed. princ.*: *l' ᶜlw ydy ṭwm'tn*).
D. And it is permitted to pick them on the Sabbath.
E. [If] they have taken root among each other in the dirt (*qrqᶜ*) of an attic [cf. M. 5:2M],
F. lo, they are in their [prior] status regarding [the removal of] tithes and [laws restricting the use of produce grown in] the Seventh Year.
G. But if they were unclean, they have left their unclean status.
H. And it is forbidden to pick them on the Sabbath.
I. But if he picked them [anyway], he is exempt [from punishment as a violator of the Sabbath].
J. [*If*] *debris collapsed about them and they were exposed* [*to the sky*], *lo, these are considered planted in the field* [= M. 5:2 N-O].
K. [And they are] forbidden [from being tended] in the Seventh Year, and are liable to tithes [if they are picked during the six years of the Sabbatical cycle].

T. 3:9 (p. 239, ls. 23-28)
(A-I: cf. y. Ma. 5:2[51d])

T. offers a pericope worthy of M. Building upon the obscure foundations of M. 5:2M-O, the pericope shows that the full complement of laws regarding the tithing of agricultural produce applies only when the onions return entirely to the status of a field-planted crop. The onions at A have sprouted in a bin, and in no way are to be viewed as having received nourishment from the earth. They therefore remain in the status of picked onions, and their

disposition is governed by all laws appropriate to plucked produce. If they had already been tithed, they need not be tithed
again; or if they had been harvested in the sixth year and sprouted
in the Seventh Year, Sabbatical restrictions do not apply to them
(B). Similarly, if they had become unclean, they remain so, for
they are not deemed to have returned to the earth (C). If follows
as well that Sabbath restrictions against plucking produce do not
apply (D: cf. M. Bes. 5:2).

E-I parallels M. 5:2M, which specifically addresses the
problem of produce growing in the attic. The house itself is
considered to be firmly attached to the ground. The onions taking
root in the dirt of the attic, therefore, share that status. Thus
they become free of their former uncleanness (G), as M. has said,
and may not be plucked on the Sabbath (H). I, a gloss, points out
the ambiguity of the case. Its point is simply that even though
the onions may be technically rooted in the ground, they are in
fact simply sitting in an attic. Therefore, even though the householder ought not pluck these onions on the Sabbath, he incurs no
penalty if he does so. The important point is at E-F, which repro-
duces B. Although the onions are rooted in the earth, they remain
in the status of produce growing in the house. Since the agricultural laws of tithes and the Sabbatical Year apply only to produce
of the field, the onions remain in their former status regarding
these laws.

J-K brings us to M. 5:2F-H. Once the roof collapses and the
onions are exposed to the sky, they are in all respects like produce which has been growing in the field. If the householder
picks them, he is required to tithe, even if they were tithed at
their original harvest. Similarly, if it is the Sabbatical Year,
the produce is subject to all appropriate restrictions regarding
produce of the seventh year of the Sabbatical cycle.

5:3

A. A man shall not sell [a field inclusive of]^{10} his produce which
    has reached the period of its tithing ($m\check{s}b\,'w\ l^cnt\ hm^csrwt$) to
    one who is untrustworthy concerning [the removal] of tithes
    [i.e., an ^{c}am ha'ares].

B. And [he shall] not [sell a field of produce] in the Seventh
    Year to one who is suspected of [violating laws regarding the
    consumption or sale of] Seventh Year [produce].

C. But if [some produce] ripens [prior to the rest of the crop],

he takes the ripe [produce for his own use] and sells the rest
[to whomever he wishes as long as it remains unripened].

M. 5:3 (A-B: cf. T. Sheb. 4:5,
6:20)

The "period of tithing" referred to at A is the point at which
produce has ripened in the field and is subject to the law of
tithes (cf. M. 1:2-4). As we recall, this is the point at which
the produce is deemed edible. The prohibition against selling a
field of ripened produce to an *ʿam ha'ares* is intended to ensure
that all produce which becomes subject to the law of tithes will
eventually be tithed. It follows that prior to the ripening of
the crop, the field may be sold to whomever the farmer wishes.
Since the produce growing in the field is not deemed food until
it ripens, the farmer as yet bears no responsibility for preserving
it for eventual tithing.

A similar restriction is imposed, at B, upon the sale of produce grown in the Seventh Year of the Sabbatical Cycle. During
the Seventh Year, fields belonging to Israelites may not be worked,
and all produce found in them is deemed public property, to be
enjoyed by all passers-by (Lv. 25:1-7). Landlords, it follows,
may not harvest their produce in quantity, nor may they market it
in commercially profitable fashion (cf. M. Sheb. 7:3, 8:3). B
simply points out that the sale, in the Seventh Year, of a field
inclusive of its produce, is permitted only if the customer is
known to respect the restrictions regarding the consumption and
sale of such produce.

C refines A, pointing out that the whole field of produce is
not subject to the status of its part. If the crop is unripened,
with only a small amount of early-ripening produce, the latter
alone may not be sold with the rest of the field. If the farmer
wants to sell the whole field, he must first pick the ripened produce, taking care to tithe it as he normally would. We may note
at this point that C begins a series of formally independent, but
conceptually related, glosses (M. 5:4C-D, M. 5:5I, M. 5:6F-H)
which consistently raise problems regarding the disposition of
fields or mixtures containing various proportions of liable and
exempt produce.

A. One who [publicly] relinquishes ownership of his field (*hmpqyr
    't sdhw*)--
B. [within] two or three days he may retract [his declaration][11]
    [and the field remains in his possession].
C. If he said, "I hereby declare my field ownerless (*hry sdy*

mwpqrt) for one day, for one week (*šbt*), for one month, for
one year, for one Septennate (*šbw*^{c})"--

D. before [the field] is claimed,

E. either by himself or another (*bynw lbyn 'hr*),

F. he may retract his declaration [and the field remains in his
possession].

G. Once [the field] is claimed,

H. either by himself or another,

I. he may not retract [his declaration] [and the field is considered to have been appropriated while ownerless, regardless
of the claimant].

T. 3:11 (p. 240, ls. 32-35)
(A-I = b. Ned. 43b; cf. y. Pe'ah
6:1[19b], y. Ned. 4:10[38d])

The apparently simple ruling at A-B generates C-I, which
explores unforeseen issues arising from the former. Substantively,
T. bears no connection to our tractate, for its interest is the
elucidation of ambiguities regarding both the status of land which
has been declared ownerless, and the rights of the former owner
himself once he has made such a declaration.[12] Thus, T.'s sole
point of contact with M. 5:3 is that, like the latter, T. regulates
the householder's rights regarding the disposition of his field.[13]

A-B establishes a grace-period of three days for retracting
a declaration that one's field is henceforth considered ownerless.
On the surface, the law is straightforward. However, as C-I will
show us, the law raises some interesting problems. In effect, it
gives the householder the right to evict the claimant of the abandoned field within three days of the original declaration. Yet, if
the householder does *not* do so within the stipulated period, the
claimant is considered to have acquired an abandoned field from
the moment he takes possession--even a day after the original
declaration--and may not be evicted by the former owner thereafter.
Paradoxically, then, for a period of three days after the declaration of ownerlessness, the field is both abandoned *and* the property
of the householder, *if* he chooses to exercise his right of retraction. After three days, of course, the householder loses all
rights to the field, and it is abandoned in all respects. If it
remains unclaimed, the former owner may claim it himself.

This latter point is where C-I joins the issue, for its primary assumption is that the former owner of a field acquires the
rights of any other passer-by to claim the field, once it has been
abandoned. The issue, however, is made more complex. The householder has declared the field ownerless for a limited time only,

after which the field shall revert to his possession if it remains
unclaimed. He is, then, in an unusual position. On the one hand,
as at A-B, he is the owner of the field as long as it remains unclaimed; yet, at the same time, he has the rights of the passer-by
to claim the same field during the period for which it has been
declared ownerless. The problem is to adjudicate his use of conflicting rights, for one man cannot act as passer-by and householder
at the same time. D-F states that if the former owner has not
acted as a passer-by in claiming the field, he may exercise his
owner's right to retract the declaration of ownerlessness, provided
that no one else has claimed the field in the interim. If the
field has already been claimed by a passer-by, the new claimant is
understood to have acquired the field while it was ownerless, and
the former owner's subsequent retraction is ineffective. G-I
presents the second logical possibility within the limits of the
case. If the former owner has acted within his rights as a passer-
by and claimed the field for himself, he loses the owner's pre-
rogative of retracting the declaration which rendered the field
ownerless. This loss is meaningless, however, for in all events,
the man has regained possession of his field. His only risk is
that some other passer-by will lay claim to the field before he
himself has the opportunity. In that event, as at D-F, the first
claimant has the right to the field. In sum, then, C-I makes the
simple point that as long as the field is unclaimed, the former
owner can exercise *either* the rights of the passer-by or those of
a householder, but *not* both. Once the field has been claimed by
a second party, however, the problem evaporates, for the field is
now firmly in the possession of another.

A.   (G omits: *w-*) He tethers his beast in the vicinity of (*^{c}l gby*)
     [produce which has been declared] ownerless,
B.   but not in the vicinity of gleanings, forgotten sheaves, or
     [produce left unharvested in] the corner of the field, [for
     these are the property of the poor: Lv. 19:1, Dt. 24:19-22].
C.   Yet he uproots [produce to which the poor are entitled], and
     casts it before her [i.e., the beast], [for now he is disposing
     of what he himself has gathered].
D.   [If] late-ripening figs [remained on the trees] (*'šypt t'nym*),[14]
     but [the householder] was tending his field for [its] grapes,
E.   [or if] late-ripening grapes [remained on the vine], and [the
     householder] was tending his field for [its] greens--
F.   if workers were passing among them [i.e., the late-ripening
     fruit],

G. [and] if the householder scrutinizes their [activities while
   they are in his field] (*mqpyd* ^c*lyhm*)--

H. lo, these [late-ripening fruit] are liable [to the removal of
   tithes].

I. But if not [i.e., if the householder does not scrutinize the
   workers' activities], lo, these [late-ripening fruit] are exempt [from the removal of tithes].

T. 3:12 (p. 240, ls. 35-39)
(D-I: cf. y. Dem. 1:1[21d],
b. Pes. 6b)

A-C adds to T.'s random observations concerning ownerless
produce, but reveals no interest in M. The distinction between
ownerless produce (A) and produce which is considered the property
of the poor (B) is that the former is deemed the property of whoever happens to consume it--including beasts (cf. T. Pe'ah 3:1)--
while gleanings, etc., are specifically designated for the use of
the poor. It follows that a man may tether his beast near abandoned
produce, for whatever the beast eats is considered hers by right.
But the beast, for obvious reasons, does not qualify as a "poor
man." Her owner is therefore forbidden to tether her where she
might by chance nibble at the offerings which belong to the poor.
HD adds that even if the beast's owner is himself a poor man, he
is robbing his fellow paupers by permitting the beast to consume
its fill. C qualifies the above. If the owner--in this case,
certainly a pauper--wishes his beast to eat of the offerings of
the poor, he simply gathers the produce himself and then feeds the
beast. Once he has taken possession of the produce as a poor man,
he may do with it what he wishes.

D-I is autonomous of both A-C and M., but at last shows some
interest in relating the question of abandoned property to the
tithing matters which preoccupy M. The problem is whether late-
ripening produce, which is normally of poor quality and allowed to
rot on the vine after the harvest (cf. Rashi, b. Pes. 6b, s.v.,
whtny'), is considered to be ownerless once the field itself is
being cultivated for a new crop. As we would expect, all depends
upon the intentions of the householder. If he scrutinizes the
activities of workers among the late-ripening fruit, he clearly
demonstrates his intention to maintain control over the disposition
of the produce. Thus the produce remains subject to the law of
tithes, for the householder has not relinquished possession of it.
It follows that if he ignores the worker's actions, he no longer
has any interest in the late-ripening produce, and intends to let
it rot untended. Despite its presence in a tended field, the fruit

in question is considered ownerless, and no longer subject to the
law.

5:4

A.   A man shall not sell his straw, olive-peat or grape-pulp to
     one who is untrustworthy concerning [the removal of] tithes,

B.   [if the purchaser intends] to extract the [potable] liquid
     [remaining in the olive-peat or grape-pulp].

C.   And if [prior to the sale the householder] extracts [edible
     produce from the above waste-products, the extract] is liable
     to [the removal of] tithes, but is exempt from [the separation
     of] heave-offering.

D.   For one who separates heave-offering has in mind [the edible
     produce found among] that which is improperly threshed, and
     that [found] along the edges [of the pile], and that which is
     [found] in the straw.

M. 5:4 (C-D: cf. T. Ter. 3:6)

A carries forward the formulary pattern of M. 5:3A, an apodic-
tic prohibition (*l' ymkr 'dm*), and, according to B, makes the same
point. The manufacturer, like the farmer, must ensure that all
edible produce over which he has control is eventually tithed.
A-B is clear that the liability of a product to the law of tithes
depends upon whether or not its owner deems it to be a food. This
must be borne in mind by anyone seeking to turn a profit from the
sale of agricultural or manufacturing wastes (e.g., for use as
fodder). While straw or mash may indeed be of no use as food to
the processer of grain, wine or oil, he must nevertheless be sure
that anyone to whom he sells these wastes is reliable in the matter
of tithing, for kernels remaining in the straw, or liquid remaining in the mash, may be used as food by the purchaser himself
(cf. M. 5:6). Should the latter consume these without tithing,
the seller will have caused forbidden produce to be consumed as if
it were common food.

A secondary development of A-B, C-D points out that the seller
has the option of extracting the edible substances from the straw
or mash before the sale. Presumably, he may then sell the waste
to whomever he pleases. The problem now, however, is the method of
tithing the edible extract. Since the grain, for example, has
presumably had its heave-offering and tithes removed as soon as it
was piled on the threshing-floor (cf. p. 181, n. 3), we want to
know how to tithe the kernels now removed from the straw, for these

may be considered a separate batch of produce. C's claim, that
only tithes need be removed from the second batch, is explained at
D (cf. M. 1:6U). Heave-offering was separated from the entire
batch of grain--including what is mingled with the discarded
straw--at the time the processing of the batch was completed. The
result is that the heave-offering of the present batch (removed
from the straw) has already been removed on its behalf, and may not
be removed a second time (cf. M. Ter. 3:1). The tithes, however,
are a separate problem. While tithes have been removed from the
original batch of grain, we assume that the householder intended
his tithing to release for use only that batch of grain which he
intended to use as food. Now that he has designated a second
batch of grain for use as food, however, he must remove tithes
from this batch as well.

A. One who winnows his straw without special concern [for removing
    edible kernels] (*štm*),

B. and another purchased it--

C. even [if he purchased the straw] in order to extract [edible
    kernels] from it,

D. he is exempt [from tithing the extracted kernels].

E. Said R. Simeon b. Gamaliel, "The House of Shammai and the House
    of Hillel concur that a man shall not sell a stack of grain,
    or a basket of grapes, or a vat of olives unless [he sells it]
    to a *ḥaber* or (*w-*) one who prepares [his food] in cleanness."

F. He [i.e., a *ḥaber*] sells him [i.e., an *ᶜam ha'areṣ*] wheat,
    even though [the *ḥaber*] knows that [the *ᶜam ha'areṣ*] does not
    knead his dough in cleanness.

G. And similarly, a man shall not give his neighbor a dish [of
    food] (*tbšyl*) to cook [E, G add: for him], or dough to bake
    for him, unless he indeed knows that [the neighbor] removes the
    dough-offering for him (*qwṣh lw ḥlh*), and prepares [the food]
    in cleanness.

H. And similarly, a Levite [shall receive no tithes unless it is
    known that he prepares his food in cleanness: Lieberman] (*wkn
    bn lwy*).

I. (Lieberman emends: Lo,) he [i.e., a *ḥaber*] acquired (*ntmnw lw*)
    tenant-farmers [who were *ᶜamei ha'areṣ*], and they were preparing
    olives--

J. lo, this one [i.e., the *ḥaber*] removes a tenth of the [un-
    tithed] olives and of the untithed oil from [the produce be-
    longing to] his household

K. (Lieberman emends: "and says,") "Whatever these olives [of the

tenant-farmer] are capable of producing, its tithe is in the
southern [portion of the olives which I have separated from my
own produce], and its heave-offering of the tithe is in the
southern-most [tip of the same batch]."

T. 3:13 (pp. 240-41, ls. 39-46)
(E-F: cf. y. Dem. 6:7[25c])

A-D, E-H, and I-K offer materials supplementary to M. 5:3-4's
prohibitions of trade with those who are untrustworthy regarding
tithes. The three units are autonomous of each other, and only
A-D exhibits any literary relationship to M. The case at A-D
differs from that of M. 5:4A-B only in that here the householder
has not winnowed the straw with great care. The consequence, that
perfectly good grain will remain trapped in the straw, indicates
that the householder is unconcerned that the grain will be sold at
the same low price as the straw. In other words, he makes no distinction between the grain and the straw. Therefore, when someone purchases the straw *as straw*, the law takes no account of the
grain purchased along with it. It follows that whatever grain the
purchaser happens to extract is not considered food, and may be
eaten without tithing. T., it appears, takes issue with M. for we
have seen that M. considers the waste products subject to the law
as long as the purchaser intends to derive food from them. T.
argues, to the contrary, that only the intentions of the householder determine the status of the edible produce found within
discarded materials. Since the seller of the straw takes no note
of the grain, the purchaser, regardless of his own evaluation of
the grain in the straw, need not tithe.[15]

The rulings at E-H control the transfer of produce between
those who eat their tithed food in a state of priestly cleanness
(*ḥaberim*) and those who neither tithe nor observe the laws of
cleanness (*ᶜamei ha'areṣ*). While not directly relevant to the law
of tithes, the rulings nevertheless supplement M. 5:3-4's interest
in relations between *ḥaberim* and *ᶜamei ha'areṣ*. The concern of E
is that the *ḥaber* permit none of his produce to leave his possession unless he can ensure that it will be prepared in cleanness.
The point is parallel in principle to that of M., even though it
is under dispute between the Houses at M. Dem. 6:6. F certainly
contradicts E, for it permits precisely what E forbids. I cannot
explain the contradiction.[16] The point of G is that one must
supervise the preparation of one's meals unless the person doing
the preparation can be trusted to preserve the food's cleanness.[17]
The text of H is corrupt, and I have simply supplied, in brackets,
Lieberman's suggested interpretation.

I-K assumes the responsibility of a householder to make sure
that all produce of his fields is properly tithed. The problem at
hand is simply the means by which the householder makes sure that
produce earned by his tenant-farmers is properly tithed. Since
they themselves harvest the produce and take their own portions,
the householder has no opportunity to tithe the produce himself,
for he cannot remove the tithes from what has already become theirs.
He solves the problem by tithing from his own produce on behalf
of the produce belonging to the tenant-farmers. He separates a
quantity of produce from his own stock which is equal to one-tenth
of the quantity taken by the tenant-farmers, and then designates
a portion of it as tithe and heave-offering of the tithe on behalf
of the produce earned by the tenant-farmers. After removing the
sanctified portion, he may consume the rest.[18]

5:5

A. One who purchases a field of greens in Syria--
B. if [he purchased it] before [the produce] reached its period
    of tithing, [he] is required [to tithe the entire harvest],
C. but [if he purchased the field] after [the produce] reached its
    period of tithing, he is exempt [from tithing the entire har-
    vest].
D. And he gathers [late-ripening produce] as he pleases.
E. R. Judah says, "Also: let him hire workers to pick [the pro-
    duce for him]" (*llqt*, following O[2]).
F. Said R. Simeon b. Gamaliel, "Under what circumstances [must he
    tithe produce of a Syrian field which he purchased prior to
    the crop's period of tithing]? When (*bzmn š-*) he acquired the
    land [along with the produce].
G. "But when (*'bl bzmn š-*) he did not acquire the land--
H. "if [he purchased the produce even] before it reached its
    period of tithing, he is exempt [from tithing the harvest]."
I. Rabbi says, "Also: [if he purchased the field after most of
    the produce reached its tithing season, he tithes] according
    to the percentage [which ripens after his purchase]" (*'p lpy
    hšbwn*).

                    M. 5:5 (A-F = y. Ma. 1:4[49a])

    Produce of fields in Syria is subject to the law of tithes
only if the field is owned by an Israelite.[19] A-C assumes this
postulate, but adds an important refinement based upon M.'s
notion that produce becomes subject to the law of tithes only when

it ripens (M. 1:2-3, cf. M. 5:3). An Israelite who acquires a
field in Syria need tithe the produce of that field only if the
produce was unripe at the time of purchase and later ripened under
his ownership (B). Produce ripening before the Israelite acquires
the field (C) need never be tithed, for at the time at which it
could have become subject to the law it was beyond Israelite
jurisdiction.

The series of glosses to this ruling may be grouped into three
independent units, D+I, E, and F-H. D+I offers a dispute concerning the purchaser's obligation to tithe late-ripening produce,
which reaches maturity after the field of ripe produce at C has
been purchased (so T. 3:14). D permits the purchaser to make
tithe-free use of the late-ripening produce, even though it has
ripened under his ownership.[20] The point seems to be that the
status of the smaller percentage of the produce is judged by the
status of the field as a whole. This notion is disputed by Rabbi
(I), whose opinion, unaccountably, has been placed at the end of
the pericope. Rabbi holds to the literal meaning of A-C, that
Syrian produce ripening under Israelite ownership must be tithed.
He maintains, therefore, that the purchaser of a field containing
both ripe and unripe produce must tithe that percentage of the
crop which was unripe at the time of the purchase.

Of the remaining glosses, E and F-H, only E presents a difficulty. I cannot determine what is at stake for Judah, for I do
not know why someone would object to the hiring of workers to
harvest either the crop of B or that of C (but cf. MR).[21] Simeon
b. Gamaliel's gloss of A-C (F-H) is obvious. If the crop alone
was purchased, but not the land, the produce remains exempt
regardless of when the purchase took place, for it is the ownership
of the land which imposes liability upon the crop.

A. *One who purchases a field of greens in Syria--if* [*he purchased
    it*] *before* [*the produce*] *reached its period of tithing,* [*he*] *is
    required* [*to tithe the entire harvest*] (*ḥyyb*, following
    Lieberman). [*If he purchased it*] *after* [*the produce*] *reached
    its period of tithing, he is exempt* [*from tithing the entire
    harvest*] (*pṭwr*, following Lieberman) [= M. 5:5A-C].
B. "*He gathers* [*late-ripening produce*] *as he pleases,* and is
    exempt [from tithing]"--the words of R. Aqiba [cf. M. 5:5D].
C. But Sages say, "Also: [if he purchased the field] after [the
    produce] reached its tithing season, he is required [to tithe]
    according to the percentage [which ripens after the purchase]"
    [cf. M. 5:5I].

D. Sages concede to R. Aqiba that if he [i.e., the Syrian] sold to
    [the Israelite] grain [ready] to reap (*lqṣwr*), or grapes [ready]
    to harvest (*lbṣwr*), or olives [ready] to pick (*lmṣwq*), he [i.e.,
    the Israelite] gathers as he pleases and is exempt [from tith-
    ing that which ripens after the harvest].

                              T. 3:14 (p. 241, ls. 46-50)
                              (D: cf. y. Ma. 5:4[51d], b. Hul.
                              136a)

    T. not only makes important formal improvements of M. 5:5,
but, further, attributes to Aqiba the basic position of M. After
citing M. at A, B-C recasts, as a dispute between Aqiba and Sages,
the disconnected stichs of M. 5:5D and I (attributed in M. to
Rabbi).[22] Formally, the fact that Sages, D, concede to Aqiba
indicates that Aqiba emerges the victor in the dispute. Yet,
substantively, the concession is no concession at all, but simply
points out a case in which none of the concerned parties would
have reason to disagree. Sages state that if the Israelite buys
produce ready for the harvest, he is exempt from tithing that which
he harvests, and may pick late-ripening produce as he pleases
thereafter. This is simply an exemplfication of the point made by
Simeon b. Gamaliel at M. 5:5 F-H.[23] Since the Israelite has
bought the produce, *not* the land, the harvest is by definition
exempt, for it is grown from land owned by a non-Israelite. Note
that T. accounts for all of the positions cited in M., except the
obscure gloss of Judah (M. 5:5E).

                              5:6

A. One who steeps grape-pulp in water [to form a beverage]
    (*ḥmtmd*),[24]
B. and added a fixed measure of water,
C. and [then] found the same measure [of liquid in the tub after
    pressing the water from the pulp]--
D. [the liquid] is exempt [from the removal of tithes].
E. R. Judah declares [the liquid] liable.
F. [If] he found more [liquid] than the measure [of water he
    originally poured over the pulp],
G. he removes [tithes] on behalf of [the beverage] from another
    batch (*mmqwm 'ḥr*)
H. according to the percentage [of the liquid which exceeds the
    original quantity of water].

                              M. 5:6 (A-E = y. Ma. 5:5[52a],
                              y. Dem. 1:1[21d], y. M.S. 1:3[52d],
                              b. Pes. 42b, b. Hul. 25b)

The pericope carries forward M. 5:4, sharing the latter's
assumption that potable liquid extracted from the waste of wine
production is deemed food and must be tithed. Under dispute at
A-D+E is whether such liquid has indeed been extracted from the
pulp. A-D argues that since the liquid pressed from the pulp is
equal in volume to the water poured over it, we assume that the
water has simply passed through the pulp without carrying any of
the pulp's liquid with it. The beverage is deemed to be water and,
like water, is exempt from the removal of tithes.[25] Judah's point
is that, even though the volume of liquid is equal to the original
volume of water, the liquid has absorbed both the color and the
flavor of the grape-pulp. Since the householder, having gone to
the trouble of steeping the pulp, clearly wants the water to
absorb the flavor, the liquid must be tithed as if it were wine
(cf. M. Ter. 10:1, 3).[26]

F-H must be interpreted in light of A-D. The water in the
mixture is distinct from the liquid extracted from the pulp, and
may not be removed as tithe on behalf of the liable liquid (cf.
M. Ter. 1:10). It follows that tithes for the pulp-liquid may
not be removed from the mixture before us, for exempt water will
inevitably be removed on behalf of the liquid. Rather (G), the
householder removes tithes on behalf of the pulp-liquid from
another batch of untithed liquid which has not been mixed with
water. Secondly (H), the quantity of liquid removed as tithe from
the second batch will be only a percentage of that quantity of
liquid which exceeds the original quantity of water. If, for
example, the owner poured a gallon of water over the pulp and
extracted five quarts of liquid, only one quart of the liquid is
subject to the law of tithes, for we assume that the quart represents the actual quantity of liquid pressed from the pulp. The
owner, then, removes tithes from another batch in a quantity equal
to that required from a quart of liable liquid. From Judah's
perspective, the problem so carefully worked out at F-H could never
arise. Judah, who holds that the water is indistinguishable from
its flavoring agent, will have no difficulty in determining how
to tithe liquid exceeding the original quantity of water added to
the pulp. Tithes are simply removed from the mixture itself, just
as if it were a new batch of wine.

5:7

A. Ant-holes which remained overnight beside a stack [of grain]
    from which tithes had yet to be removed (*rymh hhybt*)--

B. lo, these [i.e., kernels found in the ant-holes] are liable
    [to the removal of tithes],
C. for clearly [the ants] have been dragging [grain] from a pro-
    cessed batch (*dbr gmwr*) all night long.

                              M. 5:7 (A-B = y. Ma. 5:6[52a],
                              y. Hal. 1:8[58a])

    C explains A-B. The stacked grain has been processed and is
therefore liable to the removal of tithes (M. 1:6Q-R). Any grain
found in adjacent ant-holes is also assumed to be liable, for we
suppose that the ants have taken the grain from that very pile.

                              5:8

A. Baalbekian garlic,[27] onions of Rakhpa,[28] Cilician split-beans,[29]
    and Egyptian lentils[30]--
B. R. Meir says, "Also: *qirqaś*";[31]
C. R. Yose says, "Also: *qoṭnym*"[32]--
D. are exempt from [the law of] tithes, and are purchased from
    anyone in the Seventh Year.
E. The seeds of the higher pods of arum (*lwp*),[33] the seeds of
    leeks, the seeds of onions, the seeds of turnips or radishes,
F. and all other garden seeds which are not eaten,
G. are exempt from [the law of] tithes, and are purchased from
    anyone in the Seventh Year.
H. For (*š-*) even though the plants from which they were gathered
    ('*byhn*: lit., "their fathers") [were designated as] heave-
    offering, lo, these [seeds] may be eaten [even by non-priests,
    for they are not considered food].

                              M. 5:8 (A-B = y. Dem. 2:1[22b];
                              E-F: cf. Sifra Beḥuqotai 12:9,
                              Sifre Dt. 105c, y. Ma. 1:1[48c],
                              y. Ma. 5:7[52a]; H = y. Ma. 5:7
                              [52a])

    The rulings at A+D and E-G share identical apodoses, each
giving examples of produce which, for reasons based upon M. 1:1A-B,
are exempt from the law of tithes. The items of A+D are exempt
from the law because they do not grow in the Land of Israel (cf.
M. 5:5). They may therefore be imported into the Land and consumed there without removing tithes. It follows that Seventh Year
prohibitions do not apply either, for these prohibitions apply
only to produce grown in the Land. The interpolated items of B-C
are unidentified, but presumably refer to types of produce which
are exempt from the law by virtue of being foreign to the Land of

Israel. The items at E-G, as F makes clear, are exempt because
they are not used as food (M. 1:1B1). H carries forward the point
of E-G. Since only food may be designated as heave-offering, the
inedible seeds of plants which have been so designated remain
permitted for the use of non-priests, even though the plants
themselves are permitted only to priests. The ruling stands
within Aqiba's assumption (M. 4:6K-L) that only the part of the
plant which is normally eaten can become subject to the law of
tithes, even if a secondary part of the plant is in fact consumed.
So here, the status of heave-offering is conferred only upon that
part of the plant which is normally used as food.

A. What is [considered] *garlic of Baalbek* [cf. M. 5:8A]?
B. Any [garlic] which has only a single corolla (*dwr*) surrounding
    the central stem [rather than individual cloves: Lieberman].
C. What is [considered] *onion of Rakhpa* [cf. M. 5:8A]?
D. Any [onions] the stalks of which are not disintegrated within
    the [bulb].
E. Rabban Simeon b. Gamaliel says, "Any [onions] which have only
    a single husk."
F. What are [considered] *Cilician split-beans* [cf. M. 5:8A]?
G. (following E:) These are large and square.
H. Rabban Simeon b. Gamaliel says, "There has never been a square
    bean since the six days of Creation [i.e., such beans receive
    their shape during processing: Lieberman].
I. What are [considered] *Egyptian lentils* [cf. M. 5:8A]?
J. Those which are pointed on top.
K. Rabban Simeon b. Gamaliel says, "Any [lentils] which have no
    seeds in them.
L. *R. Meir says,* "Also *qilqas,* for their stalks are small and
    their seed-pods (*hlqt*: Jastrow, p. 346) are numerous [cf.
    M. 5:8B].

T. 3:15

M. *R. Yose says,* "Also the *qantyn*[34] which are beneath them [cf.
    M. 5:8C].
N. Such as these [i.e., the items of A-K], Sages stipulated,
    should be clearly marked (*kgwn 'lw srkw hkmym*: following E),
O. for no similar types [are found] in the Land of Israel.
P. But [in regard to] hazelnuts, and peaches, and cedar nuts
    [imported from outside the Land of Israel], [Sages] did not
    stipulate that they be clearly marked.
Q. for similar types [are found] in the Land of Israel.
R. [Regarding the tithing status of mixtures of foreign and

domestic] produce, Sages ruled neither according to taste, nor
fragrance, nor appearance, nor price, but solely according to
[the geographical origin of] the major portion [of the mixture].

S. *And all other garden seeds* [= M. 5:8F]:

T. for example (*kgwn*), seeds of cucumbers and gourds, and seeds
    of turnips and radishes.

U. *And all other garden seeds which are not eaten are exempt from
    [the law of] tithes, and are purchased from anyone in the
    Seventh Year* [= M. 5:8F-G].

V. R. Judah says, "They stated [the ruling with respect to] garden
    seeds only."

W. R. Yose says, "Also: [they stated the ruling with respect to]
    seeds of the field, such as the seed of woad and vetch."

                              T. 3:16
                              T. 3:15-16 (pp. 241-42, ls. 51-64)
                              A-M: cf. y. Ma. 5:7[51d],
                              H = y. Ned. 3:2[37d], y. Shebu.
                              3:9[34d]; N-O: cf. y. Dem. 2:1
                              [22b]; R = T. Dem. 4:11; T-O:
                              cf. y. Ma. 5:7[52a])

      T. concludes its tractate with a series of citations, glosses,
and supplements to M. 5:8. A-K provides identifying characteristics of the foreign produce listed at M. 5:8A. L-M cites and
glosses M. 5:8B-C, but the point of the added material is unclear.
The characteristics of the stalks and seed-pods of *qilqas* do not
explain why M. exempts it from the law, nor does the explanatory
information added to Yose's lemma (M) add to our understanding.
y. makes better sense of matters by recasting L-M into the form
of A-K: "And what are [considered] *qryqaś*? Whatever has small
stalks and numerous pods. And what is similar to it? Said R.
Yose, "For example, *qunyaṭa*." Thus, at least on the surface,
Meir and Yose are made to add to A-K's list of foreign produce
receiving description, a position supported by N.

      The point of N-Q is obscure as well. We are told that the
foreign produce of A-K should be marked upon importation into the
Land of Israel, for there are no similar types of produce grown
in the Land. Further, produce which is grown on both sides of
the border need not be marked when that grown abroad is imported.
In the absence of further information, the first problem before us
is to interpret the reason for marking the produce. If we assume,
as have the copyists and commentators cited by Lieberman, that the
point of marking the produce is to distinguish this non-tithable
produce from tithable produce grown inside the Land, then we would
like to correct the text to read that the items of A-K *should* be

marked, for produce similar to these in appearance *do* grow in the
Land of Israel, while the items of P need *not* be marked, for these
do not grow in the Land. By marking imported produce of a type
which grows in the Land as well, we insure that heave-offering and
tithes will be removed only from domestic produce, which alone can
become sanctified. Similarly, failure to mark imported produce of
a type which does not grow in the Land will result in no harm at
all, for no one will assume that such produce needs to be tithed.
The problem with this correction, as HD (followed by Lieberman)
points out, is that T. 1:1c assumes that the items of P are indeed
native to the Land, for it defines the point in their growth at
which they become subject to the law. We must, then, deal with
the text before us, for it shares assumptions attested elsewhere
in T. The text says that precisely the produce which is in danger
of being mistaken for tithable produce need not be marked. Clearly,
if T. is to make sense, there must be some reason for marking
foreign produce other than to distinguish it from domestic produce
for tithing purposes. In absence of other information, however,
the text remains unintelligible.[35]

R is identical to T. Dem. 4:11, and clearly has been taken
from a larger unit, T. Dem. 4:11-12, which discusses the status of
mixtures including domestic and imported produce. The rule simply
states that the status of such mixtures is determined solely by
the status of the major portion of produce composing the mixture.
If the major portion is domestic, the whole mixture is subject to
the law, while if the major portion is imported, the entire mixture is exempt. The ruling does not help us interpret N-Q, for
marking imported produce of a type also grown domestically would
certainly facilitate determining which type constitues the majority
of the mixture.

S-T and U-W are independent citations and glosses of M. 5:8E-F.
S-T simply provides examples of the kinds of seeds M. has in mind.
At U-W Judah and Yose dispute the kinds of seeds which M. specifies
as inedible, and therefore exempt from the law.

šlyq pyrq' wkwl' mškt bšyyt' dšmy'

INTRODUCTION

[1]The primary scriptural sources for Mishnah's law of tithes
are Lv. 27:30, Nu. 18:8-13, 19-32, Dt. 14:22-27 and Dt. 26:12-15.
There is little unanimity among the various sources regarding the
precise names of the various offerings, or even to whom they are
presented. The classic discussion of the problem is O. Eissfeldt,
Erstlinge und Zehnten im Alten Testament (Leipzig, 1917). For
more recent discussions, see Bunte, pp. 27-28, Guthrie, "Tithe,"
Weinfeld, "Tithes" and Sarason, *M. Demai*, pp. 3-9.

[2]Whatever the difficulty of harmonizing Scripture's various
notices, Mishnah is clear that the following six offerings are
included among the taxes which must be removed:

  a. heave-offering--a sanctified offering of unspecified
     quantity which is designated for the use of priests (see
     Peck, *M. Terumot*)
  b. first tithe--a charity offering for the Levite, compris-
     ing one tenth of the crop remaining after the removal of
     the heave-offering
  c. heave-offering of the tithe--a tenth of the first tithe,
     sanctified by the Levite for the use of the priest (see
     Sarason, *M. Demai*)
  d. second tithe--an offering which the householder himself
     must sanctify and consume at the culmination of a pil-
     grimage to Jerusalem. This tithe consists of one tenth
     of what remains after the removal of first tithe (see
     Haas, *M. Maaser Sheni*).
  e. poorman's tithe--a final tenth, given to the poor in years
     in which the farmer is not obliged to make pilgrimage
  f. dough-offering--a sanctified portion of all dough used in
     the preparation of bread. The offering is for the priest
     alone (see Havivi-Eisenman, *M. Halah*). .

The Division of Agriculture's main interest is in those offerings
sanctified for the priests and pilgrim, for it is to these alone
that it devotes tractate-length studies, i.e., M. Terumot (Heave-
Offering), M. Halah (Dough-Offering), M. Demai (Doubtfully Tithed
Produce [i.e., produce which contains heave-offering of the tithe]),
and M. Maaser Sheni (Second Tithe). Neusner, *Judaism*, and Sarason,
"Mishnah and Scripture" both point out that Mishnah's principle of
selection is guided by the problematic of living according to holy
rules in a Land which remains holy. My own analysis of M. Maaserot,
which does not discuss any of the offerings in particular, entirely
confirms the conclusions of Neusner and Sarason. I might add here
that there is no basis to the oft-repeated suggestion that M.
Ma^{C}aserot is at all or even tangentially concerned with problems
specific to first tithe (cf. Strack, p. 32, Schürer-Vermes-Millar
I: 71). The opinion apparently is based upon the erroneous title
of T. Ma^{C}aserot in the Erfurt MS.: "First Tithe" (*m^{C}sr r'šwn*),
Zuckermandel, p. 81.

[3]Mishnah thus carries forward a notion of tithes which has
deep roots in Near Eastern antiquity, particularly in the Temple-
states of second-millenium Mesopotamia and Syria-Palestine. For
discussions of ancient Near Eastern views on tithing, and their
influence on those of Scripture, see Eissfeldt, *BZAW*, Eissfeldt,
RGG^3, Oppenheim, "Temple," Wright, "Temple," and the articles
cited in n. 1 above. The extent to which mishnaic law regarding

tithing reflects common structures of Mesopotamian mythic imagination remains to be explored.

[4]Cf. the recent formulation of Sarason, "Mishnah and
Scripture":

> God, as owner of the Land, has a prior claim on its
> produce. But man must acknowledge God's ownership
> and validate God's claim through actively designating
> and separating God's portion .... Sacrilege thus is
> conceived as a violation of God's property rights.

My own formulation of matters, obviously, is indebted to Sarason,
even though I differ regarding specific details. In general, however, Sarason's essay is a reliable and penetrating analysis of
the dynamics of the tithing law in Mishnah.

[5]The notion that agricultural offerings are to be eaten in
the meals of their recipients appears to emerge from a close
reading of Dt. 26:1ff., in which first-fruits are contrasted with
the tithes for the Levite. The former are eaten by priests after
the offering is waved before the altar, i.e., in the course of a
ritual, while the latter is eaten in daily, non-cultic surround-
ings. Similarly, offerings which Mishnah understands Scripture
to assign to the priesthood (cf. Nu. 18:8-13, 15:17-21), for
example, are not ritually consumed, but are rather eaten in the
course of the priest's daily meals, as a privilege of his sacred
office. The only tithe which in Scripture has any cultic over-
tones is the pilgrim offering of Dt. 14:22ff, which must be eaten
"before the Lord" in the Temple. In Mishnah, however, which
equates this offering with second tithe, the farmer is simply
required to eat the produce within Jerusalem. M. Maaser Sheni,
which is devoted to second tithe, prescribes no ritual for the
consumption of the offering, simply stipulating that all produce
designated as second tithe must be eaten as produce of that type
is normally eaten (M. M.S. 2:1; see Haas, *M. Maaser Sheni*). In
general, there is little in Tractate Maaserot or elsewhere in
Mishnah which would indicate any interest in sacred or cultic
meals.

[6]Mishnah comes to completion toward the end of the second-
century A.D., some 60 years after the failed messianic uprising
against Rome under the leadership of Bar Kokhba (132-135) and the
persecutions which followed under Hadrian. On the devastating
social and economic impact of this war during the subsequent
decades upon the Jewish population of Palestine, see Allon,
History II: 48-83 (esp. pp. 53-59) and Avi-Yonah, *Jews*, pp. 15-31.
To be sure, by the turn of the century, the social and economic
conditions of Palestinian Jewry under the patriarchate of Judah
the Prince (Rabbi) appear to improve markedly (cf. Lieberman,
"Palestine" and, more recently, Levine, *Caesarea*, pp. 61-79).
Nevertheless, we cannot conclude that increased economic security
carried with it solutions to issues of imagination which, in the
course of time, remain pressing and unresolved. I argue that the
details of Tractate Maaserot, as well as the structural and
substantive outlines of Mishnah as a whole, are themselves important evidence that, despite material well-being, a significant
sector of the Palestinian Jewish population continued to reflect
upon the theological meaning of the disasters suffered by immediately preceding generations. For the most exhaustive formulation
of this interpretation of the mishnaic evidence, see Neusner,
Judaism, Chapters Five and Six. Thus one may well accept suggestions such as those of Applebaum, "Severan Empire," p. 36, that
the efficient cause of Mishnah's compilation is a result of
Severan encouragement of provincial peoples to formulate indigenous

codes of law. It remains necessary to acknowledge, however, that
the *product* of this effort of compilation deeply reflects an
attempt on the part of Mishnah's framers, undoubtedly the circle
of the Patriarch, to achieve clarity on the nature and meaning of
the Jewish future in a world--at least for the time being--without
Temple and cult.

[7]Compare Bunte's dissection of M. into the following units:

a. Zehntpflichtige Bodenerzeugnisse und der Termin ihrer
   Zehntpflichtigkeit (M. 1:1-8).
b. Beginn und Dauer des zehntfreien Genusses von Bodenerzeug-
   nissen (M. 2:1-4)
c. Kauf und Verkauf zehntpflichtiger Bodenerzeugnisse und
   ihr Genuss (M. 2:5-6).
d. Bedingungen, unter welchen der Bodenerzeugnisse Bear-
   beitende und seine Familie Zehntfrei essen oder tauschen
   dürfen (M. 2:7-3:4).
e. Gebaude und Zehntpflicht (M. 3:5-7).
f. Pflücken, Kauf, Verkauf, Verpflanzen und sonstige Behand-
   lung von Bodenerzeugnisse und die Zehntpflicht (M. 3:8-
   5:7).
g. Zehntfreie Bodenerzeugnisse (M. 5:8).

While Bunte's analysis is, on the whole, justifiable in terms of
content, it does not reflect the formal divisions which the edi-
tor(s) of M. impose upon their units, nor do the topic rubrics
lay open, as I have attempted to do, the logical unfolding of the
tractate's issues. Bunte analyzes the tractate as if it were an
encyclopedia; I approach it as if it were an essay. The reader
may determine which is the more productive approach.

[8]For the original explication of this proposition, see
Neusner, "Form and Meaning," anthologized in Neusner, *Method and
Meaning in Ancient Judaism* (Missoula, 1979), pp. 155-181. My own
exposition supplements Neusner's, for I attempt to describe the
concrete exegetical processes by which meaning is brought forth
from form.

[9]The argument has most recently been reformulated by Neusner
in Neusner, "Redaction," pp. 2-7. Clearly, no one would assert
that the text of Mishnah as we have it is in all respects identical
to the "original." To the contrary, the text-critical work of
Jacob Epstein has shown that the text of Mishnah remained relatively fluid for some time after its publication. The point is
that the literary traits of the text, however much we allow for
fluidity of content, are imposed upon Mishnah at the outset and
remain unchanged.

[10]Green's remarks are made in the context of a discussion of
the problem of rabbinic biography. See William S. Green, "What's
in a Name?--The Problematic of Rabbinic 'Biography,'" in Green,
Approaches I, p. 80.

[11]For a full catalogue of Mishnah's repertoire, see Neusner,
Purities XXI:196-246.

[12]More explicit examples may be found throughout Mishnah,
particularly where materials attributed to pharisaic figures have
been appropriated for the purposes of Mishnah. See J. Neusner,
*Development of a Legend: Studies in the Traditions Concerning
Yohanan Ben Zakkai* (Leiden, 1970), pp. 57, 61-64, and *idem.,
Pharisees* III:89-119.

[13]My discussion of the construction of the pericope differs in
some detail from that of Neusner, who proposes the theoretical
construct of the "cognitive unit" as a means of defining Mishnah's
smallest whole unit of meaning. For his latest formulation, see
"Redaction," p. 10.

[14]Neusner, *Purities* XXI:165 defines a "form" as a word or
words "which function in, but bear no meaning distinctive to, a
particular cognitive unit." That is, a form adds no *content* to
a pericope. Rather, it defines the terms in which the information
of the pericope is to be grasped. The principal forms in Mishnah
as a whole are identified by Neusner as the attributive (i.e.,
the ascription of an opinion to a named authority by the use of
Authority + '*MR* ["said"]), the dispute, the *ma*^{c}*aseh* (a stock
phrase introducing a precedent), and the list. For discussion
see Neusner, *Purities* XXI:165-196. Below I discuss only the dispute and the list, the most prevalent of forms in Tractate Maaserot.
The *ma*^{c}*aseh* appears only once (M. 2:5) and the attributive, precisely because it is ubiquitous, loses true exegetical significance.

[15]Neusner, *ibid.*, p. 165, defines a "formulary pattern" as a
"grammatical arrangement of words distinctive to their subject
but in fixed syntactical patterns serviceable for a wide range
of subjects." The principal formulary patterns of Mishnah are
all variants of the declarative sentence (subject + verb + predi-
cate). For discussion of the various patterns themselves and
their functions, see *Purities* XXI:196-246 and "Form and Meaning,"
pp. 156-157.

[16]I should add, however, that at no point in my exegesis of
the tractate have variant MS. readings solved any particular
formal problem. In general, Mishnah's copyists are insensitive
to its formulaic character.

[17]These formal-thematic units are the true "chapters" of the
tractate. The present division of Maaserot into five chapters
is the result of the work of copyists and printers, not the plan
of Mishnah's editor(s). While the judgment of the former is
often acute, there are important errors which confuse interpretation of the law. See my discussions of M. 4:5-6 and M. 5:1-2.

[18]For a preliminary discussion of rabbinic exegesis of Mishnah,
see Joel Zaiman, "The Traditional Study of the Mishnah," in J.
Neusner, ed., *The Modern Study of the Mishnah* (Leiden, 1973).

[19]On the work of particular individuals see the essays in
ibid.

CHAPTER ONE

[1]On this point, see Introduction, pp. 1-2. Relevant literature is cited at p. 165, n. 1 and p. 166, n. 4.

[2]The core rulings of each catalogue conform to the following
pattern: substantive + *mš-/ᶜd š-* + imperfect. There is no effort,
however, to balance the catalogues, either in number of stichs or
in pattern of glossing.

[3]It is possible to argue (though, to my knowledge, no one has)
that M. 1:2-3 and M. 1:5-8 present contradictory conceptions of
the law. The former claims that produce must be tithed as soon
as it is ripe, while the latter claims that produce must be tithed
only after it is processed. Indeed, the two notions are somewhat
out of joint, requiring efforts at harmonization such as I have
provided. My solution is substantially in agreement with that
arrived at in earlier commentaries, and recently reformulated by
Lieberman in *TK*,II:666.1. If this harmonization is deemed artificial, it is important to note that not only has the redactor
of Chapter One read the pericopae as complementary, but nowhere
in M. do we find any indication that the harmonistic reading of
Chapter One is ever questioned. The point, then, is that the
Ushan notion of the law of tithes, reflected in Chapter One, is
the presupposition of all pericopae in M. which address the same
topic.

[4]So Sammter (p. 137), who translates "gehütet." Perhaps the
best translation of *nšmr* would be "cared for" or "tended." This
sense informs the discussions of b. Shab. 68a, s.v. *lmᶜwty hpqr*
and y. Ma. 1:1 (48d), both of which exclude from the law of tithes
all produce grown in untended fields.

[5]I discern three senses in the participle *ḥyyb* as it is used
in M. The first defines a general class or status to which unharvested produce belongs. *Ḥyyb* has this sense in M. 1:1 and
M. 1:2A, where it indicates that a given batch of produce is
"among those things to which tithing laws apply." The second use
of the term, as at M. 3:4, refers to items which are already
harvested. In these cases *ḥyyb* means that produce is "liable to"
or "requires" removal of tithes forthwith before the produce may
be eaten. The third usage, as in M. 2:2 and M. 4:1, refers to
the man who owns the produce. That is, the owner of a given
batch of produce is *ḥyyb*, "required to tithe" whatever he eats.

[6]Cf. Danby (p. 67): "Whatsoever is used for food either in
its earlier or later condition (of ripeness)." I follow KM
(*Tithes*, 2:5) and MR (M. 1:4) in interpreting *thltw* to indicate
the point at which the fruit is recognizable as a member of its
species.

[7]Failure to meet any one of the three criteria at B exempts
the produce in question from the law. For example, produce growing wild is edible, but the fact that it is not cultivated by
human beings means that tithes need not be removed from it. The
locus classicus for determining the range of produce *excluded*
from the law of tithes is b. Shab. 68a where M. is cited and
glossed. The passage is the foundation for all later commentaries

to M.   Cf. as well as Sifre Dt. 105 (translated and discussed,
pp. 56-57) and y. Ma. 1:1(48c), which is based upon Sifre.

[8]Sarason, *M. Demai*, p. 9, observes that in any given year
nearly 22% of the harvest is to be offered as heave-offering and
tithes.

[9]Both of these criteria have clear precedents in Scripture's
discussion of tithing rules. On the specification that tithes
must be removed from all agricultural produce in particular, cf.
Dt. 14:22: "You shall tithe all the yield of your seed which
comes forth from the field year by year." On the notion that
tithes are due from the land because the land itself is God's
gift, cf. Dt. 26:14-15 which requires the farmer to remove his
tithes and confess: "I have obeyed the voice of the Lord my God,
I have done according to all that thou hast commanded me. Look
down from thy holy habitation, from heaven, and bless thy people
Israel and the ground which thou hast given us, as thou didst
swear to our fathers, a land flowing with milk and honey." To be
sure, B3 does not specify that, in order to be subject to the law,
produce must grow from the earth of the *land of Israel*. Nevertheless, this notion is attested everywhere in Mishnah, and must be
read as the meaning here as well. On the stipulation that tithes
come only from the land of Israel, see M. 3:10, M. 5:5, M. Dem.
6:11, and, at length, Maim., *Heave-offering* 1:1-9.

[10]Lv. 25:23 is clear that the land is owned by God: "The land
shall not be sold in perpetuity, for the land is mine." Lv. 27:30
is equally clear that the fruits of the land also belong to God:
"All the tithe of the land, whether of the seed of the land or of
the fruit of the trees, is the Lord's; it is holy to the Lord."
We must note here that B entirely ignores the fact that, according to Lv. 27:32, cattle as well must be tithed as offerings for
the Temple sacrifices. Mishnah's discussion of the cattle-tithe
(M. Bek. 9:1-8) is found in The Division of Holy Things, in a
tractate devoted to the problem of cattle offerings for Temple
sacrifices. The tithe of cattle, then, is deemed to fall under
problems relevant to the cult rather than those applicable to
agriculture.

[11]I translate *yrq* as "green vegetable" for lack of a better
term, even though M. 4:5 uses the term to refer to the green leaves
of herbs. More generally, the term is applied to anything which
grows on a creeping vine or stalk (see p. 171, n. 17). M.-T.'s
inclusive use of the term *yrq* to subsume a number of different
species is paralleled in Theophrastus, for whom the term "herb"
defines items such as marjoram and basil (*Enquiry*, VII.ii.1) as
well as lettuce, cabbage, cucumber, or gourd (*ibid.*, VII.ii.9).

[12]Unless specified otherwise, M. assumes that seed will be
used for planting instead of food (cf. M. 5:8 and T. 3:16).

[13]At y. Ma. 1:1 Yonah observes that vegetables kept for their
seed become so hard that they are as wood regarding tithes, i.e.,
they are exempt (cf. M. Sheb. 2:10). But cf. White, *Roman Farming*,
p. 187, who cites Theophrastus' opinion that seed must be taken
from plants "in their prime."

[14]Sifre Dt.'s exegesis of Dt. 14:22ff. is important in the
history of M.'s exegesis. Accordingly, I offer a translation and
commentary to the relevant passages of Sifre Dt. 105, which I
have divided into three units, b-d. Unit a, irrelevant to M., is
not discussed, while units c and d are translated and discussed

in relation to their respective pericopae of M. For a quite independent version of Sifre Dt. 105, cf. y. Ma. 1:1 (48c).

[15]Cf. T. 3:16 where Yose exempts woad and vetch (*bqy'*) from
the law. In M. Sheb. 7:1 woad and madder are designated "types
of dye" which are subject to the laws of the Sabbatical Year.

[16]*Rubia Tinctiosum* (Löw, p. 311), a plant yielding a red dye.

[17]In the technical vocabulary of M.-T. there are three general
types of produce subject to the laws of tithe: *prwt* (fruit),
tbw'h (grain) and *yrq* (greens). A fourth item, *qtnyt* (pulse), is
normally categorized with grain. In general, *prwt* refers to anything which grows from a climbing vine, a tree or bush (M. 1:2-3).
Tbw'h, according to M. Hal. 1:1, includes wheat, barley, spelt,
rye, and oats. *Yrq*, as at T. 1:1b (see p. 170, n. 11) and M. 1:4,
refers to produce which grows from a creeping vine or stalk (T.
Uqs. 2:11). *Qtnyt* refers to a wide variety of items ranging from
sesame to various types of legumes (M. Sheb. 2:7-8). The common
characteristic of *qtnyt* is that all items in this class require
hulling before they may be eaten.

Mishnah's classification of grains and pulses is closely
parallel to that of Theophrastus, and indicates that Mishnah's
authorities knew a common Hellenistic science of taxonomy.
Theophrastus remarks (*Enqiry*, VIII,i.1): "There are two principal
classes [of corn and corn-like plants]: there are the corn-like
plants such as wheat, barley, one-seeded wheat, rice-wheat, and
the others which resemble the first two; and again there are the
leguminous plants, as bean, chick-pea, pea, and in general, those
to which the name of pulses is given." On this passage and other
parallels between Mishnaic and Hellenistic taxonomy, see S.
Lieberman, *Hellenism*, pp. 180-193.

[18]C and M record the verb in the imperfect, *mśybhylw*. MSS.
reveal no pattern in the use of perfect and imperfect forms in
this pericope. Thus, while the forms change from stich to stich
and MS. to MS., I consistently translate as future perfect.

[19]S reads *b'wśym*, "sickly grapes" (cf. Ribmaṣ, Lieberman, *TK*,
II:667.5-6, Jastrow, p. 135, and Sacks-Hutner, p. 200). In light
of M. 1:1B, which stipulates that only agricultural produce is
subject to the law, S is to be preferred, for its grapes are
domesticated.

[20]On the meaning of *B'Š* cf. y. Ma. 1:1(48d), Maim., *Tithes*
2:5 and Jastrow, p. 137.

[21]*Rhus Coriara* (Bunte, p. 57). According to Bunte, the fruit
is used in pickling.

[22]*Morus* (Löw, *Pflanzennamen*, p. 395).

[23]*Punica Granatum* (Löw, *ibid.*, p. 312).

[24]See Sacks-Hutner (p. 201) for the numerous MSS. traditions
for this word. Bunte (p. 59) notes that all closely resemble
the Greek word for peach (*persikon*).

[25]So Jastrow, p. 234, s.v., *GYD*.

[26]*Juglans Regia* (Low, *op. cit.*, p. 84).

[27]S appears to have added "and almonds" in order to balance
I with J. The addition, however, upsets the division of the

pericope into 10 items per unit, with J the dividing line. For
discussions of the "original" reading, see Albeck, p. 394, and
Lieberman, *TK*, II:668.7.

[28]*Crustiminum pirum* (Löw, *op. cit.*, p. 208). Also known as
"pippin."

[29]*Pirus Cydonia* (Bunte, p. 61). I follow Löw, p. 144, and
Bunte in translating "medlars," but see Danby (p. 67) and Blackman
(p. 352) who translate "quince." Löw documents the error which
led to the identification of *pryš* with quince.

[30]*Crataegus Azarolus* (Löw, *op. cit.*, p. 288).

[31]The reference is unclear. TYY explains that the reference
is to other tree-fruits which are neither red nor black.

[32]*Trigonella Foenum Graecum* (Löw, *op. cit.*, p. 316).

[33]The items at M. 13-16, we may point out, appear elsewhere in
M.-T. in numerous contexts, yet always in the same order (cf.
M. Uqs. 1:6, M. Kil. 1:4, T. Uqs. 3:7, T. Sheb. 7:16). Thus the
list, "pears-crab apples" is a standard unit of material providing
a fixed protasis for numerous apodoses. Only at T. Uqs. 3:7 is
there any interest in the point at which these items are subject
to the law. There we are told that the items in question impart
food uncleanness from the point of their "tithing season" and
thereafter. The point, that the produce imparts uncleanness as
food only after it has become food, is congruent with the view of
A, that edibility determines when produce is subject to the law.

[34]Cf. M. Sheb. 4:7-9 which attests the fact that figs, grapes,
grain and olives are all ripe enough to be eaten *before* they have
reached the stages enumerated here at B-C and P.

[35]See Q. Jones, "Fenugreek," *EB*, 9:176.

[36]The meaning is obscure. T. Ter. 2:14 claims that grain
which has not "reached a third," will not sprout if sown. This,
however, does not explain the meaning of the term. I know of no
sustained discussion of the term, but cf. the remarks of J. Feliks,
Ḥaqla'ut, p. 125.

[37]Maimonides' interpretation of M. 1:2-3 departs considerably
from the clear intentions of the redactor. Maimonides ignores
the issue of edibility entirely and stipulates that the signs all
refer to the point in the growth of the produce at which its seeds
are fertile. Thus, he reads the entire pericope in light of O.
See *Tithes* 2:5 (tr. I. Klein, p. 189): "When is the season of
tithing? When the produce reaches the stage that makes the seed
thereof fit to be sown and to sprout ...."

[38]See Lieberman, *TK*:667.5.

[39]*Corylus Avella* (Löw, p. 48).

[40]*TK*:667-68. There is no MS. evidence for Lieberman's suggestion, even though the context thoroughly supports it.

[41]Fruit of the cedar tree, *Pinus Cedrus* (Löw, p. 58).

[42]The opinion is analogous to Yose's ruling about connection
in regard to uncleanness in M. Toh. 8:8 (cf. Neusner, *Purities*
XI:198-200 and XII:154-57), and we can therefore take Ishmael's

attribution as reliable. In M. Toh. 8:8, Yose holds that still
water trapped between balls of dough--each of which is less than
an egg's-bulk in size--is sufficient to join the balls together
in a size requisite to receive food uncleanness (i.e., an egg's-
bulk). Thus, the fact of connection renders parts which are exempt
from the law of purities into a whole which is subject to it. In
T. Yose's conception is perfectly complementary. The connective
of the common stem renders the whole subject to the law which now
applies to the part. On the general Ushan provenance of issues
regarding connection in the transfer of uncleanness, see Neusner,
Purities III:298-305, XII:196-97.

[43] *šy'h = Satureia thymbra* (Löw, p. 135).

[44] *'zwb = Origanum majorana* (*loc. cit.*). Also known as hyssop.

[45] *qwrnyt = Calamantha officialis* (*ibid.*, p. 330).

[46] Theophrastus (*Enquiry*, VI, ii, 3-4) discusses the development of berries upon the herbs mentioned in A: "Savory, and still
more marjoram, has a conspicuous fruitful seed, but in thyme it
is not easy to find, being somehow mixed up with the flower; for
men sow the flower and plants come up from it." Theophrastus
further observes that "most herbs wither with the ripening of
their seed" (VII, i, 7).

[47] I translate following Jastrow, p. 2, s.v., *'B*, *'YB*, (*'WB*).
Aruch Completum, I:3, s.v. *'B*, derives the word from the Syriac
'b', "fruit."

[48] y. treats T. 1:4 and T. 1:5a(A-B) as a single unit.

[49] Lieberman (*TK*, II, p. 670, ls. 13-14) notes that a version
of A-B appears in y. Sheb. 7:6 where it is joined to T. 1:4.
This indicates that A-B was read as a statement about the herbs
cited in T. 1:4.

[50] In his discussion of T. Sheb. 2:6, Neusner (*Pharisees*,
II:79) theorizes that "... the Houses serve as convenience names
to which to attribute the two possible opinions on any intermediate
or ambiguous stage of an issue. Simeon may on his own have fabri-
cated the Houses-dispute, in conformity with a prevailing literary
convention."

[51] In general, contrary to A-B, M.-T. seems clear that there is
no single standard for determining the tithing year of produce.
M. Bik. 2:6 is clear that green vegetables are tithed according
to the year in which they are picked, and that only citrons are
like them in this regard. T. Sheb. 4:20 says that the tithing
year of fruit trees is established by the year in which the fruits
first form (*HNT*), and does not mention harvest. M. Sheb. 2:7's
discussion of pulse likewise ignores the harvest and says that
pulse is tithed according to the year in which it takes root. I
have found no clear statement in M.-T. regarding other types of
fruit, but compare the *baraita* cited at y. Ma. 5:4(50d) in the
name of Jonathan b. Yose, which indicates that grain is tithed
according to the year in which it reaches a third of its growth.
In light of all this, we may understand A-B in one of three ways.
Either (1) it simply contradicts other rulings in M.-T. by claiming a single standard applies to all crops, or (2) the rule refers
only to green vegetables (M. Bik. 2:6), or (3) it claims that the
herbs of T. 1:4 are subject to the same criteria as are green
vegetables (HD). As I shall argue, this latter view is probably

that of the redactor of T. 1:5a, but cannot be shown to be the original meaning of A-B.

[52]Lieberman (*TK*, II: 670.16-17) argues that Simeon b. Gamaliel knows A-B. Further, Lieberman asserts that the dispute of D-F concerns the herbs of T. 1:4. He thus sees T. 1:4 + T. 1:5a as a unitary pericope which discusses at what point the tithing year of herbs is determined. As my analysis indicates, this view is correct only on the redactional level of meaning. But since T. 1:4 + T. 1:5a is a series of three formulaically independent units (T. 1:4 + T. 1:5a[A-B] + [C-F]), it is not likely that one tradent formulated the whole or even that a single conception of the law informs each unit.

[53]Lieberman's emendation, which simply transposes the w and the y of the text's '*wbyn*, is highly plausible since the two letters are easily mistaken in MSS. Further the context of D calls for a stage of development between blossoming and maturity. The stage of sprouting recorded in the printed text does not qualify, while the point at which berries develop is such an intermediate point.

[54]Concerning the question of whether a single phenomenon can establish both the onset of liability to the law and the year in which the produce must be tithed, see MR to M. Sheb. 2:7 and Maimonides, *Seventh Year and Jubilee* 4:9.

[55]Kosovsky's concordances to Sifra, Sifre and Mekhilta d'Rabbi Ishmael contain no other references to the words y'*mr zh* in an exegetical context. The sense seems to be similar to the later Babylonian Amoraic term *sryk'* ("it is necessary"), which is used to show that a word or passage in a Tannaitic text is not superfluous and in fact contains a concept essential to the proper understanding of the law.

[56]Löw, p. 102, gives no positive identification for *prgym*, except to say that despite the traditional identification of *prgym* as poppy seed, it is more likely a type of millet in the family *Panicum*.

[57]Löw, p. 336, identifies pulse (*Hülsenfrucht*) as any type of plant whose edible part is a berry or bean found in a hull. The types of pulse listed at O all require some kind of preparation. P must have in mind items such as peas or lima beans, which can be eaten raw. See Krauss (*TA*, I:115) who asserts that many types of pulse were used as substitutes for grain in the baking of bread.

[58]*Lupinus Termis*. Also known as Horsebean (Löw, p. 394).

[59]*Shlyym = Lepidum Sativa* (Jastrow, p. 1548).

[60]*Grgyr = Eruca Agrestis* (Jastrow, p. 264).

[61]Probably a reference to *Ficus Sycomorus*, a popular shade tree in the Middle East. Its fruit is edible only after the apex is cut open so that the insect which normally inhabits the fruit can no longer survive. See Löw, p. 176, Condit, and S. Klein.

[62]Acacia pods are used in the tanning process. See Feliks, *Plant World*, p. 98.

[63]As I have indicated at n. 55, y'*mr zh* is an oddity. Moreover, the particle $\check{s}$- never appears before the formulaic phrase "if so, I should say" insofar as I have been able to check these instances

in Kosovsky's concordances to Sifra, Sifre and Mekhilta d'Rabbi
Ishmael. In fact, N-P appears to be a truncated exemplum of a
rhetorical form frequently found in Sifra but which appears only
here in Sifre (Kosovsky, *Sifra*, I:188 and *Sifre*, I:161-63). The
form has four essential components: I. Scriptural citation;
II. *'ynw dyn š-* (isn't it logical that ...?); III. *'ylw kn hyy ty
'wmr* (if so I could say ....); IV. *tlmwd lwmr* (Scripture says ....).
II is a faulty deduction from the Scriptural citation. III makes
this clear by deducing a further implication from II which Scripture (IV) clearly contradicts. Sifre's version omits part II.
M forces us to read L's citation of Scripture as the introduction
to N. But this turns the Scriptural rule into a false proposition!
As I have indicated in the translation, some MSS. try to remedy
this by substituting *'lml'* (if it were not) for *'ylw* (if). While
this is indeed the only way of making sense of what is before us,
it is an obvious fabrication. The phrase *'lml' kn* never appears
in any Tannaitic midrash, insofar as I can see from a survey of
the standard concordances.

[64] *qšw'ym* = *Cucumis Sativa* (Löw, *op. cit.*, p. 334).

[65] *dlw^c ym* = *Cucurbita Pepo* (*ibid.*, p. 351).

[66] *'btyhym* = *Citrullus Vulgaria* (*ibid.*, p. 352).

[67] *mlppwnwt* = *Cucumis Melo* (*ibid.*, p. 351).

[68] *'trgyn* = *Citrus medica cedra* (*ibid.*, p. 46).

[69] On these items, see Bunte, p. 66.

[70] Lieberman (*TK*, II:666.2), on the basis of y. Ma. 1:4, argues
that A-B is understood by the Palestinian Amoraim as a gloss
appended to M. 1:3P, yielding the following reading: "Olives and
grain--when they reach a third of their growth. And among green
vegetables: cucumbers, gourds, chatemelons, and muskmelons."
Thus these green vegetables are subject to the law upon reaching
a third of their growth, while all other greens mentioned in
M.-T. (e.g., T. 1:1b) are subject to the law at all points in their
growth. As Albeck points out (p. 394), Lieberman's solution fails
to solve the literary problem, for A-B in its present form does
not follow conventional glossing patterns common in M. See Albeck's
discussion of M. 1:4 in the appendix of his commentary to the
Division of Agriculture, p. 394.

[71] F-G has in fact been excerpted from its original location in
M. Hul. 1:6, where it appears in the midst of a catalogue of
thematically diverse rulings sharing only a common, and striking,
pattern of formulation. The contrast between the role of F-G in
M. Hul. 1:5-6 and its present function in M. 1:4 is instructive in
regard to the possible redactional principles available to M.'s
formulators. In M. Hul. 1:5-6, formal criteria alone determine
which materials are to be placed together. In M. 1:4, formal
criteria are subordinated to content.

[72] So Lieberman, *TK*, II, 669.9-10. Cf. Löw, *Flora* III:215,
s.v. "Apfel," who indicates that the fruit, known in Greek as
melimela, is the fruit of an apple tree grafted on to quince
stock.

[73] Lieberman (*TK*, II:669.12) explains that Simeon exempts melons
even after they have reached a third of their growth, as long as
they have not yet become smooth. This interpretation follows from
his analysis of M. 1:4A-B as a gloss of M. 1:3P (see my comment to

M. 1:4, p. 175, n. 70). Lieberman, however, ignores the formulary
identity of A and M. 1:4E (... *pṭwr* ... *bqṭnn*) which suggests that
Simeon is indeed responding to a claim that melons are tithable
whether large or small.

[74]MS. Erfurt's version of A is cited anonymously.

[75]I follow Lieberman and *ed. princ.* against y. Ma. 1:4, HY
and HD. See *TK*, II:669.10-11.

[76]Note, however, that B agrees with the anonymous rule of
T. 1:1c(N), as PM suggests by his gloss of B with the explanatory
remark of T. 1:1c(O). See PM, y. Ma. 1:4, s.v. *ᶜd štprš qlyptn
hhyṣwnh.*

[77]The *baraita* reads:

   A. *That which is subject [to the law] among bitter almonds
      is exempt among small sweet [ones]. That which is subject
      to tithes among sweet almonds is exempt among large
      bitter ones.*
   B. *tny:* R. Ishmael b. R. Yose in the name of his father:
      "Bitter almonds are exempt, and sweet ones are not subject
      until (*ᶜd š-*) the outer shell separates."

A interpolates T. Hul. 1:24A-B's distinction between large and
small almonds into its citation of M. B = T. 1:2, save for the
substitution of "exempt" for T.'s "subject" (see note 75). Compare b. Hul. 25b which cites T. Hul. 1:24 in its entirety and
adds a different version of Ishmael b. Yose's lemma.

[78]Translated from Zuckermandel, p. 501.

[79]The translation is paraphrastic, for I can produce no literal
translation of A which yields readable English. Literally, the
passage reads: "What is the [stage in processing for] storage at
which [the requirement to remove] tithes [is binding]?" Cf. Danby,
"When is their tithing season?" (p. 68), and Cohen, "When are the
fruits fixed to be tithed?" (p. 257). The key problem of translation is the word *goren*, which literally means "threshing floor"
(cf. Nu. 18:27), the place where grain is threshed and winnowed
in preparation for storage (cf. Maim., *Comm.*). On the semantic
range of *goren* in M.-T. and the Talmuds, see Feliks, *Haqla'ut*,
p. 235. Feliks does not refer to our passage, and none of his
citations is perfectly applicable to the use of the term in the
present context. Following T. 1:5a, we may define *goren* as the
point at which produce is processed for storage and is therefore
rendered liable to the removal of tithes. Neither the suggestion
of Jastrow ("harvesting season," p. 227, s.v. *GWRN*) nor that of
Krauss ("completion of harvest," *TA*, II:575, n. 271; followed by
Bunte and Sammter) is adequate to the present context, for the
produce listed in our pericopae has already been harvested. At
issue, as T. points out, is the completion of the processing and
the storage of the produce.

[80]O1, O2, B, G5 read *myšpqš*, "when *he* ...." For discussions
of various readings see Lieberman (*TK*, II:670.18), Sacks-Hutner
(p. 200, n. 69) and TAS (M. 1:5).

[81]Throughout M. 1:5-6 MSS. are indiscriminate in dropping or
preserving the *w-* before *'m* (see Sacks-Hutner, pp. 205-09). Therefore, I have translated Albeck's text without noting variant
readings.

[82]Seven MSS. read ^cd $\check{s}$- instead of $m\check{s}$-. Since the use of the particles is inconsistent in all MSS. and editions, I have simply translated Albeck's text. The meaning, in any case, is substantially the same; "Tithes are removed *after*" ($m\check{s}$-) or "Tithes need not be removed *until*" (^cd $\check{s}$-). Cf. the discussion of this phenomenon, and its exegetical possibilities at b. B.M. 88b.

[83]So Lieberman (*TK*, II:671.18) for $\check{S}LQ$. Cf. Albeck, pp. 394-95.

[84]See Krauss (*TA*, II:197 and 581, n. 327) for the term *muqṣeh*.

[85]So Danby, p. 67.

[86]So Jastrow, p. 1358, s.v., $QYṬ^c$.

[87]So b. A.Z. 56a: "Learn from this [i.e., M. 1:7B] that we are discussing the skimming [which takes place in] the vat [rather than the skimming which takes place in] a jar."

[88]So Jastrow, p. 1106.

[89]I follow the witness of eleven MSS. Albeck reads *wmbyn*, "and from between."

[90]So Jastrow, p. 795.

[91]In M.T.Y. 1:1 the word *hmyth* refers to a kind of thin cake. Interpretations of the word as it appears at F generally follow this meaning. The context, however, and the evidence of T. 1:7b(C) and M. Shab. 3:5 both argue for the translation I have suggested. Cf. Maim., *Comm.* and Lieberman, *TK*, II:674.30.

[92]So Maim., *Comm.* for $DW\check{S}$.

[93]The etymology and original meaning of the term *tebel* are unknown. See Krauss, "TBL" for a review of Amoraic, medieval and modern philological research.

[94]I cannot explain why G-H and J-K repeat the pattern twice, or why J-K simply cites G-H. The important stich in each case is the last, H and K, both of which repeat that at issue is the point at which the owner has stored enough produce for his own use.

[95]Opinion is divided concerning the referent of L-M. Maimonides, *Tithes* 3:1-3 indicates that L-M applies to all the produce of M. 1:5-8, certainly a plausible interpretation. Nevertheless MS, following the observation of Joseph Ashkenazi, notes that the items of M. 1:6-8 are all glossed by qualifications specific to the types of produce enumerated in those pericopae. This yields the hypothesis that L-M refers back to B-K alone. As I argue below, Maimonides is probably correct, for L-M is placed in its present location for literary and substantive reasons relevant to the redactor's glossing agendum rather than to the meaning of the rulings at B, D, F and I.

[96]b. B.M. 87b-88a understands matters differently. Yannai, basing himself upon Dt. 26:12 ("I have removed the holy thing [i.e. the tithes] from my house"), claims that the tithes become sanctified only upon entry into the householder's dwelling. Untithed produce, therefore, may be eaten prior to that point because the holy portion is not yet active. Yannai's point is well taken, but his exegetical basis is farfetched. Requiring explanation is why

the house functions as a terminus for the removal of tithes. M.
itself is clear that this is the point at which the man is deemed
to have effected final acquisition of the produce, i.e., the point
at which God's claim to the tithes is provoked.

[97]The only difficulty is that the ruling at N unexpectedly
receives no gloss at all. This is due to the substance of the
ruling itself. All items at N are dried, i.e., processed, before
they can be used or stored. If N were cast in the pattern of the
other rulings, it would yield an absurdity: "Dried split-pomegranates, etc.--when they are dried. But if he does not dry them, when
they are stacked up." The absurdity is that if the pomegranates,
etc., are piled without drying, they will rot.

[98]Translated by Neusner, *Appointed Times* I. See his comments
loc. cit. and in his introduction to M. Shab. Chapter Three, in
the same volume.

[99]Maimonides, *Uncleanness of Foodstuffs*, 12:2-3. See also
Neusner, *Purities*, XVII:19-22 for the interpretation of M. Makh.
1:1 which I follow.

[100]On the divisibility of intention regarding susceptibility
to uncleanness, and Judah's position regarding the matter, see
Neusner, *ibid.*, pp. 15-44, 60-63, 91-92, and 185-98.

[101]The reader will note that I have translated *grnn lmᶜsrwt*
differently than at M. 1:5. As at M. 1:5, my concern is to convey
the sense of this untranslatable term in the context within which
it is employed. In T., the term itself is simply cited and then
glossed by the definitional remarks of B-C. Therefore I have
provided, at A, the most literal translation. See M. 1:5-8, n. 79
(p. 176).

[102]This is Maimonides' understanding of the rule, *Tithes* 3:8.
But compare *Tithes* 3:4 where Maimonides says that if the melons
were in the owner's house and only *then* did he begin to process
them, they are all rendered liable with the completion of the first
melon. Presumably, since they have already entered the owner's
home the first indication of his desire to process them renders
them all liable immediately. Cf. KM and RDBZ to *Tithes* 2:8 as
well as the entirely different development of the matter at b.
B.M. 88b. See also MH, y. Ma. 1:5, s.v. *hyh mpqś*.

[103]V lacks "he has not" (*šl'*), but the reading appears both in
E and *ed. princ.* Furthermore, the context clearly requires the
negative. Lieberman includes the words in brackets in his text
of T., p. 228, 1. 19.

[104]Although T. specifies that this is the case only for the
four items mentioned, M. Ter. 1:10 suggests that the rule is
generally applicable: "They [may] not separate heave-offering ...
from something which is not completely processed for something
[else] which is not completely processed. But if they separated
heave-offering [despite this], their separation of heave-offering
is considered valid heave-offering (*trwmtn trwmh*). See Peck,
M. *Terumot*, HD and HY.

[105]See Lieberman's discussion of the rare term *mhpwrt* (*TK*, II,
p. 672, 1. 24).

[106]Here I follow Lieberman's understanding of the case (*loc.
cit.*, 1. 23). But see HD who understands the ears to have fallen

from the pile onto the threshing floor. In his reading, T. contradicts M. rather than providing a further exemplification of the same principle.

[107]For other interpretations of the matter, see y. Ma. 1:6 and Sirillo, s.v. *qwlṭ hw' mtḥt hkbrh w'wkl.*

[108]Lieberman (*TK*, II, pp. 673-74, 1. 26) attacks the problem by arguing that the crucial difference between A-C and E-G is that at A-C the former owner has completed the manufacturing of the Temple's wine while at E-G the Temple treasurer himself performed the labor. While the observation is important, Lieberman can interpret its legal implications only by resorting to an Amoraic legal principle. Citing the opinion attributed to Simeon b. Laqish (y. Ma. 5:6), Lieberman explains that if a man completes the processing of another's produce without the owner's knowledge, then the processing does not effect liability to tithes. That is, since the owner had no intention of completing the processing at that particular time, the unauthorized act is null and void. The tithing status of the produce remains unaltered until the owner authorizes the processing explicitly. Lieberman applies this principle to A-C, surmising that the former owner has skimmed the wine without the knowledge of the Temple treasurer who represents the Temple as the wine's owner. The resulting situation is that the conditions required at H, which exempts wine processed under Temple auspices, do not apply to A-C. That is, the wine at A-C has not undergone a *legitimate* stage of processing while in a state of exemption from tithing regulations, and therefore cannot be considered in any sense to have been processed while exempt from the law. Unlike the wine of E-G, it remains subject to the law after it is redeemed, for the owner must then authorize the processing which will render the wine liable. While this account resolves the contradiction between the two rulings, it must be regarded with the greatest suspicion since it imports into the exegesis of T. a principle attested only in b. Secondly, the explanation presumes the ignorance of the Temple treasurer regarding the owner's actions, a fact which can hardly be seen as central--if it is even present at all--in T.'s articulation of the case.

[109]See *TZ*, p. 229, variant readings 1. 26, and *TK*, II, p. 274, 1. 26.

[110]In Lieberman's text the word *whwlk*, translated as "continual," appears in brackets. The insertion is based upon the readings of *ed. princ.*, E and Sirillo.

[111]*Anigaron* is a kind of broth (Lieberman, *TZ*: 229.33).

[112]See Peck, *M. Terumot.*

[113]*Ibid.*

[114]This point is made at M. 4:1G-I.

[115]Alternatively, as at M. 4:1D-F, the issue is whether the action of crushing is interpreted as making a random snack or a regular meal. If one crushes in the hand, this is a snack, and the juice is exempt. If one crushes into a cup, this is a meal, and the juice is rendered liable. Cf. Maimonides, *Tithes* 5:17, RDBZ, *loc. cit.*, and Lieberman, *TK*, II:675.36.

[116]Cf. Lieberman, *TK*, II:676.39 and y. Ma. 1:8, end.

[117]Krauss, *TA*, II:189 affirms that the threshing was commonly done in the fields.

[118]Quoted by Finkelstein, p. 165, l. 2.

[119]On the stalls of Beth Ḥanan see Freedman's translation of b. B.M. 88a (p. 508, n. 8): "These were stores set up on the Mount of Olives for the supply of pigeons and other commodities required for sacrifices, and owned by powerful priestly families, to whom they proved a source of wealth."

[1] Cf. y. Ma. 2:1(49c), s.v., *šmw'l 'mr*.

[2] For other interpretations of the meaning of F's rather obscure point, see Maim., *Tithes* 5:6, MR and Albeck. Cf. y. Ma. 2:1(49c), s.v., *bmqwm šrwb*.

[3] The procedure for tithing *demai*-produce, and its rationale, are described by Sarason, *M. Demai*, p. 10:

> This procedure ("tithes of *dema'i*") is far less rigorous [than normal tithe-removal]. To begin with, we do not now separate heave-offering at all, since we assume that it already has been separated at the threshing-floor, viz., the point at which produce becomes liable to this obligation. The *ᶜam ha'areṣ* is deemed to take seriously the taboo against eating and selling *tebel*, and will not violate it .... We also do not have to separate first tithe from *dema'i*, but merely designate, i.e., localize, it in the produce. It is up to the Levite to prove that the produce certainly was not tithed if he wishes to claim his portion. We must, however, separate heave-offering of the tithe, i.e., one-hundredth part of the whole, from *dema'i*-produce and give it to the priest, for heave-offering of the tithe carries the same stringent taboo as does heave-offering (i.e., it may not be eaten by a non-priest), and is treated in every way like the latter. Second-tithe, too, must be accounted for in the case of *dema'i*, but this tithe simply may be designated in the produce, since in any case it can be redeemed with coins, the value of which will be eaten in Jerusalem by the owner of the produce. In the third and sixth years of the sabbatical cycle, poorman's tithe need only be designated in the produce. It is up to the poor man who would claim the tithe to prove that the produce has not previously been tithed. In the case of bread, dough-offering also must be separated from *dema'i*, since this is a priestly gift which cannot be eaten by a non-priest. Taken as a whole, only those tithes which a non-priest is forbidden to eat (heave-offering of the tithe and dough-offering) must be separated from *dema'i* produce and given to their rightful recipient. The preeminent concern expressed in this tithing procedure, then, is not to violate the taboo against eating a priestly offering. The tithing and purity preoccupations of the *ḥaber* are thus seen to be complementary in focus. On the one hand, only priests may eat unconsecrated food. On the other, non-priests are to eat their unconsecrated food in conditions of cleanness, i.e., as if they were priests eating priestly gifts.

[4] y. Ma. 2:2(49d), s.v., *hd' 'mrh šbytw ṭwbl lw 'bl l' l'ḥrym*.

[5] Printed editions read: *wkn byhwdh*, "and [this is] also [the case] in Judea." Thirteen MSS. and y. Ma. 2:3(49d), however, record the reading which I translate (cf. Sacks-Hutner, p. 214, l. 8, n. 8, and remarks by Albeck and MS to M. 2:3).

[6]Neusner, *Purities* III:336-42, V:213-16 and VIII:200-02, observes that contrasting positions on "form vs. function" underlie numerous pericopae in which Meir and Judah appear in dispute with each other. Neither authority, however, appears consistently "formalist" or "functionalist" from tractate to tractate, although within the limits of a *single* tractate each will consistently represent one view over against the other. See in particular Neusner's discussion in *Purities* III, *loc. cit.*

[7]MR, who assumes that the man is bringing the produce to Judea in order to sell it, stipulates that since the man has no intention of selling the produce until he reaches his destination, the produce is not rendered liable to the removal of tithes until the owner brings it to the market of his destination. At D the man has changed his destination in mid-journey, given up the thought of selling the produce in Judea, and returned to Galilee. Since he has given up his commercial interest, his produce remains permitted to him as a random snack until he arrives home or actually markets the produce elsewhere. Similar approaches may be found in MS, TYY and Bert. The solutions are all ingenious, but seem to me to over-interpret what is before us. Maimonides' version of the ruling (*Tithes* 4:11), which preserves D without explanation, is still the clearest presentation of the ruling: "While a person is conveying his produce from one place to another, it does not become designated for tithing, even if along his way he brings it into and out of houses and courtyards. He may therefore eat occasionally of it until he reaches his final destination. And the same applies to his return journey" (tr. I. Klein, p. 200).

[8]In Mishnah the term *rwkl* generally describes a seller of perfumes and spices (e.g., M. Kel. 2:4, cf. Jastrow, p. 1459, s.v., *RWKL*). As Maimonides (*Comm.*) points out, the subject of the present case is *not* produce which the peddler is offering for sale, but rather the untithed produce he has brought with him for his own personal use.

[9]Judah apparently contradicts M. 2:2J-L, which permits people found within a man's place of business, i.e., the surrogate for his own home, to make a snack of untithed produce. In fact, the two issues are unrelated. Judah's ruling at M. 2:2 N-O reveals that, for him, the problem is whether a place of business, i.e., a place not used as a dwelling, can be deemed a surrogate for the owner's own home. Judah concludes that it is deemed a surrogate only if the formal requirement of privacy is met; and even then, the privacy only establishes the "at homeness" of the owner, not that of the customers in his shop. In the present pericope, however, the problem is whether the *home* of one man can be a surrogate for the home of another. Judah now claims, on formalist grounds, that since the dwelling is *already* a home, anyone given permission to enter it is deemed to have entered the equivalent of his own dwelling. Cf. MR's probing discussion of M. 2:3.

[10]E reads: *'pylw lšty š^cwt*, interpreted by Lieberman as "at two hours," i.e., at 8 a.m. (*TK*, II:677.6).

[11]Lieberman (*ibid.*, ls. 5-6) considers E's reading a scribal error, for it makes nonsense of Meir's opinion. There is also another textual difficulty at L-N. Note that L, which employs the plural imperfect (*hgy^cw*), is out of phase with N, which employs the singular present participle (*hyyb*). Since M. 2:3E, upon which L-N is based, employs the singular (*mgy^c*), L must be considered a scribal error which has imported H's correct use of the plural imperfect *hgy^cw*.

[12]For further remarks on the use of Meir's traditions in M.-T.,
see R. Goldenberg, *The Sabbath Law of Rabbi Meir* (Missoula, 1978),
pp. 12-14.

[13]Heave-offering, the first agricultural offering to be
removed from produce, is normally separated at the completion of
processing (cf. T. Ter. 2:11-13), for this is the point at which
the owner incurs the obligation to tithe. The notion that the
completion of processing, apart from all other considerations,
renders produce liable is, of course, the unadorned thesis of
M. 1:5-8. M. 2:4 is entirely uninterested in further complexities,
introduced by M. 1:5-8's redactor, regarding the storage of produce or otherwise effecting appropriation. In M. 2:4's view, produce must be tithed as soon as it is desirable as food. The
question of appropriation, read into the pericope by T. and all
later commentators, is foreign to the problems before us.

[14]MR argues that A-C and E-G in fact address separate issues.
Of concern at A-C is whether removal of heave-offering indicates
the owner's decision to complete processing with the produce in
its present condition. At E-G the problem is whether figs in a
basket are processed or unprocessed. From this point of view
Sages are consistent, as I shall explain in my commentary. Cf.
Albeck, p. 395. MR's solution, as we shall see below, is little
more than an elaboration of T. 2:2, which offers an essentially
identical solution to the Sages' self-contradiction.

[15]Neusner, *Eliezer*, I:355.56, lists this pericope among those
"not demonstrably part of the traditions about Eliezer ben
Hyrcanus." The reason is that, in its redacted context, Eliezer
is placed in dispute with Simeon, an Ushan. Since Eliezer b.
Hyrcanus is a Yavnean, it is therefore likely that the Eliezer at
B is an Ushan Eliezer.

[16]See Sarason, "Mishnah and Scripture":

> The farmer, by his act of separation, determines how
> much of the produce actually has been consecrated as
> *terumah* [heave-offering]. That the holiness of produce
> is not immanent, but the result of man's act of consecra-
> tion, further is illustrated by the ruling that *terumah*
> and tithes for a particular batch of produce need not be
> separated from that batch itself. They may be taken from
> any tithable batch of produce, so long as natural taxonomic
> categories are not violated .... *For Mishnah, then, it is
> man who consecrates produce by his word and deed* [italics
> supplied].

Sarason's point, as he later states, is that Mishnah's theory
of holiness—at least as it applies to agricultural produce—is
"transactional rather than immanentist," i.e., that sanctification
occurs in the world by virtue of man's consecrating activity,
rather than by virtue of some created holy substance which inheres
within things irrespective of human agency. From this perspective,
at issue between Eliezer and Simeon is whether man's acts of
consecration, which require his complete attention and concentra-
tion (M. Ter. 1:1-3), may be broken by periods of inattention,
such that a snack may be made of the produce in the midst of its
tithing.

[17]So Lieberman, *TK*, II:679.18, citing y. M.S. 3:6, b. B.M. 88b.

[18]GRA (*Shanot Eliahu*, M. 2:4; cited by Lieberman, *ibid.*,
p. 678, 1. 11) explains Sages' agreement in the following way.
As M. 1:5K states, a basket of produce is completely processed as

soon as the owner picks all he needs. The fact that the separation
of heave-offering prevents the owner from adding completely untithed produce to the basket (i.e., mixing untithed with partially-
tithed produce), indicates that he has now picked the desired
quantity. Therefore the work is complete and the produce forbidden until the tithes are removed. This explanation is ingenious,
but ignores the fact that the produce at A is no less susceptible
to the addition of untithed produce after the heave-offering has
been separated, yet there the Sages do not consider the produce
forbidden.

[19]In y. Ma. 2:4(49d) our pericope is cited according to the •
version which reads, "and he removes tithes [as he would for]
certainly-untithed produce." The ensuing discussion begins with
the observation, "We have [another version] written in the notes
(*pynqś*) of Hilfai [which reads], 'He makes a chance meal of them
and removes tithes [as he would for] doubtfully-tithed produce.'"
b. Bes. 35b and MS Erfurht concur with Hilfai's version. I follow
the version of y., which offers a superior mnemonic for the
apodoses of the dispute: *l' y'wkl- dmyy/'wkl- wdyy*. Cf. Lieberman, *TK*, II:678.15-16.

[20]An *issar* is worth 1/24th of a *dinar* (T. B.B. 5:11). Cf.
Krauss, *TA*, II:406-08. The most recent study of currency in
Roman Palestine is D. Sperber, *Roman Palestine 200-400: Money
and Prices*. Sperber's work is far more sophisticated than Krauss's
in the use of rabbinic and other sources, and is more exhaustive
in scope as well. See especially his Table of Values (p. 29) as
well as his chapters on the *dinar* (pp. 31-34) and comparative
prices (pp. 1-25).

[21]Eleven MSS. read *ᶜsrym*, "twenty." On the strength of K-M,
which doubles the quantities cited at G-I, the translated reading,
that of the printed edition, is most likely.

[22]Judah's opinion, that the operative act is the buyer's
gathering of the produce, is congruent with the anonymous ruling
which introduces M. B.M. 4:2. Meir stands with Simeon, whose
gloss of M. B.M. 4:2 indicates that whoever holds the coin determines whether the purchase is binding. If the buyer holds the
ccin, the purchase is not deemed binding even if he has gathered
the produce. If, on the other hand, the seller holds the coin,
whatever the buyer gathers is deemed to be purchased. This is
precisely Meir's position at A-B. Cf. Neusner, *Damages* II.

[23]y. Ma. 2:5(49d), s.v., '*mr rby mn*' has an entirely different
view of matters, and an appropriate solution. According to Manna,
the buyer at A-B, unlike that of E-I, has not picked his figs,
but has rather received them from the seller in a handful. The
figs, which are *already* gathered before the buyer in the hands of
the seller, are therefore liable to tithes (cf. T. 2:11). Judah,
at C, maintains that even under these circumstances the buyer may
eat one fig at a time from the seller's hand. Manna reads the
problematic *maᶜaseh* at D as further support for Judah's position.
Judah now reports that the owner of the rose garden would not
permit people to enter it in order to purchase figs. Rather, he
would bring them to the buyers himself. Since these figs were not
tithed, Judah holds that any purcahse need not be tithed if the
buyer gathers fewer than five (cf. PM, *loc. cit.*). Manna's solution is ingenious but unsupported by the text.

[24]See Lieberman's explanation for reconstructing the text
(*TK*, II:234.43). Cf. also GRA's notes on the text of T., in which
he suggests the reading, *l' y'kl ᶜd šyᶜsr*, "he shall not eat

unless he tithes." Lieberman's emendation is to be preferred as
more plausible.

[25]The roots *QSY* and *QS^c* can refer either to harvesting fresh
figs, drying harvested figs, or packing pressed figs. I follow
the translations of Cohen (p. 264) and Danby (p. 69). For philological notes on these roots see Jastrow (p. 1405, s.v., *QSY*, *QSH*,
QS^cH), *Aruch Completum* II:169, s.v. *QS*, III:176, s.v. *QS^c*) and
Krauss (*TA*, II:197).

[26]Neusner, *Damages* II, translates M. B.M. 7:2 as follows:

   A. And these [have the right to] eat [the produce on which
      they work] by [right accorded them in] the Torah:
   B. he who works on what is as yet unplucked [may eat from
      the produce] at the end of the time of processing;
   C. [and he who works] on plucked produce [may eat from the
      produce] before processing is done;
   D. [in both instances solely] in regard to what grows from
      the ground.
   E. But these do not [have the right to] eat [the produce
      on which they labor] by [right accorded them in] the
      Torah:
   F. he who works on what is as yet unplucked, before the
      end of the time of processing;
   G. [and he who works] on plucked produce after the processing
      is done,
   H. [in both instances solely] in regard to what does not
      grow from the ground.

The Talmuds (b. B.M. 87a, y. Ma. 2:6[50a]) link the ruling
exegetically to Dt. 23:24-25, which permits a man to pick and eat
produce while in another's field, but forbids him from putting it
in a basket or cutting it with a scythe. Latter actions are
deemed trespassing or thievery. The Talmuds point out that field-
workers alone are exempt from this ruling. According to b. B.M.
87a, "When you are putting [the produce] in the householder's
basket [i.e., working for him], you eat [by authority of Dt.
23:24-25]; but when you are not putting it in the householder's
basket, you do not eat [by authority of Dt. 23:24-25]." Cf. also
Sifre Dt. 266 (Finkelstein, p. 286) and y. Ma. 2:6(50a), s.v.
ktyb ky tb' bqmt r^ck.

[27]Neusner, *op. cit.*, translates:

"And in all instances they have said [that he may eat from
the produce on which he is laboring] only in the time of
work" (M. B.M. 7:4).

[28]So y. Ma. 2:6(50a), s.v. *lmh ly ^cl mnt*.

[29]See Sacks-Hutner, p. 219, 1. 29, for the numerous variant
readings. The identity of these figs is uncertain (Löw, p. 392).
b. Ned. 50b, which cites A-B, reads *klwpsyn* for M.'s *lbsym*, and
identifies these as "a kind of fig from which pap is made." I
follow b. in translating *lbsym* as "cooking-figs." Cf. Jastrow,
p. 640, s.v. *KLWPSYN*.

[30]As above, the exact species is unclear. I translate following y. B.B. 2:14 (cf. Maim., *Comm.*, M. 2:8), which discusses "a
tree of white *brt swb^cyn*." *brt swb^cyn* is simply the Aramaic
equivalent of *bnwt sb^c*. Cf. Jastrow (p. 198, s.v. *BRT*, p. 200,
s.v. *BT*) and Bunte (p. 95).

[31]Neusner, *Damages* II, translates:

    A. [If the laborer] was working on figs, he [has] not [got
        the right to] eat grapes,
    B. [if he was working] on grapes, he [has] not [got the
        right to] eat figs.
    C. But [he does have the right to] refrain [from eating]
        until he gets to the best produce and then [to exercise]
        his right to eat.

Except for minor differences concerning the produce involved, M.
B.M. 7:4A-C is identical to M. 2:8A-C.

[32]*Ed. princ.* reads *ly*, "for me," where both M and P read *lk*,
"for yourself."

[33]The attribution to Eleazar b. R. Simeon is also supported
by y. Ma. 3:8(50d). M. knows two authorities named Eliezer b.
R. Sadoq, one of Yavneh and the other of Usha. Eleazar b. R.
Simeon, on the other hand, lived in Rabbi's generation.

[34]A *se'ah* equals six *qabs*.

[35]My interpretation of A-C + D-F differs substantially from
that of Rashi (b. Erub. 32a), MB, HY, HD, and Lieberman (*TK*,
II:679.20-21ff.). These commentators read the issue raised by
the gloss at G-L back into our rulings, and understand the matter
as follows. The problem of the rules is to determine whether the
owner of the figs is likely to have already tithed the figs by
removing tithes from another batch of produce on their behalf
(J-L). At A-C the recipient tithes the figs as certainly-untithed,
because the owner has not specified a particular amount of figs as
a gift. Consequently, he cannot have known the proper proportion
of tithes to remove on behalf of these figs from a separate batch
of produce. At D-F the recipient tithes the figs as if they are
doubtfully-tithed, because the basket is a fixed quantity, making
it possible for the owner to remove the proper proportion from a
separate batch as tithes for the basket. Full discussions of
these rulings are found in b. Erub. 32a-b and y. Ma. 2:1(49c),
s.v., *s' wlqt lk*. Cf. also Maimonides' revision of the pericope
in *Tithes*, 10:10, with the comments of KM.

[36]This point is assumed in M. 5:3A-C, below.

[37]While I mistrust my own interpretation of the case, I am
even less satisfied with those offered by HD, MB, PM, and
Lieberman (*TK*, II:681-82.30-31), all of which stem from the
following discussion of our pericope in y. Ma. 2:1(49c):

    "Rabbi Bun bar Ḥiyya inquired before Rabbi Ze[c]ira [concerning
    the obligation of the recipient of the twenty figs]: 'But
    is it not true that a man eats one by one and is exempt
    [from tithing]?' He [Rabbi Ze[c]ira] answered him, 'Yes.'
    'Then why is he required [to tithe]?' He answered him,
    '[The case assumes that] he has gathered [them together].'
    [Rabbi Bun replied], 'But if [the case assumes that] he has
    gathered [them together], then even the one who eats his
    fill should be required [to tithe]: And [furthermore], is
    he not forbidden [to eat without tithing] on the ground
    that exchange [is the same as a purchase]?' Said Rabbi
    Simi, 'He has not participated in an exchange, for this
    fellow only intended to encourage his [friend] to eat [by
    saying the equivalent of, 'Here, do not be ashamed of
    eating these twenty figs, for I shall take many of yours':
    PM].

The commentators cited above concern themselves with interpreting the enigmatic opinion of Simmi which, whatever it might in fact mean, does not solve the problem of why one man's produce is liable and the other's is exempt. MH (y. Ma. 2:1), after refuting all the options made available by y. concludes, "These matters have no solution, and there is no point in going on at length about them."

[1]On the root *QSY* refer to M. 2:7, p. 185, n. 25. Figs are routinely sun-dried in order to preserve them and to process them further into pressed cakes (cf. M. 1:8, M. 3:4).

[2]MSS. and *rishonim* know numerous versions of D-E. MS. Kaufman is identical to D-E as I have translated it, with the exception of D, where the word *ᶜlyw* appears instead of the *'wklyn wptwryn* of the printed versions. In context, MS. Kaufman's reading means: "The responsibility for tithing rests upon the employer." Bunte (p. 97), who uses MS. Kaufman as his primary text, interprets the law in this fashion as well. The point is that since the workers eat with the employer's permission, it is his responsibility to tithe the gift. MS. Kaufman, therefore, does not understand the workers to be eating by right of the Torah, a position with which I concur. Another variant, however, cited by MS, reverses the order of D and E, such that in a case in which the workers are dependent upon the employer for their board, they eat and are exempt, and if not, they must tithe. As Sacks-Hutner (pp. 221-22, n. 7) suggests, this reading must be interpreted to indicate that the workers of D-E are eating by right of the Torah, i.e., from produce which is in the midst of processing, while those of F-G are eating produce which is already processed. For further discussion, see MS, Sens, Sirillo and MR.

[3]The term *muqṣeh* (*QṢY*) applies to the drying figs as well as to the place in which they are dried. See Krauss (*TA*, II:197).

[4]Maimonides (*Comm.*, cf. *Tithes* 5:13) reads the issue in light of M. Dem. 5:8, which forbids one from selling *ṭebel*. Since the exchange of produce for labor is regarded as a ṣale, Maimonides says that the workers of F-G may not eat because "the owner may not defray his debt with *ṭebel*." This, of course, is correct, but there is little indication that M. is interested in bringing this principle into operation. Maimonides here makes the error, rare for him, of interpreting the ruling apart from the context created by M.'s redactor.

[5]The common translation of the *qal* construction of the root *ŠKḤ* is "to forget," a rendering which is confusing in the present context. The man has forgotten nothing, rather he has inadvertently brought his produce through a place which he should have avoided, had he his wits about him. To render this sense, I have chosen the word "careless."

[6]The readings for P are not unanimous. I have indicated the readings of *ed. princ.* and E in my translation. The paraphrase of our case in y. Ma. 3:1(50c) reads: "[If] he brought figs from the field [= M], and brought them through *his courtyard* in order to them on the roof--Rabbi declares [the figs] liable. R. Yose b. R. Judah declares [them] exempt" [italics supplied].
No reading is without its problems. In order to make sense of Lieberman's text or its MS. variants, we must assume that, contrary to M. 2:2, a man's produce can be rendered liable by passage through his fellow's home, even though the owner of the produce is not on a journey. Even if we so assume, the next problem is, as KM (*Tithes* 4:13) asks, Why should the fellow's home effect liability while the owner's own house (A-E, F-I) does not?

If we appeal to the version of y., which specifies that the man
has brought the produce through his *own* courtyard, we are still
left with the problem of understanding the discrepancy between A-F
and G-L, on the one hand, and M-Q on the other. Lieberman (*TK*,
II:683.37-38) suggests the following emendations as a solution.
In accordance with the version of y., he deletes O ("if he was
careless") as a copyist's error. This changes the case to one in
which the man *intentionally* brought the produce into a private
courtyard. Lieberman next suggests an eclectic reading for the
problematic stich at P: "and he brought them *through the courtyard of the house*." He explains that the man originally intended
to bring his figs to the roof via the *back* of the house which does
not face the courtyard. He then changed his mind and brought them
through the courtyard. Since his change of mind is deliberate,
the courtyard renders the figs liable. I would follow Lieberman
in deleting O, for the ruling at Q requires a deliberate act in
order to conform to the general rule worked out at A-F and G-L.
However I do not see how Lieberman's emendation of P is necessary,
or his explanation of it plausible.

[7]See also Maimonides, *Tithes* 5:13: "But if they are dependent
upon him for their board, they shall not eat even though the processing is not complete, for one does not defray a debt with
ṭebel." Lieberman (*TK*, II:684.39) follows Maimonides' understanding of the matter. At n. 4 above, I discuss the difficulty of
interpreting the present issue as a matter of defrayment of debts.
Here, as in M. 3:1, we are simply presented with an issue of sale.

[8]The roots *NKŠ* and *ᶜDR* can both bear the sense of "pruning"
(so Jastrow, p. 904, s.v. *NYKWŠ*, and Lieberman, *TK*, II:686 n.53).
If that is the case here, the point is that even though the workers
are actually removing fruit, they do not eat it by right of the
Torah, since the removal is not for the harvest, but rather for
the benefit of the other fruit on the tree. In my commentary I
have interpreted each root in the sense of "weeding."

[9]Here I follow Lieberman's emendation of K.

[10]b. B.M. 89a-b understands the point to be that use of salt
or bread encourages the worker to eat more than is proper, in
which case what he eats comes under the category of stolen property (cf. Rashi, b. B.M. 89b, s.v. *l' yšpwt* and *Nemuqei Yosef* to
Alfasi B.M. 52b, s.v. *kᶜnbym wdbr 'hr*). This interpretation of
T. would be legitimate if the pericope did not appear in our
tractate, but rather in T. B.M., which shows no interest in the
tithing laws. Since the pericope is presently located in our
tractate it is legitimate to read the issues of tithing into the
law, as I have indicated in brackets of my translation.

[11]M and Sa read: *qṣyᶜwt*, a reading attested as well in b.
B.M. 21b. See Sacks-Hutner, p. 233, n. 22, for citations from
Geonic and medieval halakhic sources. Cf. Cohen, p. 267, n. 6.

[12]T. Ket. 8:3 defines abandoned property (*hefqer*) as property
"the location of the owner of which is not known." For a general
discussion of the issue, see S. Albeck, "Ye'ush," *EJ* 16:774-75.

[13]Cf. b. B.M. 21b, Rashi, *loc. cit.*, s.v., *y'wš šl' mdᶜt*.

[14]So Raba, b. B.M. 21b, but cf. Maimonides, *Tithes* 3:24, who
does not see the issue in terms of theft at all:

> If one finds olives under an olive tree, or carobs under
> a carob tree, they are liable to tithing, because the

presumption is that they had dropped off from that same
tree. If one finds figs under a fig tree, there is cause
for doubt, seeing that figs are likely to change their
appearance by getting soiled in the dust, as to whether
they had dropped off from this fig tree or from some figs
that have already been tithed (tr., Klein, p. 197).

Given the fact that E is integral to C-D+E-F, Raba must be preferred to Maimonides on this point.

[15]On the general characteristics of this form in Mishnah, see
Neusner, *Purities* XXI:217ff.

[16]On the basis of T. 2:19I it is possible to argue that underlying the ruling is the notion that produce which may be used
either as human food or as cattle fodder is subject to the law of
tithes by virtue of its human value, even if actually used for
cattle. Maimonides explicitly assumes that this is the case in
Tithes 3:20. This assumption permits the following explanation
of M. at *Tithes* 3:18:

> In the case of carobs, as long as they have not yet been
> taken up to the roof-top, one may fetch some of them
> down for his cattle, and he is exempt, because he is
> likely to take the remainder back for drying, *so that*
> *he is thus providing only a casual feed for his beasts*
> (tr. Klein, p. 195, italics added).

The cattle are understood to have rights similar to those of the
householder's dependents. That is, they may eat unprocessed produce as a snack, sharing in this regard the privileges of the
householder himself. Cf. M. 3:1A-B.

[17]"Private domain" (*rṧwt hyhyd*) and "public domain" (*rṧwt
hrbym*) are common technical terms. In M. Shab. 11:1-2 and M. Erub.
10:4-9 the terms are used to distinguish separate realms of space
for the purpose of defining Sabbath limits on carrying. In M. Toh.
4:7, 4:11 and chapters 5-6, the adjudication of the status of
objects, about which there is doubt concerning their cleanness, is
determined by whether the objects were found lying in the private
or public domain (cf. Neusner, *Purities* XI:10-11, 112-18, 126-57).
As T. Shab. 1:3-5 makes clear, the terms primarily define a kind
of enclosed space.

[18]At b. B.M. 22b (s.v., *krykwt brhr hry 'lw ṧlw*) Rabbah and
Raba understand the issue to be the likelihood that the owner of
the lost object will despair of recovering it if it is lost in
the public domain.

[19]Cf. HY, HD, MB and Lieberman (*TK*, II:680.57-58).

[20]HD understands the rule to mean that the finder can declare
the produce to be heave-offering and tithes for his *own* produce.
Thus HD is able to read N in reference to both K-L and M. Since
the strewn grain (M) was smoothed before it was abandoned, it
remains subject to the law. Thus the finder may offer it as
heave-offering, etc., for other produce in his possession and need
not worry about being considered a thief. If stacked grain was
found (K-L), HD says that the finder may not use the produce himself unless he estimates the value of the produce and sets the
money aside for the former owner. The finder then removes the
offerings and eats the rest of the produce. HD here reads the
gloss at S-T back into this entirely separate case.

[21]See Peck, *M. Terumot*, for further discussion of M. Ter. 1:1ff.
The fact that the finder ought to have no right to dispose of
another's produce in any case brings Lieberman (*TK*, II:688.60-61)
to accept the reading of MS. Erfurt, which I have cited in my
translation. Lieberman's explanation is substantially that of
HD, cited above. S-T is read back into our rule. After having
estimated the cash value, the finder then "removes heave-offering
and tithes on their [i.e., the produce in the stack's] behalf
from the householder's produce; i.e., *from the produce itself*
[which has been found] (*mtwkm*) ... and gives heave-offering and
tithes to the Priest and Levite without fear of robbing the
householder." I do not see how N's directions to remove offerings
from produce belonging to the householder can possibly be understood to refer to the stack itself. MB, HY and GRA are able to
interpret N only by emending it to conform to the version of N
found at y. Ma. 3:3: "In either case, [the produce] is liable
[to the removal] of tithes, but exempt [from the separation of]
Great Heave-Offering (*trwmh gdwlh*), for it is not possible that
processed produce (*gwrn*) would be removed [from the threshing
floor] unless heave-offering had been separated." The rule avoids
the issue of robbery entirely and substitutes a plausible ruling
applicable to both K-L and M.

[22]My formal analysis of M. concurs almost entirely with
earlier analyses offered by Primus, *Aqiba*, pp. 71-72 and Porton,
Ishmael I: 46-47. See, however, n. 23, below.

[23]Porton, *loc. cit.*, does not distinguish B and C as separate
literary elements. There can be no doubt, however, that B-C as
a unity exemplifies the larger principle of the pericope.

[24]I have not been able to locate any archaeological evidence
illuminating the ways, if any, in which Tyrian courtyards differ
in structure from other types. According to W.L. MacDonald
("Tyrus," *Princeton Encyclopedia of Classical Sites*, p. 944),
remains stemming from Imperial Rome and the early Byzantine period
have been uncovered in Tyre, but are limited to colonaded avenues
and public buildings. No domestic dwellings have been found
which could confirm the assertion of y. Ma. 3:5(50d) and b. Nid.
47b that Tyrian courtyards have a guard posted at the entrance
protecting the utensils.

[25]Cf. M. Erub. 6:1-10 which assumes that a courtyard shared by
two or more householders constitutes a public domain separate
from the private domains of each household. The requirements of
Sabbath observance necessitate an agreement on the part of each
householder to place a commonly owned quantity of food (*crwb*)
within the courtyard on Sabbath Eve, so that the residents of
each house may consider the courtyard, in which their food is
kept, to be their household for the Sabbath. They may then carry
their utensils from house to house via the courtyard during the
Sabbath without violating the prohibition of carrying, on the
Sabbath, utensils from the private to the public domain. On the
importance of food in the establishment of the household, see
Nehemiah (F).

[26]Cf. M. Erub. 9:2. Eliezer points out that a courtyard
leading into the public domain (e.g., a street) is itself deemed
part of the public domain, such that it is forbidden on the Sabbath
to carry from such a courtyard into the private domain.

[27]Cf. y. Ma. 3:5(50d), which is identical to A-C, but at D
reads: "but *not* two tenants." The point, then, is that since

the courtyard is the domain of a single individual--the landlord--
the tenants' control of access is ceded to them by him. This
does not constitute a violation of his personal domain, for the
presence of the tenants is solely the landlord's decision. Therefore the courtyard retains its ability to render produce liable.

[28]The gate-house is a separate structure built into the wall
surrounding the courtyard. Normally a watchman is posted within
the gate-house to control access to the courtyard (Krauss, *TA*,
I:52, 365, n. 674).

[29]*kṣdrh* (pointed as *'akhṣadrah* by Yalon in Albeck, p. 231) is
a loan word from the Greek *exedra*. Krauss (*TA*, I:366, n. 675)
notes that in Greek usage the word denotes a covered colonnade
leading to the entrance of the house, while in Latin (*exedra*)
a kind of ante-room is indicated. In M. the structure is apparently similar to the Greek colonnade, leading from the entrance
of the courtyard to the doorway of the house (cf. T. Ah. 8:5,
where the normal exit from the *'kṣdrh* is assumed to be the gate-
house). In a *baraita* attributed to Eliezer (b. B.B. 25a-b) it is
assumed that the *'kṣdrh* is enclosed on three sides and open on
the fourth. Cf. T. Erub. 5:23 (*TM*, p. 116, ls. 59-60) and
Lieberman's remarks in *TK*, III:407.59-60.

[30]Balconies are attached to the house itself (see n. 32 below).
It should be noted that M. Erub. 8:4 considers these three structures to be domains distinct from the courtyard, such that if food
is placed in one of these structures on Sabbath Eve, it is not
permissible for the residents of the courtyard to carry utensils
from their homes to the courtyard on the Sabbath (cf. p. 192,
n. 25). Clearly, then, M.'s discussion of private and public
domains--so crucial in the construction of Sabbath law--are
immaterial in determining the status of produce regarding the
law of tithes. For example, a courtyard may be deemed public
domain regarding the Sabbath, yet private property regarding the
law of tithes. As far as I can determine M. makes no attempt to
harmonize or relate the two bodies of law (but cf. T. 2:17).

[31]The notion that the roofs of houses form a domain distinct
from those occupied by the houses upon which they are constructed
appears as well at M. Erub. 9:1. All roof-tops are deemed a
single domain regarding the Sabbath, such that objects kept on
roofs belonging to householders who have not co-operated in the
placing of an *ᶜerub* may be moved from roof to roof without
violating the Sabbath prohibition (see Neusner, *Appointed Times* I).

[32]C's balcony is somewhat out of phase with the point of the
ruling. If the balcony is built onto the house, why should its
status depend upon that of the courtyard? Since the householder
is free to step onto the balcony from his house, the balcony
ought to be deemed part of the domain of the house. Maimonides
(*Comm.*) suggests that balconies have a staircase leading to the
courtyard as well as an entry into the house. The balcony,
therefore, is considered part of the courtyard's contained space
and shares its status regarding the law of tithes. A literary-
critical solution is also possible. The series "gate-house,
portico, balcony" appears to be a formulaic protasis serving
cases in a number of different contexts (cf. M. Erub. 8:4,
M. Sotah 8:3). Apparently it has provided a protasis for C-D
as well, despite the fact that "balcony" is somewhat unsuited to
the ruling's principle.

[33]A make-shift structure used for storage (Bunte, p. 108, n. 1).
The notion that the *ṣryp* is cone-shaped appears in all commentaries,
and gains support from T. Suk. 1:10, which assumes that the roof
of a *ṣryp* may be less than a handbreadth in width. Krauss (*TA*,
I:275, n. 71) suggests that *ṣryp* is borrowed from the Greek
sarpos, defined in Liddel-Scott (p. 1311) as a kind of wooden hut.

[34]A loan-word, pronounced "borgan." The Greek *purgos* simply
means "tower" (Liddel-Scott, p. 1284), while the Latin *burgus*
refers more specifically to a watch-tower used for military
purposes (Krauss, *TA*, II:327). See now D. Sperber, "Pyrgos,"
in *AJSR* 1 (1976).

[35]Maimonides (*Comm.*, M. 3:6 and M. Oh. 18:10) implausibly
derives the word from the Aramaic *qyyṭ*, "summer," yielding the
meaning "summer hut." Krauss (*TA*, I:276, n. 81) suggests several
Greek candidates, all of which bear the sense of shed or shack.

[36]Gennasar refers to the region surrounding Lake Kinneret in
the Northern Galilee. For appearances of the term in the literature of Greek and Jewish antiquity, see Bunte, p. 108, n. 5.

[37]B and O^2 read *dyrt hmh 'w dyrt gšmym*, "*either* a summer
dwelling *or* a winter dwelling." According to this reading, the
dwelling need serve as a home only for an entire season, in order
to be deemed permanent. On the substitution of *w-* by *'w* in MSS,
see Epstein, pp. 1062-64.

[38]So Rashi, b. Suk. 8b, s.v. *šty šwkwt šl hywṣrym*. In b. the
inner hut is deemed a permanent dwelling, and is therefore required
to have a *mezuzah* attached to its doorpost, and may not serve as
a Festival Hut during the Festival of Tabernacles. The outer hut,
to the contrary, needs no *mezuzah* and may be used as a Festival
Hut.

[39]For further discussion, see Lieberman (*TK*, II:691.71).

[40]*Coriandrum* (Löw, p. 209).

[41]On the translation of *nšmr* as cultivated, see M. 1:1B and
p. 169, n. 4.

[42]M. Ter. 8:3 assumes with the present pericope that produce
picked for immediate use is rendered liable as soon as it enters
the courtyard, even if it is unprocessed. As far as I am aware,
my interpretation of M. as an exercise in defining a means of
eating produce without harvesting it in the courtyard is not shared
by any commentator to M. Maimonides, in both his *Commentary* and
Tithes 4:15-18, simply cites M. without interpretation; and he
is followed in this silence by Mishnah's later exegetes. RDBZ
(*Tithes* 4:18), however, argues that the point of our pericope is
to permit making a random snack of unprocessed produce in the
courtyard (cf. M. 3:1A-B). The dispute between Tarfon and Aqiba,
from this perspective, concerns only the quantity deemed permissible
as a random snack. As I have argued throughout this essay, however, "eating one by one" is not identical to "making a random
snack." The two notions are brought together for purposes of
analysis in M. 4:3 and M. 4:5A-D.

[43]Cf. Primus, *Aqiva*, p. 73 on the literary history of the
dispute: "The grapecluster, the pomegranate and the melon are
linked elsewhere without attribution to Aqiva, in ... M. Ma. 2:6;
although such evidence is not decisive, it does suggest that
[K-L] has been added on to Aqiva's saying in [J]. [H-I] are in

turn added on to Tarfon's opinion in order to balance the content, although obviously not the literary form, of [K-L]." According to Primus, then, the original dispute between Tarfon and Aqiba consisted of F+G vs. J.

[44]Compare my discussion of the identical materials at M. 2:6F-I. The different contexts within which the unit appears require different exegeses.

[45]An illustration of coriander, bearing out our exegesis of M.'s problem, may be found in Britton-Brown, II:646-47.

[46]See T. Ter. 2:12 (translated and discussed in Peck, *M. Terumot*) for the borders of the Land in Israel in regard to the law of tithes. The question of the sanctity of the land is made more complex by the fact that in certain locations outside the Land of Israel, such as Syria, an Israelite is required to offer tithes from produce growing on land which he has purchased. As elsewhere in Mishnah, the notion of "intrinsic sanctity" is modified, and sanctification is made relative to the needs and actions of human agents. Cf. M. 2:4, p. 183, n. 16 on this problem. The Talmud's discussion of sanctification and the borders of the Land of Israel is found at b. Git. 8a-b, and excellent discussions of this passage may be found in Maimonides, *Heave-Offering* 1:1-6 and MR (M. 3:10).

[47]MR adds that if the tree is rooted within the city, with a bough extending beyond it, the manslaughterer is protected if he takes shelter under the bough. It seems to me, however, that such a state of affairs more closely conforms to the principle of the entire tree sharing the status of the roots.

[48]Discussion of these laws may be found in Haas, *Maaser Sheni*.

[49]T. M.S. 2:12 adds that if the roots are within the city and the bough without, the entire tree is considered outside the city. Fruit picked within the walls, therefore, may be brought outside the city and exchanged for coins (so Lieberman, *TK* II:730.62-63). Both M. and T. M.S. 2:12 contradict M. M.S. 3:7, which states that produce growing within the wall is deemed to be within the city, while produce growing from the bough is deemed to share the status of produce brought from afar. b. Mak. 12a-b and later commentators have proposed numerous ways of resolving the contradiction. Representative, and valuable for its clarity, is the discussion of Maimonides, *Second Tithe and Fourth Year's Fruit* 2:15 (tr. I. Klein, p. 251): "In the case of a tree standing within the wall of Jerusalem with its foliage extending outside, *one may not eat second tithe underneath its foliage* [for regarding the eating of second tithe, one beneath the bough is deemed to remain outside the city: KM, *loc. cit.*]. *Second tithe that has come under its foliage may not be redeemed*, inasmuch as it is accounted the same as if it had entered Jerusalem" [italics supplied]. Maimonides, as interpreted by Joseph Caro (KM), claims that we rule according to the location of the bough in one set of circumstances and according to the location of the roots in another, in order to impose the greater stringency in either case.

[50]Lieberman (*TK*, II:692.75) seeks to harmonize A-D with M. 3:10 D-E. The problem, then, is why the man should be able to eat as he pleases from a bough extending into his home, when he may eat only one by one in the courtyard. Lieberman's answer appears to be *ad hoc*, with no textual evidence to support it:

"Perhaps ... the explanation is that he picks as much as he pleases--even two by two--as long as he has not completed picking." In other words, we do not consider the harvest (and processing) complete until the owner has picked all he desires. For another harmonistic interpretation, see HY's citation of RTBA, who says that since the figs have been brought into the house through the window, rather than the door, the unusual mode of entry exempts the produce from liability.

[51]It should be noted that M.-T. is not univocal on this point, for T. 2:19A-H clearly permits unprocessed produce to be brought to the table without the necessity of removing the tithes.

[52]This is by far the simplest explanation of the dispute. For further discussion in the light of the laws applying to dough-offerings and trees bearing fruit for less than three years, see y. ^COrl. 1:1, b. Git. 22a, b. B.B. 27b and Lieberman, *TK*, II:692-93.77-78.

CHAPTER FOUR

[1]"In the field" (*bsdh*) appears in eighteen MSS, and is included in Albeck's text. The phrase is absent from the standard printed edition reproduced in Sacks-Hutner (p. 232, n. 4).

[2]*hmtbl*. Cohen, p. 272, n. 8, explains, "If he dipped it in salt, brine or vinegar."

[3]I interpolate "a ladle of wine" on the basis of T. 1:9A-C (p. 58), which points out that wine skimmed in a tub or other small vessel is not rendered liable to the removal of tithes. For further remarks, see n. 5 below.

[4]My interpretation of M.'s issue, which denies that E-H's concern for processing may be read into A-D, differs dramatically from that of most commentaries. These follow Maimonides' view of matters. Maimonides, in an effort to rationalize M.'s diverse criteria by which produce is rendered liable to the removal of tithes (*Tithes*, 3:3-4; cf. y. Ma. 4:1[51a], b. Bes. 35a), offers the following account of the law (tr. I. Klein, pp. 191-92):

> Each one of the following six things designates produce for tithing: courtyard, purchase, fire, salt, heave-offering, and Sabbath. *And all of them are effective only upon produce whose preparation [i.e., processing] has been completed.* How so? ... [P]roduce sold, boiled over a fire, pickled with salt, subjected to heave-offering, or overtaken by the Sabbath--one may not eat thereof until he has tithed it, even if it has not yet reached the house [italics supplied].

Note Maimonides' insistence that *only* processed produce can be rendered liable to tithes. The data of M. do not support this interpretation, for the grapes of M. 3:8-9, for example, are rendered liable in the courtyard without any processing whatsoever. M.'s concern for processing, rather, is a function of its conviction that a man is only likely to appropriate produce in its most desirable form (cf. my discussion of M. 1:5-8, pp. 45-48). It is in no sense, however, a *sine qua non* for determining whether or not produce can be rendered liable. Should a man, as in M. 4:1, make appropriation of the produce despite its unprocessed condition, the produce is rendered liable immediately. At issue in M. 4:1A-D, therefore, is not whether the cooking or pickling completes the processing, but whether these acts indicate preparation for use in a meal. In other words, M. simply wants to know whether or not the man intends his actions to effect appropriation of the produce prior to the normal act of appropriation (e.g., bringing the produce home, etc.).

[5]Cohen (p. 272, n. 14), following Bert., argues that the wine has been skimmed *after* it has been poured into the stew: "Liability to tithing is not fixed here by this skimming, since the wine has already been mixed before the skimming." The point, I assume, is that since the wine was not food when it was added to the stew, the later skimming is inconsequential, for now there is indeed no possibility of skimming the wine in its pure condition. The circumstances, however, seem implausible to me, for which reason I have interpolated at G the factor of the ladle of wine.

[6]Mishnah understands Ex. 16:23's prohibition against preparing food on the Sabbath to include as well a prohibition against
tithing on that day. Cf. M. Shab. 2:7, M. Bes. 5:2 and Maimonides'
Commentary to M. Bes. 1:1 and M. Ter. 2:3. Tithing, it appears,
is understood as part of the food's preparation.

[7]D-F appears at M. Ed. 4:10 as part of a catalogue of Houses
disputes having the common element of a strict Hillelite ruling
and a correspondingly lenient Shammaite ruling. For discussion
see Neusner, *Pharisees* II:93-94, 331-40 and *Damages* IV.

[8]b. Bes. 34b. s.v. *my 'mrynn* (cf. Rashi, *loc. cit.*, s.v.,
tynwqwt) seems to suggest that at issue between the Houses is
whether an untithed basket of Sabbath fruit may be eaten on the
Sabbath without the removal of tithes. The Shammaites, in this
view, would argue that since the produce is designated for the
meal, it need be tithed only if it is used in the meal. The
householder, therefore, may *snack* during the Sabbath without
tithing. The Hillelites, however, differ, arguing that *all* produce consumed on the Sabbath is deemed a festive meal (cf. Sens,
M. Ed. 4:10), and must therefore be tithed. Since this is
impossible on the Sabbath, the produce remains forbidden. The
problem with this interpretation is that the apodoses of the
dispute do not support it. If matters are as b. suggests, we
should expect the dispute to be *mtyryn* vs. *'wśryn* (permit vs.
forbid), i.e., the Shammaites *permit* use of the produce on the
Sabbath, while the Hillelites *forbid* its use. Instead we have
pwtryn vs. *mhybyn* (declare exempt vs. declare liable). The
question can only be whether the produce is exempt from the
removal of tithes under all circumstances or liable under all
circumstances. Such a question can only arise if at issue is
the status of the produce on a day *other than* the Sabbath. As
I suggest, the true exegetical problem of the dispute is to
determine whether the Houses refer to the status of the produce
before the Sabbath (as at G) or after the Sabbath (A-C).

[9]MR rejects Maimonides' claim that G refers specifically to
a Sabbath basket, preferring instead to read G in light of M.
Dem. 3:3. That rule forbids a man from sending untithed produce
to a friend, lest the latter assume that tithes have been removed,
and consequently eat forbidden produce. MR argues that as soon
as one resolves to send such a gift it is rendered liable, so
that even the sender, who knows it is untithed, must tithe before
eating. MR's exegesis is, however, implausible. The point of
M. Dem. 3:3 is to relieve the recipient of doubt regarding the
status of the produce. The sender, who has no such doubts,
should therefore be permitted to snack without tithing until he
actually sends the gift. M. Dem., then, appears to have no bearing upon Judah's ruling. Similarly, it is hardly likely that
Judah requires a person to tithe all produce he offers as a gift,
for at M. 2:2 he assumes just the opposite. Clearly, then, Judah
must have a Sabbath basket in mind, as Maimonides suggests, and
as the context of M. requires. Cf. M. 5:1E-F and discussion.

[10]It is by no means unusual for a dispute attributed to the
Houses in the period before 70 A.D. to depend upon conclusions
attested, in their earliest formulation, to Usha (135-180 A.D.).
For the classic discussion of this phenomenon, see Neusner,
Purities XI:203-19 and XII:133-43 (M. Toh. 9:1-7): "Where we
have an Ushan attestation, therefore [i.e., Simeon, T. Toh. 10:10],
we must take seriously the possibility that Ushans have phrased
the problem in terms of principles important to Ushans and have
assigned opinions to the Houses congruent to larger general

rules ... subject to dispute by them ...." (*ibid.*, XII: 141).
Strikingly, the issue at M. Toh. 9:4 is identical to that of
M. 4:2, the problem of whether intentions or actions regulate
how we determine the status of food regarding susceptibility to
uncleanness (M. Toh.) or liability to the removal of tithes.

[11]Lieberman's emendation of V; see *TK* II:694.3-4 for discussion. V, which Lieberman prints as his text, reads: "doubt
[concerning the identity of the figs renders them] forbidden;
doubt [concerning] the preparation [of the figs specifically for
the Sabbath renders them] forbidden" (*špyqn 'šwr špq mwknn 'šwr*).
Cf. the version in Zuckermandel, p. 84, ls. 18-19, which follows
MS. Erfurt: "lo, these are forbidden, for doubt [concerning
their identity renders them] forbidden." This is followed by an
independent stich which reads: "doubt [concerning] preparation
[of the figs specifically for the Sabbath renders them] forbidden."
Lieberman argues that MS. Vienna has added this independent stich
to its own tradition, thus conflating two texts. He therefore
harmonizes the two by inserting the conjunction *mpny š* between
MS. Vienna's original tradition (D) and that of MS. Erfurt (E).

[12]Lieberman (*TK*, II:694.2-4), following all commentaries,
interprets the pericope within the framework of the tithing laws.
In his view the figs are liable to tithes if they have been
designated for the Sabbath. The problem of the case is to determine tithing procedure in cases where there is doubt as to whether
the produce has in fact been designated. Presumably, if the figs
have not been designated, the advent of the Sabbath should have
no effect upon them. The point of D (+E), then, is that doubt as
to whether the figs have been designated for the Sabbath requires
us to treat them as if they have been designated. Thus the figs
are forbidden unless they are tithed. I have not taken this
route because the apodoses at D and E employ the term "forbidden"
(*'šwr*) instead of the term which is standard regarding produce
which is liable to tithes, *ḥyb*. Since, in M. Bes. 1:4, "forbidden"
signifies nothing more than that the produce may not be prepared,
I have understood its use here in the same way.

[13]M. Bes. 1:4A-B: *zmn šḥwrym wmṣ' lbnym, lbnym wmṣ' šḥrym.*
T. 3:2b/A-C: [*ṭmnw*] *šḥwrym wmṣ' lbnym, lbnym wmṣ' šḥwrym.*

[14]But cf. Rashi, b. Bes. 35a, s.v., *ḥll ʿṣmw*, and Lieberman
(*TK*, II:694-95.5-8), who argue that the point of the gloss is
to show that *only* Hillel held to the prohibition. Further proof
is adduced by Lieberman from MS. variants of b.'s text which
indicate that Hillel enacted the rulings for *himself* alone (*ḥll
lʿṣmw hyh 'wśr*). If this is the case, the point of Judah's
glosses is to show that the rulings are a minority opinion. This
is unlikely, however, for the anonymous ruling cited at J is
attributed to none other than Judah at M. 4:2G. At K Judah
glosses this ruling with the observation that Hillel himself used
to forbid it. If the point of Judah's gloss is to say that only
Hillel held the opinion at J, it is necessary to explain why T.
cites Judah against his own words in M.

[15]See n. 10 above. For further discussion of the probable
provenance of M. 4:2 and related materials see my remarks in
Neusner, *Judaism*, "Appendix II" and Neusner's earlier discussion
in *Pharisees*, I:230.

[16]y. and major commentaries to T. read M. 4:2A-C and T. 3:5a
as pericopae deriving from the same hand and exhibiting the same
principle, i.e., that the intentions of minors cannot be inferred

from their actions (see y. Ma. 4:2[51b], s.v. *r z^c̆yr b̆ṣm rb hmwn'*
and Lieberman, *TK* II:695-96.9). I do not see that the issue is
of any importance to either M. or T.

[17]In light of F, the batch of salted olives is liable because,
having been salted, it can no longer be returned to the bin. The
olives in the bin, we recall, are being softened for eventual
pressing. If the salted olives are returned to the bin, the
resulting oil will be salty and devoid of commercial value.
Clearly, then, the householder has removed the olives permanently
and intends to use them in a meal.

[18]Alternatively, B-C and D-F are independent rulings, each of
which is served by the protasis at A. The issues of both B-C
and D-F, while certainly related, are quite independent of each
other, for while F is essential to the exegesis of D-F, it offers
only a secondary level of meaning to A-C (see above note). I
would argue that redactional skill alone is responsible for the
fact that D-F appears to be such a natural and appropriate gloss
of A-C.

[19]The chain of contamination presupposed by the ruling may be
found at M. Toh. 2:2-7, a pericope in which Eliezer, incidentally,
plays an important role. On the presumed second-remove uncleanness of the hands, see M. Yad. 2:3-4. In the present case, the
transfer of uncleanness from the hands to the olives occurs in the
following manner. The hands, presumed to be in the second remove
of uncleanness, render unclean in the first remove the liquid
coating the olives. The olives, coated by the liquid, are then
unclean in the second remove. When these olives are returned to
the batch of clean olives, they render unclean in the first remove
that liquid coating the remainder of the olives. Now *all* the
olives of the bin are unclean in the second remove.

[20]Lieberman deletes *thwr* ("clean") from the end of the stich,
despite its presence in both E and V. The deletion is sound,
for it makes no sense to return the unclean olives to a clean bin.

[21]For interpretations of the Houses dispute in light of M. Bes.
1:8, see Lieberman, *TK* II:703.31-32. While E-G may plausibly
be understood to reflect the issues of M. Bes. 1:8, Simeon b.
Eleazar's phrasing of matters is clearly dependent upon A-D's
refinement of M. 4:3A-C. Therefore, the Houses opinions trans-
mitted by him are most probably the result of Ushan efforts to
depict the Hillelites in accord with M. 4:3A-C. See p. 198, n. 10
and p. 199, n. 15.

[22]A is an imperfectly formulated protasis for this dispute,
for the present apodoses at C and D do not smoothly follow from A.
As it stands, A is simply a declarative sentence stating a rule,
to which are appended "it is exempt" and "declares liable."
Normally, such apodoses should refer to a protasis phrased as
conditional clause, e.g., "If one drank wine at the press" (*s̆th
c̆l hgt*), or "One who drinks wine at the press" (*h̆s̆wth c̆l hgt*).
MSS. cited at C attempt to achieve a smoother reading by adding
w-, "and," to the first apodosis. This yields a somewhat better
reading: "They drink ... *and* it is exempt." One may speculate
that A has been reformulated in order to create a better sentence
in conjunction with B, for together they appear to be a single
ruling: "They drink ... whether ...." Even this reading, however,
leaves C and D poorly connected to their protasis.

[23]Both b. Shab. 11b and b. Erub. 99b (followed by G[4] and G[5])
cite A-E with the additional stich, "since he returns the surplus"

(= M. 4:3F). Either this shows exceptional sensitivity to the
redactional program of M.'s redactor, or M. at one time circulated
in the form cited at b. Epstein does not discuss the pericope.

[24]Meir's position is represented as well by the glossator of
M. 1:5-6 (C, E, G-H, J-K, P, R, T). For comment, see pp. 45-46.
above.

[25]Read outside the context of M. 4:3, Sages' distinction between hot and cold mixtures makes a different point entirely.
Wine mixed with hot water is understood to have been cooked (M. 4:1),
and must be tithed on that account alone. While this is in fact
a far simpler interpretation of M., I follow b. in permitting the
redactional context of the pericope to impose its own logic on
the materials.

[26]So Bunte, p. 126, n. 1.

[27]Eleven MSS. and b. A.Z. 7b read, "Eliezer." See Epstein,
p. 1177, for a discussion of the frequent confusion between Eleazar
and Eliezer in MSS. As I shall argue, evidence internal to the
pericope suggests that at G we should read "Eliezer," as the
majority of textual witnesses attest.

[28]See Sifre Dt. 105c/T, p. 39, and p. 174, ns. 59 and 60.

[29]So fifteen MSS. and Albeck vs. the printed text's "Rabban
Simeon ben Gamaliel." See Sacks-Hutner, p. 129, n. 5.

[30]*Vicia Faba* (Löw, p. 312, Bunte, p. 129, n. 5).

[31]*Capperis Spinosa* (Löw, p. 264, Bunte, p. 130, n. 1).

[32]See Sacks-Hutner, p. 236, ns. 58 and 70. Of all sources I
have consulted, only Sirillio, in his commentary to y., divides
the pericope into its natural units, A-D and E-L.

[33]Compare M. 1:1D-F and discussion, pp. 29-30. Both E-J
and M. 1:1E assume that produce deemed food is not subject to the
law until it is actually edible (although the assumption is only
implicit at E-J). M. 1:1E, however, is explicit that once a
person intends his crop for use as food, objective criteria of
edibility govern the point at which it is actually subject to the
law. We may assume that Aqiba, at K-L, would agree on this point.
E-J, on the other hand, is concerned with a separate, and logically
prior matter, i.e., the role of the farmer's intention in determining first of all that a crop is to be the kind of produce which
is considered to be food. Thus, once the subjective factor of
intention determines that a crop shall be food (E-L), objective
criteria of edibility determine when it actually becomes subject
to the law of tithes (M. 1:1D-F).

[34]So y. Ma. 4:5(51b), s.v. *kyny mtnyt'*.

[35]The fact that Aqiba, a Yavnean, glosses J suggests that if G
and J are attributed to a single authority, that authority is
Eliezer b. Hyrcanus, a Yavnean. Cf. Neusner, *Eliezer* I:71.
Neusner lists this pericope among the "fair" traditions (*Eliezer*
II:175), i.e., "those attested at Bet Shearim, in the circle of
masters around Judah the Patriarch" (*ibid.*, p. 90).

[36]On the use of originally independent materials to create
"artificial" disputes, see the important article of G. Porton, "The
Artificial Dispute: Ishmael and Aqiba," in Neusner, *Cults* IV:18-29.

[37]Cf. M. Ter. 10:5-6 where the stalks of fenugreek are deemed
to be heave-offering (i.e., food) only if the householder has
specifically designated them as such. Peck's remarks to the
pericope, in the forthcoming *M. Terumot*, are most interesting from
the perspective of E-J: "... The stalks [of fenugreek] are not
deemed to be liable to the separation, or to have the status of
tithes, for the householder normally does not eat them. If,
however, he designates them as such, the designation is valid,
for he *shows his intent to use the stalks as food*" [my italics].

[38]Primus, *Aqiba*, pp. 73-74, stresses this point as well.

[39]Lieberman explains T.'s distinction on the basis of the
relative sizes of the two types of kernel. Since wheat kernels
are smaller, one may gather more of them without being suspected
of intending to make a formal meal (*TK*, II:697.11). For an
attempt to read T. 3:6 in light of M. 4:3F ("for he returns the
surplus"), see y. Ma. 4:5(51b), s.v., *'mr lyh šnyy' hy' hk'*.

[40]Cf. T. Dem. 1:14 (= T. Makh. 3:15) where a related formulary
pattern is employed for the transmission of Joshua b. Qebusai's
tradition (*mymy l' gš lyby* vs. *kl ymyy hyyty qwr'*).

[41]Jastrow (p. 355, s.v., *HMTLY'*) identifies *hemtalia* ("liver-
wort") as a loan-word from the Greek, *hepatorion*, "Herbs used for
cooling the blood." Cf. *Aruch Completum* V:122, s.v. *MTLY'* which
describes the product as a type of white bean.

[42]For discussion of M. Ter. 2:4's ruling concerning the
proper separation of heave-offering, see Peck, *M. Terumot*.

[43]y. Ma. 1:1 (s.v., *w^cwd mn hd' dtny*) revises the ruling to
more clearly support Gamaliel's position: "Said R. Joshua [y.
deletes patronymic]: 'Never in my life did I presume to tell a
man, "Go and pick *stalks of fenugreek, of mustard, and of white
beans*, and boil them in order to exempt them from tithes." The
italicized portion cites M. 4:6I.

[44]b. A.Z. 38b (tr. Cohen, p. 188) gives the following recipe:
"Take the seeds of parsley, flax and fenugreek, soak them together
in lukewarm water and leave them until they begin to sprout. Then
take new earthenware pots, fill them with water and soak therein
red clay into which the seeds are planted. After that go to the
bathhouse and by the time of coming out they will have blossomed,
and on eating of them you will feel cooled from the hair of the
head down to the toenails."

[45]y. Ma. 4:6(51c) knows a discussion of M. 4:6J which appears
to have been formulated in light of C: "The blossoms and the
stalks [of the caper-bush] are a single kind. One tithes the
blossoms on behalf of the stalks, and the stalks on behalf of the
blossoms--but [one does] not [tithe either] of them on behalf of
the berries, or the berries on their behalf."

NOTES

CHAPTER FIVE

[1]So have matters been viewed by the copyists and printers responsible for the present chapter divisions. For a somewhat different analysis of the place of Chapter Five's materials in the structure of the tractate, see my outline of M. in the Introduction to this volume, pp. 11-12.

[2]Cf. Pa, O[2], P and R: *lqḥ*, "purchased." The reading is accepted as well by Maimonides (*Tithes* 5:2) and other commentators, including Epstein, pp. 229-30. If we accept this reading the point of E-F is that since the purchase is designated for another, the produce remains permitted to the one who actually purchased it. If this is the correct reading, however, then the point made by Eleazar at G-H seems hardly *a propos*.

[3]On the problem of translating *grn*, see p. 176, n. 79. In the present context the word "harvest" seems most appropriate.

[4]I follow the witness of twelve MSS. over against the printed text's and Albeck's *bslym mšhšryšw*. See Sacks-Hutner, p. 240.

[5]As at M. 4:5-6, the infelicitous division of the pericopae is the responsibility of copyists and printers. In the present case only Sirillio, as before (cf. p. 201, n. 32), recognizes the natural units, A-L and a pair of declarative sentences at M-O.

[6]Cf. Theophrastus, *Enquiry* VII, v. 3: "All herbs grow finer and larger if transplanted; for even the size of leeks and radishes depends upon transplantation. Transplanting is done especially in view of collecting seeds."

[7]The ruling entirely ignores the intentions of the farmer, a surprising fact in view of the crucial role played by intention in the cases of Chapter Four.

[8]Cf. Sarason, *M. Demai*, *passim*.

[9]For a completely different evaluation of Eleazar's contribution, see T. Zahavy, *Eleazar b. Azariah*, p. 28.

[10]Cf. y. Ma. 5:3(51d), s.v. *kyny mtnyt'*, and PM (M 5:3). The context requires the sale of the field with the produce growing in it. Otherwise, the seller would simply tithe the produce on behalf of the purchaser prior to the sale. If the field itself is included in the sale, however, the seller has absolutely no control over the produce from that point on.

[11]So Freedman (b. Ned. 43b, p. 139) for *ykwl lḥzwr bw*.

[12]Lieberman observes that the unit serves the interests of T.'s redactor, rather than those of M. We recall that T. 3:8C(1) has already introduced the issue of ownerless produce, and we shall see that the matter is carried further at T. 3:12. Thus, the matter of ownerless produce, which is totally ignored by M., appears as a running sub-theme in T. Interestingly, the two most substantial units on this subject, T. 3:11 and T. 3:12, have no interest in the subject of tithing whatsoever.

[13]Both y. Pe'ah 6:1 and b. Ned. 43b-44a assume that the point
of the householder's activity is to avoid the necessity of removing tithes from the produce of the field. If he reclaims the
field as a passer-by, he is considered to have claimed an abandoned
field, the produce of which is exempt from the law. If he simply
retracts the declaration of ownerlessness, however, the field remains his as before, and he is responsible for tithing the produce
(cf. Greenstone and Albeck, "Hefker"). Within this context,
standard in all commentaries (cf. Freedman, b. Ned. 44a, pp. 139-
140, ns. 2-5), Lieberman provides the most cogent interpretation
of the ruling before us (*TK*, II:704): "Bavli [i.e., b. Ned. 44a]
explains that the Sages passed such an ordinance to hinder dis-
honest landlords, so that they would not relinquish their fields
and then reclaim them [as passers-by], thereby exempting themselves
from the law of tithes. Thus they said that for three days the
householder may retract his declaration. Now, by definition, any
act of laying claim to the field could be considered a retraction
[of the original declaration of ownerlessness]. Thus the field is
not rendered exempt from the law of tithes [for it is considered
to have been in the continuous possession of the householder]. The
fact that the householder is prevented from claiming the field for
three days permits the word of the field's release to spread, and,
in turn, arouses the householder's fears that someone else will
preceed him in claiming it. The fact that he has refrained from
making an outright retraction of his declaration for three days
proves that he is not acting deceptively [when, after three days,
he in fact lays claim to the field as a passer-by]." This is an
ingenious interpretation of our rule, and shows its relevance to
a tractate on Tithes, but receives no support from the text of T.
Indeed, even if we accept the context outlined above, the rulings
of C-I are extremely difficult to follow. As G-I, in particular,
shows, the householder may simply claim the land as a passerby,
and exempt the field's produce from the law. If the Sages are
intent on preventing circumventions of the law, we must explain
why they apparently permit it here. See Freedman's discussion,
cited above, for a survey of later thinking on the matter.

[14]See Lieberman, *TK*, II:704.36-37.

[15]Lieberman, who argues that A-D furthers T.'s particular
interest in ownerless produce, offers the following plausible
interpretation. "If he winnowed carelessly, and was unconcerned
with extracting the wheat from the straw, the wheat is simply
ownerless produce and is exempt from tithes--even if the purchaser
acquired the straw in order to remove the wheat" (*TK*, II:705.39).

[16]y. Dem. 6:7 (s.v., š'yn) explains the rulings as an expression of concern for one who is starving for lack of bread. The
explanation is not entirely implausible. T. Sheb. 6:20 forbids
the sale of large quantities of Seventh Year produce to an ʿam
ha'areṣ, but permits the sale of a quantity sufficient for three
meals. Presumably, the smaller quantity is not useful for trade,
and will support the life of the purchaser.

[17]Cf. T. Dem. 4:31 and Sarason's comments, in *M. Demai*, p. 149.
See also the slightly different view of matters offered by
Lieberman (*TK*, II:706.43), who views the prohibition as one for-
bidding the *gift* of food to one who does not remove the necessary
offerings, or prepare food in purity. Lieberman's view is based
upon a varient reading found in MS. Erfurt and in G.

[18]For further discussion, see Lieberman (*TK*, II:706.44-45).
Cf. also GRA's emendations and the subsequent comments of MB on
the emended text. A large block of materials treating the problem

of the householder who must share his produce with his tenant-
farmers appears in T. Dem. 7:1-15, of which T. Dem. 7:11-12 are
particularly relevant to our problem. Sarason's comments may be
found in *M. Demai*, pp. 221-25.

[19]Although governed in the past by Israelite kings, Syria is
not deemed part of the original gift of God to Israel, a fact
which raises a number of ambiguities regarding the application
in Syria of certain laws specific to the Land of Israel. The
problem is discussed at b. Git. 8a, and is summarized in regard
to agricultural law by Maimonides at *Heave-Offering*, 1:2-5. For
a recent contribution toward determining those portions of the
Land of Israel which were subject to tithing laws, see Sussman,
"Inscription," pp. 97-104.
    The status regarding the law of tithes of produce grown in
Syria is under dispute by Yavneans at M. Hal. 4:7. There Eliezer
and Gamaliel dispute whether tenant-farmers to a non-Israelite in
Syria need tithe their produce and let their fields lie fallow
in the Seventh Year. The problem is pressing, for while tenant-
farmers work the land, they do not own it. Gamaliel, who exempts
their produce from laws applicable to Israelite produce, apparently
carries forward the position which becomes normative in M.

[20]T. attributes the position to Aqiba, an attribution supported
by an independent, but parallel, *baraita* in y. Ma. 5:4(51d):

> *tny*: A field reaching a third of its growth under the
> ownership of a non-Israelite, and an Israelite purchased
> it from him--R. Aqiba says, "That which ripens afterward
> is exempt," but Sages say, "That which ripens afterward
> is liable." Cf. b. H. Hul. 136a and Lieberman, *TK*,
> II:707.47-48.

[21]MR's position is based upon b. Men. 67a, s.v. *gr šntgyyr*,
which MR understands to release from the law of tithes produce
which is processed at the hands of gentiles. He holds that the
point of Judah's ruling is to require the Israelite purchaser to
hire Israelite workers in the harvest of the crop, so that, in
cases in which the produce is purchased before it ripens, the
householder will not try to prevent the produce from being tithed
by the ploy of hiring gentile harvesters. I do not see how this
issue can be read into Judah's lemma.

[22]For extensive form-analytical comment, see Primus, *Aqiva*,
pp. 74-79.

[23]Lieberman interprets Sages' to exempt the produce only if
it was purchased *in a harvested condition*. Thus, their position
is not like that of Simeon b. Gamaliel's, for they hold that the
produce is liable if purchased while attached to the ground,
whether or not the land was included in the purchase. Lieberman
does not explain why he interprets the Sages' remark in this
manner, and I cannot see what he gains by it, since we can in no
way imagine Aqiba to hold such a position.

[24]Such grape-pulp wine is called *temed*. See Bunte, p. 149,
n. 1.

[25]M. M.S. 1:3 prohibits the purchase, with coins designated
as second-tithe, of unfermented *temed*. The liquid, in other
words, is deemed water, and cannot be sanctified as second-tithe.

[26]In Judah's view, unconsecrated produce which has absorbed
the flavor of produce designated as heave-offering, acquires the

status of heave-offering *only* if the owner of the unconsecrated
produce desires the absorbed flavor. See Peck, *M. Terumot*, M.
Ter. 10:1ff. The logic is identical in the present pericope.
Since the householder desires to use as wine the grape-flavored
water, it is deemed wine, and no longer may be used as water.

[27]Bunte points out that Baalbek was, under the name of
Heliopolis, a prosperous Roman trade center in the province of
Coele-Syria, northwest of Damascus (Bunte, p. 41, n. 2).

[28]Bunte (*loc. cit.*, n. 3) places Rakhpa ten miles south of
Baalbek.

[29]*Ibid.*, n. 5.

[30]*Ibid.*, n. 6.

[31]*qrqś* has often been interpreted as a reference to colocasia
(*colocasia antiquorum*, Löw, p. 240ff.), but Lieberman argues that
no certain identification is possible (*TK*, II:709.56). Bunte
(p. 242, n. 7) suggests that *qrqś* is the root of the Cilician
split-bean. If so, Meir is adding that the roots of the plant,
as well as the bean, are exempt from tithes. The point is superfluous, however, for if the plant does not grow in the Land of
Israel, all of it is by definition exempt.

[32]As with *qrqś*, certain identification is impossible. Cohen
(p. 278) translates, "wild lentils," in which case they are exempt
as uncultivated produce, *not* because they are foreign to the Land
of Israel. Bunte's suggestion (*ibid.*, n. 8) that the reference
is to the pods of the split-bean suffers from the same weakness
noted in n. 31 above.

[33]*Arum maculatum*, Löw, pp. 238ff. For a thorough description
of appearance and uses, see Bunte, p. 143, n. 10.

[34]The *qilqaś* mentioned by Meir and the *qanṭym* of Yose are
equivalent to the *qarqaś* and *qoṭnym* of M. 5:8B-C. The species
are unidentified. See Lieberman, *TK*, II:709.56-57.

[35]According to Lieberman, imported produce of a type which
does not grow in the Land of Israel was marked "so that people
would know the types of produce to which Mishnah referred; not in
order to prevent errors regarding the tithing of produce, but
rather for instructional purposes, in order to understand Mishnah."
Further, imported produce of a type which grows inside the Land
as well was not marked, "for the yield of the land was insufficient
for its population. Thus produce was brought from outside the
Land and remained unmarked, for everyone could recognize these"
(*TK*, II:710.58). I know of no means of evaluating Lieberman's
arguments, each of which appears rather arbitrary to me.

Abramsky, Yeḥezqel (HY), acquisition of untithed produce, 80, 87;
    barter for untithed produce, 80, 87; purchase of untithed
    produce, 80; removal of tithes, 80
Acquisition of untithed produce, 8-9, 63-105
Albeck, Hanoch, 24
Aqiba, crops not grown in Israel, 161; edible produce not deemed
    food, 11, 134, 136-37, 139; inedible produce, sale or purchase
    of, 157-58; meals, preparing untithed produce, 122, 134, 136-
    37, 139; produce subject to tithes, 35; removal of tithes,
    106-108, 113-15, 122, 134, 136-37, 139; transporting produce,
    liability for tithes, 9, 106-108, 113-15
Ashkenazi, Joseph, transporting produce, liability for tithes,
    107

Barter, acquisition of untithed produce, 8, 10, 80-98
Blackman, Philip, 24
Bunte, Wolfgang, 24

Cohen, Isadore, 24
Crops not grown in Israel, 12, 148, 160-63

Danby, Herbert, 24

Edible produce not deemed food, 11, 134-40
Eleazar, edible produce not deemed food, 134, 136-37, 139;
    harvest, produce taken before harvest, 147; meals, preparing
    untithed produce, 134, 136-37, 139; removal of tithes, 134,
    136-37, 139
Eleazar b. Azariah, harvest, taking produce before harvest, 11,
    143, 145-46
Eleazar b. Sadoq, acquisition of untithed produce, 85; barter
    for untithed produce, 85; meals, preparing untithed produce,
    9, 132-33; removal of tithes, 85, 132-33
Eliezer, acquisition of untithed produce, 8, 71-73, 75; edible
    produce not deemed food, 11, 134, 136-37, 139; gifts,
    acquisition of untithed produce, 8, 71-73, 75; meals, pre-
    paring untithed produce, 9, 122, 129-30, 136-37, 139;
    processing and storing untithed produce, 57; removal of
    tithes, 57, 71-73, 75, 122, 129-31, 136-37, 139
Elijah b. Solomon Zalman (GRA), acquisition of untithed produce,
    104; processing and storing untithed produce, 53-55; produce
    subject to tithes, 32, 38-39; removal of tithes, 53-55, 104
Ephraim Isaac of Premysla (MR), acquisition of untithed produce,
    69, 79, 93; barter acquiring untithed produce, 87; gifts,
    acquisition of untithed produce, 69; harvest, taking produce
    before harvest, 145; inedible produce, sale or purchase of,
    157; meals, preparing untithed produce, 130; processing and
    storing untithed produce, 51; produce subject to tithes,
    41; removal of tithes, 51, 69, 79, 93, 130

Gamaliel, edible produce not deemed food, 11, 134, 137; inedible
    produce, sale or purchase of, 154; meals, preparing untithed
    produce, 122, 137
Gifts, acquisition of untithed produce, 8, 10, 63-77
Goldschmidt, Lazarus, 24
Green, William S., 14

211